Praise for *Understanding SOA with Web Services*

"Finally, here's a third-generation Web services book that delivers pragmatic solutions using SOAs. Newcomer and Lomow draw from their years of real-world experience ranging from developing Web services standards to hands-on applications. Listen to them."

—*Doug Kaye, author of* Loosely Coupled: The Missing Pieces of Web Services
Host and producer, IT Conversations (www.itconversations.com)

"This book does the best job of describing not only "where we are" in the time-line of enterprise integration efforts, but also providing strategic guidance for where we need to be. The authors have worked diligently to break down the integration problem into functional areas, and send you down the path of strategic integration utilizing XML Web Services and Service-Oriented Architecture as the vehicle of choice. You will love this book!"

—*Daniel Edgar, Architect, Portland General Electric*

"E-Government needs a comprehensive guide to SOA with Web Services standards and best practices for implementation to get from the current "as is" to the future "to be" architecture. This book meets that need superbly."

—*Brand Niemann, Ph.D., Co-Chair, Semantic (Web Services) Interoperability Community of Practice, U.S. Federal CIO Council*

"There are many books on SOA available today, but *Understanding SOA with Web Services* stands out from the pack because of its thorough, outstanding coverage of transactions, reliability, and process. Where most SOA books focus on integration and architecture basics, Lomow and Newcomer fearlessly dive into these more advanced, yet critical, topics, and provide a depth of treatment unavailable anywhere else."

—*Jason Bloomberg, Senior Analyst, ZapThink LLC*

Understanding SOA with Web Services

Independent Technology Guides

David Chappell, Series Editor

The **Independent Technology Guides** offer serious technical descriptions of important new software technologies of interest to enterprise developers and technical managers. These books focus on how that technology works and what it can be used for, taking an independent perspective rather than reflecting the position of any particular vendor. These are ideal first books for developers with a wide range of backgrounds, the perfect place to begin mastering a new area and laying a solid foundation for further study. They also go into enough depth to enable technical managers to make good decisions without delving too deeply into implementation details.

The books in this series cover a broad range of topics, from networking protocols to development platforms, and are written by experts in the field. They have a fresh design created to make learning a new technology easier. All titles in the series are guided by the principle that, in order to use a technology well, you must first understand how and why that technology works.

Titles in the Series

Brian Arkills, *LDAP Directories Explained: An Introduction and Analysis*, 0-201-78792-X

David Chappell, *Understanding .NET: A Tutorial and Analysis*, 0-201-74162-8

Eric Newcomer, *Understanding Web Services: XML, WSDL, SOAP, and UDDI*, 0-201-75081-3

For more information, check out www.awprofessional.com.

Understanding SOA with Web Services

Eric Newcomer and Greg Lomow

▲▼Addison-Wesley

Upper Saddle River, NJ ■ Boston ■ Indianapolis
San Francisco ■ New York ■ Toronto ■ Montreal
London ■ Munich ■ Paris ■ Madrid ■ Capetown
Sydney ■ Tokyo ■ Singapore ■ Mexico City

The publisher offers excellent discounts on this book when ordered in quantity for bulk purchases or special sales, which may include electronic versions and/or custom covers and content particular to your business, training goals, marketing focus, and branding interests. For more information, please contact:

> U. S. Corporate and Government Sales
> (800) 382-3419
> corpsales@pearsontechgroup.com

For sales outside the U. S., please contact:

> International Sales
> international@pearsoned.com

Visit us on the Web: www.awprofessional.com

Library of Congress Catalog Number: 2004112673

ISBN: 0-321-18086-0
Text printed in the United States on recycled paper at Phoenix Color Corp. in Hagerstown, Maryland.
Third Printing: May 2007

Contents

PART II EXTENDED WEB SERVICES SPECIFICATIONS   271

Preface

The widely adopted and implemented core Web services standards (SOAP and WSDL) have achieved unprecedented interoperability across highly disparate software systems. As a result, new Web services standards have been proposed for extended features such as security, reliability, transactions, metadata management, and orchestration that extend Web services for use in a broad range of new applications.

The service-oriented architecture (SOA) has also become widely recognized for its important role in information technology projects. An SOA is a style of design that guides an organization during all aspects of creating and using business services (including conception, modeling, design, development, deployment, management, versioning, and retirement).

Despite some limitations (which we document), an SOA with Web services is the ideal combination of architecture and technology for consistently delivering robust, reusable services that support today's business needs and that can be easily adapted to satisfy changing business requirements.

Think about an SOA as an assembly line in a factory. It's an investment in the future operation of your business, so a significant amount of planning, design, and development may have to go into it before it starts to really pay off. The first car off a production line is more expensive than the thousandth. Similarly, the first service deployed in an SOA is more expensive than the hundredth. The major benefits of SOA arrive over time, although as we will see, it is possible to start small and incrementally build up to a full-fledged SOA.

SOA with Web services is important because it aligns information technology (IT) with business requirements and because it reduces the costs of IT systems and applications. An SOA gives you the ability to more easily integrate IT systems, provide multi-channel access to your systems, and to automate business processes.

Rather than relying entirely upon the skill and knowledge of certain specific individuals to implement business requirements in technology, SOA provides a foundation for rapidly assembling and composing new applications out of a library of reusable services that anyone can understand. When an SOA is in place and services are developed, developers can easily reuse existing services in their new applications and automated business processes.

Like any new investment in technology and infrastructure, it's important to understand the right way to do it and what you can and can't do. SOA and Web services are great, but they can't do everything. We hope that this book will help you achieve the benefits of SOA with Web services while avoiding the pitfalls.

Acknowledgments

The authors would like to sincerely thank series editor David Chappell for his invaluable assistance in reviewing several early drafts of the manuscript and providing unwavering clarity and vision during major rewrites to guide the book toward its current form. We would also like to thank Rich Bonneau for his help during the initial planning stages.

The authors would also like to thank the many reviewers who provided us with specific comments, suggestions, and corrections that significantly improved the quality of the book. In particular, Anne Thomas Manes for providing the most thorough review, catching many technical errors and highlighting sections whose clarity needed improvement—and doing both with concrete and helpful edits. We'd also like to thank Jason Bloomberg, Daniel Edgar, and Ron Schmelzer for reviewing the entire manuscript twice, and offering many detailed comments and overall suggestions for improving the text. And finally, we'd like to thank Steve Vinoksi for calling our attention to significant problems with the initial draft, and Max Loukianov for his many helpful comments on the final version of the manuscript. Any remaining errors, inconsistencies, and unclear text are our responsibility alone.

We'd like to thank the extremely professional and helpful editorial staff at Addison-Wesley for their fine work in producing this book, including Mary O'Brien who supported us from the beginning of the project and never lost faith, Brenda Mulligan who helped twice in arranging reviews so essential to a high-quality manuscript, and the production staff, including Sarah Kearns and Ben Lawson, who helped polish things up and ensure as much consistency as possible between the various parts that we each wrote.

I would like to thank Sean Baker for his encouragement and assistance at the beginning of the project, and the members of the senior management team at IONA for their understanding during the tough writing stages near the completion of the book. I would also like to thank Rebecca Bergersen for her assistance with the policy specifications and Wolfgang Schulze for his help with SOA concepts. And I would especially like to thank the members of my family for their patience with what they all now hope will become known as the final book project—in particular, my wife Jane and kids Erica and Alex, who have all been extremely supportive in the face of much frustration over weekends and vacation time consumed with working on the book.

—Eric Newcomer

I would like to give special thanks to Brian Unger, Marshall Cline, Joe Schwartz, Peter Cousins, and Jim Watson—you are great friends and mentors, and you continue to inspire and motivate me. I would also like to thank Ivan Casanova, Dirk Baezner, Jim Quigley, Dmitry Grinberg, Cemil Betanov, Sam Somech, Steve Marini, Ted Venema, Larry Mellon, William Henry, John Dodd, Kevin Maunz, Jeff Mitchell, and all my other friends and colleagues from Jade Simulations, Level 8 Systems, IONA Technologies, and BearingPoint—it has been a pleasure and honor working with each and every one of you. I would also like to thank my wife, Barb—thank you for all of your patience and tolerance during the writing and production of this book.

—Greg Lomow

About the Authors

In the role of Chief Technology Officer at IONA, **Eric Newcomer** is responsible for IONA's technology roadmap and direction as relates to standards adoption, architecture, and product design. Eric joined IONA in November 1999 as transaction architect, and most recently served as Vice President of Engineering, Web Services Integration Products. Eric has 26 years experience in the computer industry, including more than 15 years at Digital Equipment Corporation/Compaq Computer, where he held a variety of technical and management positions before receiving a corporate-level technical appointment. Eric received his BA in American Studies from Antioch College, with a minor in computer science.

In addition to *Understanding Web Services*, published in 2002, Eric is co-author of *Principles of Transaction Processing*, published in 1997 by Morgan Kaufman, and co-author of a chapter called "The Keys to the Highway" in *The Future of Software*, published in 1995 by MIT Press. Eric is also the author of numerous white papers and articles, co-author and editor of the Structured Transaction Definition Language specification published by X/Open (now The Open Group) in 1994, former member of the Transaction Internet Protocol working group at IETF, former member of the X/Open Distributed Transaction Processing committee that created the XA specification, former chair of the OTS RTF at OMG, and chair of the team that developed the XML Valuetype specification at OMG to map XML to CORBA. He was a charter member of the XML Protocols Working Group at W3C, where he served as an editor of the requirements document that led to SOAP 1.2. He served for nearly two years as an editor of the W3C Web Services Architecture Specification, and most recently served as co-chair and editor of the Web Services Composite Application Framework set of specifications at OASIS.

Greg Lomow, Ph.D., is a senior manager and consultant for BearingPoint, Inc. Greg has 12 years of experience as a consultant and enterprise architect working in the financial services, telecom, and federal government sectors designing business applications using service-oriented architecture, developing simulation applications using distributed object technology, and training developers in object-oriented design and programming techniques. He also worked for eight years as a product manager at Jade Simulations, Level 8 Systems, and IONA Technologies responsible for integration, web services, and middleware products. Greg co-authored *C++ Frequently Asked Questions* published by Addison-Wesley in October 1999 (1st ed.) and again in January 1999 (2nd ed.). He completed his Ph.D. in computer science at the University of Calgary, Canada, in 1988. Greg is an active member of the Web Services Interoperability (WS-I) Organization.

Introduction

In the early days of business computing, no one paid much attention to sharing application logic and data across multiple machines. The big question was how to develop systems to automate previously manual operations such as billing, accounting, payroll, and order management. Solving any one of these individual problems was challenging enough, not to mention the additional challenge of basing all systems on a common, reusable architecture, and few organizations were in a position to tackle it.

In the modern era, most operational business functions have been automated, and now the big question is how to improve the ability of these systems to meet new requirements. Adding a new user interface, combining multiple data sources into a single view, integrating mobile devices, or replacing an old application with a better one are common reasons for investing in new projects.

The paradigm of service-oriented development, although not new, is catching on as the information technology (IT) world shifts from developing new systems to getting more out of earlier investments. Developing services and deploying them using a service-oriented architecture (SOA) is the best way to utilize IT systems to meet new challenges.

A service differs from an object or a procedure because it's defined by the messages that it exchanges with other services. A service's loose coupling to the applications that host it gives it the ability to more easily share data across the department, enterprise, or Internet. An SOA defines the way in which services are deployed and managed. Using an SOA increases reuse, lowers overall costs, and improves the ability to rapidly change and evolve IT systems, whether old or new.

Supporting the shift toward service-oriented development and SOA is a large cast of characters called Web services technologies. These represent the most widely adopted distributed computing standards in the industry's history. As we'll see, Web services are an ideal platform for SOA.

The modern answer to application integration, therefore, is an SOA with Web services. An SOA maps easily and directly to a business's operational processes and supports a better division of labor between technical and business staff. Furthermore, an SOA uses a description model capable of unifying existing and new systems.

When Web services descriptions are available throughout a department or an enterprise, service-oriented integration projects can focus on composing Web services instead of dealing with the complexity of incompatible applications on multiple computers, programming languages, and application packages. Whether you use Java, C++, Visual Studio, CORBA, WebSphere MQ, or any other development platform or software system, such as J2EE or the .NET Framework, SOA provides the architecture, and Web services provide the unifying glue.

As businesses and governments continue to struggle to align IT expenditures with the bottom line to achieve strategic market objectives, software productivity gains are elusive, especially compared to gains in hardware price and performance. With the widespread adoption and implementation of Web services, products and technologies are finally in position for enterprises to realize these benefits.

Compared to the standards of the past, Web services are much easier to learn and use. The broad adoption of Web services standards makes it easy to imagine a world in which all applications have service interfaces. And from that vision, it's easy to imagine IT staff performing the bulk of their activities using Web services interfaces.

It's true, however, that someone will have to deal with the plethora of legacy technologies in order to service enable them. But the beauty of services and SOA is that the services are developed to achieve interoperability and to hide the details of the execution environments behind them. In particular for Web services, this means the ability to emit and consume data represented as XML, regardless of development platform, middleware, operating system, or hardware type.

The most important application of SOA is connecting the various operational systems that automate an enterprise's business processes. A company's operational environment can be as unique and varied as its culture because the way a company does business can be part of its competitive edge. Classic examples include Wal-Mart's inventory management system, American Airline's pioneering automated reservation system (SABRE), and Dell's on-demand manufacturing supply chain management system. Companies need IT systems with the flexibility to implement specialized operations, to change as easily as business operations change, to respond quickly to internal as well as external condition changes, and to gain or maintain a competitive edge.

In general, the evolution of the software industry has been about improving the ease with which people interact with computers, continually raising the abstraction level of languages to make them accessible to more people with less scientific training. The purpose of this evolutionary change is to adapt software systems more easily and directly to the needs of people and institutions.

Making it easier for people to tell computers what to do drives the evolution of the software industry because the easier it is to tell computers what to do, the easier it is to get more projects done quickly and cheaply. The abstraction benefit of Web services (having the ability to work with any type of implementation software) helps reduce IT's single largest cost: labor. For instance, although it might be easy enough for an office worker to create reports and spreadsheets, or for a consumer to surf the Web and order books, it is still not easy enough for the back office staff to tell those big machines (or farms of machines) what to do to service the millions of transactions a week that many businesses require to stay in operation.

When thinking about IT projects, one of the most difficult subjects is determining who will be able to bridge the business-technology gap—that is, which project member will have the right skills to ensure that the business issues are well enough understood to be implemented in the technology and that the technology issues are well enough understood to meet the business requirements. One of the great potential advantages of solutions created using an SOA with Web services is that they can help resolve this perennial problem by providing a better separation of concerns between the business analysts and service developers. The service developers can take responsibility for implementing services that meet business requirements, while the analysts can take responsibility for defining how services fit together to implement a business process.

Web services marry the ease of use of a document markup language to distributed computing concepts and apply the result to solve IT integration problems cheaply and easily. The standards are firmly in place for Web services basics and are quickly emerging for enterprise qualities of service, metadata management, and orchestration, meaning that everything is ready for businesses to start realizing the true benefits of an SOA.

Integrating existing and new applications using an SOA involves defining the basic Web services interoperability layer and the enterprise quality of service layer to bridge features and functions used in current applications such as security, reliability, and transactions. It also involves the ability to define automated business process execution flows across the Web services after the SOA is in place.

An SOA with Web services enables the development of services that encapsulate business functions and that are easily accessible from any other service. Composite services, furthermore, allow a wide range of options for combining

Web services and creating new application functionality. Web services technologies can be used to solve a broad range of IT problems, especially when used to quickly and easily join disparate pieces of software. Web services provide basic interoperability solutions and can easily be extended for use in enterprise integration architectures that lower cost and increase IT value, and they are especially valuable when used to implement SOA-enabled solutions.

What's in the Book

This book describes the best approach to designing and developing an SOA-based integration solution using Web services technologies and covers how an SOA provides a foundation for addressing other IT requirements, such as multi-channel client access, application interoperability, and business process management.

This book also provides tutorials on the advanced Web services technologies that help realize SOA solutions for enterprises, including metadata management, security, reliability, and transactions.

This book is intended for developers, technical managers, and architects interested in understanding the major principles and concepts behind SOA, how to implement an SOA using Web services, and how to achieve the business benefits of SOA. SOA is explained in the context of how it is most often used, such as enabling multi-channel access, composing applications, and automating business process management.

Organization of the Book

The book is divided into two major parts, with an overall introductory chapter. The two major parts are focused on:

- Service-oriented architecture, business process management, and how they are implemented using Web services technologies.

- Tutorials on Web services specifications for metadata management, security, advanced messaging (including reliability and notification), and transactions.

The first part introduces the major concepts behind SOA, covers how to implement an SOA using Web services, and describes the various benefits of SOA in the context of multi-channel (that is, multi-client) applications and business process flows. This part also introduces the major concepts behind BPM, explains how to implement BPM using Web services, and covers the major BPM-related specifications (WS-BPEL and WS-CDL).

The second part provides overviews and tutorial information on UDDI V3, WSDL V2.0, WS-Addressing, WS-MetadataExchange, WS-Policy, WS-Security, WS-Trust, WS-SecureConversation, WS-Federation, WS-ReliableMessaging, WS-Eventing, WS-Notification, the WS-Transactions family, the WS-Composite Application Framework, and other related specifications for the type of enterprise quality of service needed for complex, large-scale integration projects.

The book covers the motivation behind integration (why integration is so important), describes why SOA has emerged as the dominant integration approach, and illustrates the important features and functions that enable SOA for multi-channel client access and business process management.

Chapter 1—Introduction to SOA with Web Services
This chapter provides an overall introduction to the technologies and trends of SOA, BPM, and Web services that are converging to define a new, more productive, and more agile enterprise IT environment that is often called the "service-oriented enterprise." The chapter covers the definition of service, SOA, and BPM and introduces the Web services specifications that can support mission-critical integration projects, from simple interoperability to complex automated process flows and everything in between.

Part I
Chapter 2—Overview of Service-Oriented Architecture
Chapter 2 discusses the fundamental concepts that all SOAs share, including SOA governance, SOA design principles, and service contracts. It also defines the Web services platform and the features and functions it provides to support SOA-based applications. This chapter also discusses the key business and technical benefits of adopting an SOA using Web services.

Chapter 3—SOA and Web Services

Chapter 3 discusses how the core and extended Web services specifications support the facilities of a Web services platform, including service-level communication, discovery, security, data handling, transaction management, and system management. The chapter concludes with a brief comparison of various technologies that have been used for implementing SOAs, including J2EE, CORBA, and Web services.

Chapter 4—SOA and Web Services for Integration

Chapter 4 discusses two approaches that integration projects can take using Web services: Web services integration (WSI) and service-oriented integration (SOI). It begins by presenting an overview of integration business drivers, common business and technical goals, and recurring technical challenges. Next, it discusses why Web services are ideal technologies for solving integration problems. Organizations can choose between WSI and SOI, depending on their business and technical requirements, goals, and the level of formality that they wish to incorporate into the integration process. Finally, the chapter illustrates using Web services for integration by looking at integrating .NET Framework and J2EE applications.

Chapter 5—SOA and Multi-Channel Access

Chapter 5 presents a key SOA design pattern for enabling services to be delivered to customers, employees, and partners via multiple delivery channels. This chapter discusses the key layers of this architectural pattern (including the client/presentation tier, channel access tier, business service access tier, and business service tier) and how the Web services platform links them together.

Chapter 6—SOA and Business Process Management

Chapter 6 discusses the key concepts of business process management (BPM) and summarizes the business and technical benefits of BPM. This chapter discusses the complementary nature of SOA and BPM through the Web services layer. Web services provide the ideal platform for the business process layer and automating custom business process flows. This chapter also provides an overview of the major concepts and techniques involved in Web services orchestration, including flow control, compensations, correlation, and exception handling, and maps the concepts to the WS-BPEL and WS-CDL specifications with detailed examples.

Part II

Chapter 7—Metadata Management

Chapter 7 introduces the concept of managing metadata for Web services, including how to access WSDL files, what's new in WSDL 2.0, creating addressing references, using WS-Addressing, defining and accessing WS-Policy schemas associated with WSDL files, and explaining how the WS-MetadataExchange specification allows Web services developers to access the metadata they need while developing individual and composite Web services.

Chapter 8—Web Services Security

Chapter 8 introduces the main requirements of Web services security and includes a description of the additional security risks and threats opened up by using Web services, along with proposed defense mechanisms. The chapter covers message integrity, message confidentiality, authentication, and authorization. Major Web services specifications covered include WS-Security, WS-Trust, WS-Federation, WS-SecureConversation, XACML, SAML, XML Encryption, and XML Signature.

Chapter 9—Advanced Messaging

Chapter 9 introduces the concepts and requirements behind advanced messaging techniques and technologies used in Web services. The chapter explains how WS-ReliableMessaging, WS-Reliability, and ebXML Messaging work to guarantee message delivery. The chapter also provides a description of the important publish-and-subscribe message exchange pattern and how it is implemented using the WS-Eventing and WS-Notification specifications.

Chapter 10—Transaction Processing

Chapter 10 provides an overview of why traditional transaction processing technologies are not well suited for Web services, and it describes the newer designs and solutions developed for use with Web services. Specifications covered include WS-AtomicTransactions, WS-BusinessActivity, WS-Coordination, WS-Context, WS-CoordinationFramework, and WS-TransactionManagement.

Chapter 1

Introduction to SOA with Web Services

Complexity is a fact of life in information technology (IT). Dealing with the complexity while building new applications, replacing existing applications, and keeping up with all the maintenance and enhancement requests represents a major challenge.

If all applications were to use a common programming interface and interoperability protocol, however, the job of IT would be much simpler, complexity would be reduced, and existing functionality could be more easily reused. After a common programming interface is in place, through which any application can be accessed, existing IT infrastructure can be more easily replaced and modernized.

This is the promise that service-oriented development brings to the IT world, and when deployed using a service-oriented architecture (SOA), services also become the foundation for more easily creating a variety of new strategic solutions, including:

- Rapid application integration.

- Automated business processes.

- Multi-channel access to applications, including fixed and mobile devices.

An SOA facilitates the composition of services across disparate pieces of software, whether old or new; departmental, enterprise-wide, or inter-enterprise; mainframe, mid-tier, PC, or mobile device, to streamline IT processes and eliminate barriers to IT environment improvements.

These composite application solutions are within reach because of the widespread adoption of Web services and the transformational power of an SOA. The Web Services Description Language (WSDL) has become a standard programming interface to access any application, and SOAP has become a standard interoperability protocol to connect any application to any other. These two standards are a great beginning, and they are followed by many additional Web services specifications that define security, reliability, transactions, orchestration, and metadata management to meet additional requirements for enterprise features and qualities of service. Altogether, the Web services standards the best platform on which to build an SOA—the next-generation IT infrastructure.

The Service-Oriented Enterprise

Driven by the convergence of key technologies and the universal adoption of Web services, the service-oriented enterprise promises to significantly improve corporate agility, speed time-to-market for new products and services, reduce IT costs, and improve operational efficiency.

As illustrated in Figure 1-1, several industry trends are converging to drive fundamental IT changes around the concepts and implementation of service orientation. The key technologies in this convergence are:

- **Extensible Markup Language (XML)**—A common, independent data format across the enterprise and beyond that provides:

  - Standard data types and structures, independent of any programming language, development environment, or software system.

  - Pervasive technology for defining business documents and exchanging business information, including standard vocabularies for many industries.

  - Ubiquitous software for handling operations on XML, including parsers, queries, and transformations.

- **Web services**—XML-based technologies for messaging, service description, discovery, and extended features, providing:

  - Pervasive, open standards for distributed computing interface descriptions and document exchange via messages.

  - Independence from the underlying execution technology and application platforms.

  - Extensibility for enterprise qualities of service such as security, reliability, and transactions.

  - Support for composite applications such as business process flows, multi-channel access, and rapid integration.

- **Service-oriented architecture (SOA)**—A methodology for achieving application interoperability and reuse of IT assets that features:

  - A strong architectural focus, including governance, processes, modeling, and tools.

  - An ideal level of abstraction for aligning business needs and technical capabilities, and creating reusable, coarse-grain business functionality.

- A deployment infrastructure on which new applications can quickly and easily be built.

- A reusable library of services for common business and IT functions.

- **Business process management (BPM)**—Methodologies and technologies for automating business operations that:

  - Explicitly describe business processes so that they are easier to understand, refine, and optimize.

  - Make it easier to quickly modify business processes as business requirements change.

  - Automate previously manual business processes and enforce business rules.

  - Provide real-time information and analysis on business processes for decision makers.

Individually, each of these technologies has had a profound effect on one or more aspects of business computing. When combined, they provide a comprehensive platform for obtaining the benefits of service orientation and taking the next step in the evolution of IT systems.

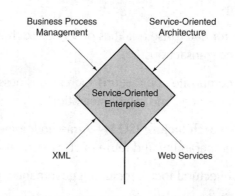

Figure 1-1   Trends converging to create the service-oriented enterprise.

Service-Oriented Development

Software vendors have widely adopted the paradigm of service-oriented development based on Web services. Service-oriented development is complementary to the object-oriented, procedure-oriented, message-oriented, and database-oriented development approaches that preceded it.

Service-oriented development provides the following benefits:

- **Reuse**—The ability to create services that are reusable in multiple applications.

- **Efficiency**—The ability to quickly and easily create new services and new applications using a combination of new and old services, along with the ability to focus on the data to be shared rather than the implementation underneath.

- **Loose technology coupling**—The ability to model services independently of their execution environment and create messages that can be sent to any service.

- **Division of responsibility**—The ability to more easily allow business people to concentrate on business issues, technical people to concentrate on technology issues, and for both groups to collaborate using the service contract.

Developing a service is different from developing an object because a service is defined by the messages it exchanges with other services, rather than a method signature. A service must be defined at a higher level of abstraction (some might say at the lowest common denominator) than an object because it's possible to map a service definition to a procedure-oriented language such as COBOL or PL/I, or to a message queuing system such as JMS or MSMQ, as well as to an object-oriented system such as J2EE or the .NET Framework.

It's also important to understand the granularity at which the service is to be defined. A service normally defines a coarse-grained interface that accepts more data in a single invocation than an object and consumes more computing resources than an object because of the need to map to an execution environment, process the XML, and often access it remotely. Of course, object interfaces can be very coarse-grained. The point is that services are designed to solve interoperability problems between applications and for use in composing new applications or application systems, but not to create the detailed business logic for the applications.

It's possible to create an aggregation of Web services such that the published Web service encapsulates multiple other Web services. This allows a coarse-grained interface to be decomposed into a number of finer-grained services (or multiple finer-grained services to be composed into a coarse-grained interface). The coarse-grained service may make more sense to publish, while the finer-grained services may make more sense as "private" Web services that can be invoked only by the coarse-grained Web service.

Services are executed by exchanging messages according to one or more supported message exchange patterns (MEPs), such as request/response, one-way asynchronous, or publish/subscribe.

At a project level, an architect typically oversees the development of reusable services and identifies a means to store, manage, and retrieve service descriptions when and where they are needed. The reusable services layer insulates business operations such as "get customer" or "place an order" from variations in the underlying software platform implementations, just as Web servers and browsers insulate the World Wide Web from variations in operating systems and programming languages. The ability of reusable services to be composed into larger services quickly and easily is what provides the organization the benefits of process automation and the agility to respond to changing conditions.

How XML Helps Simplify Systems Development and Integration

The use of XML in Web services provides a clear separation between the definition of a service and its execution. This separation in the standards is intentional so that Web services can work with any software system. The

continues

XML representation, provided through an XML Schema, of the data types and structures of a service allows the developer to think about the data being passed among services without necessarily having to consider the details of a given service implementation. This represents a change in the nature of the integration problem from having to figure out the implementation of the service in order to talk to it. Whether the service's execution environment is an object, message queue, or stored procedure doesn't matter. The data is seen through the filter of a Web service, which includes a layer that maps the Web service to whatever execution environment is implementing the service.

One way to help accomplish this significant turnaround in the way we think about how to design, develop, and deploy applications using services may be to divide the responsibility within IT departments between those who:

- **Create the services**—Dealing with the complexity of the underlying technology on which the service is being deployed and ensuring that the XML/Web services descriptions are what the service consumer needs and that they share the right data.

- **Consume the services**—Assembling new composite applications and business process flows, ensuring that the shared data and process flows accurately reflect operational and strategic business requirements.

This potential division of responsibility more cleanly separates the technical issues from the business issues.

Organizational Implications of SOA

Previously, the same individuals in the IT department were responsible for understanding both business and technical functions—and this remains a classic problem for IT, that is, getting the same person or persons to bridge business and technology domains. To gain the full benefit of Web services,

continues

SOA, and BPM technologies, IT departments should consider the best organization and skill set mix. It's important when adopting a new architecture and a new technology to identify new roles and responsibilities. Among the important considerations is that technical staff must be able to reorient themselves from thinking about doing the entire job to doing a piece of the job that will be completed by someone else. A service needs to be developed within a larger context than an object or a procedure because it is more likely to be reused. In fact, defining services for reuse is probably the most important part of service orientation. To obtain their highest value, services must be developed in the context of other services and used in combination with them to build applications. This change in thinking is likely to require someone in a departmental or corporate leadership position to help review designs and ensure that they are in line with these new IT goals.

Service Abstraction

A service is a location on the network that has a machine-readable description of the messages it receives and optionally returns. A service is therefore defined in terms of the message exchange patterns it supports. A schema for the data contained in the message is used as the main part of the contract (i.e., description) established between a service requester and a service provider. Other items of metadata describe the network address for the service, the operations it supports, and its requirements for reliability, security, and transactionality.

Figure 1-2 illustrates the relationship among the parts of a service, including the description, the implementation, and the mapping layer between the two. The service implementation can be any execution environment for which Web services support is available. The service implementation is also called the *executable agent*. The executable agent is responsible for implementing the Web services processing model as defined in the various Web services specifications. The executable agent runs within the *execution environment*, which is typically a software system or programming language.

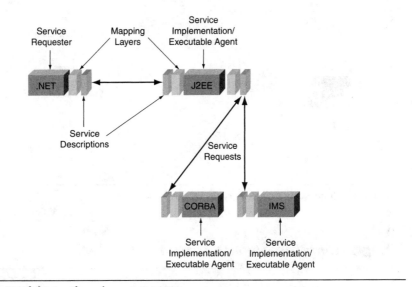

Figure 1-2   Breakdown of service components.

An important part of the definition of a service is that its description is separated from its executable agent. One description might have multiple different executable agents associated with it. Similarly, one agent might support multiple descriptions. The description is separated from the execution environment using a mapping layer (sometimes also called a transformation layer). The mapping layer is often implemented using proxies and stubs. The mapping layer is responsible for accepting the message, transforming the XML data to the native format, and dispatching the data to the executable agent.

Web services roles include requester and provider. The service *requester* initiates the execution of a service by sending a message to a service provider. The service *provider* executes the service upon receipt of a message and returns the results, if any are specified, to the requester. A requester can be a provider, and vice versa, meaning an execution agent can play either or both roles.

As shown in Figure 1-3, one of the greatest benefits of service abstraction is its ability to easily access a variety of service types, including newly developed services, wrapped legacy applications, and applications composed of other services (both new and legacy).

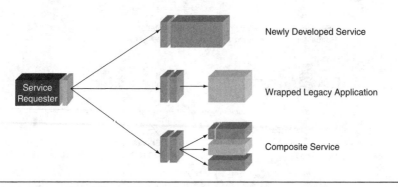

Figure 1-3   Requesting different types of services.

Separating the Service from the Product

Some software vendors still don't separate the idea of a service from the idea of an execution environment, and they continue to sell Web services implementations only as part of another, typically pre-existing product. This practice can make it more difficult to obtain the benefits of services because the products have features that may not be required to execute Web services and that may create incompatibilities if the products make the services dependent upon them.

Service-Oriented Architecture

This section introduces the major concepts and definitions for services and SOA.

What Are Services?

Before we continue to discuss technology, let's discuss the notion of services and processes from a business perspective. Most organizations (whether commercial or government) provide services to customers, clients, citizens, employees, or partners. Let's look at an example of service orientation in practice.

As illustrated in Figure 1-4, bank tellers provide services to bank customers. Different tellers may offer different services, and some tellers may be specifically trained to provide certain types of services to the customer. Typical services include:

- Account management (opening and closing accounts).

- Loans (application processing, inquiries about terms and conditions, accepting payments).

- Withdrawals, deposits, and transfers.

- Foreign currency exchange.

Several tellers may offer the same set of services to provide load balancing and high availability. What happens behind the counter does not matter to the customer, as long as the service is completed. Processing a complex transaction may require the customer to visit several tellers and therefore implement a business process flow.

Figure 1-4   Service analogy at the bank.

Behind the counter are the IT systems that automate the bank's services. The services are provided to the customer via the tellers. The services implemented by the IT systems must match and support the services provided by the tellers.

A consistent approach to defining services on the IT systems that align with business functions and processes makes it easier for the IT systems to support the goals of the business and adapt more easily to providing the same service through humans, ATMs, and over the Web.

Figure 1-5 shows how the same service can be accessed from customers at the ATM, tellers on the office network, or Web users from their PCs. The services are designed and deployed to match the services that customers need. The implementation environments for the services don't matter; it's the service that's important. This figure also illustrates how two services can easily be combined to create another service, such as how the withdrawal and deposit service are composed into a transfer service.

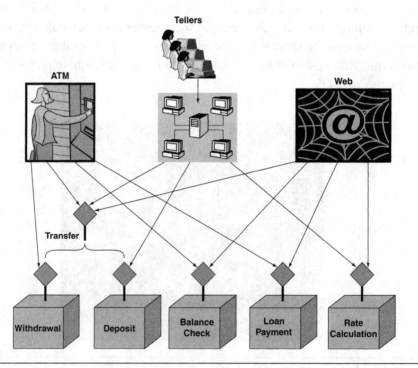

Figure 1-5   Accessing and composing services.

The definition of software services aligns with the business services that a bank offers to ensure smooth business operations and to help realize strategic goals such as providing ATM and Web access to banking services in addition to providing them in the branch office.

More complex applications can be composed from services, as we'll see, such as processing a purchase order or an insurance claim. Deploying services in the context of an SOA makes it easier to compose services into simple as well as complex applications, which can also be exposed as services that can be accessed by humans and IT systems alike.

What Is Service-Oriented Architecture?

A service-oriented architecture is a style of design that guides all aspects of creating and using business services throughout their lifecycle (from conception to retirement). An SOA is also a way to define and provision an IT infrastructure to allow different applications to exchange data and participate in business processes, regardless of the operating systems or programming languages underlying those applications.

An SOA can be thought of as an approach to building IT systems in which business services (i.e., the services that an organization provides to clients, customers, citizens, partners, employees, and other organizations) are the key organizing principle used to align IT systems with the needs of the business. In contrast, earlier approaches to building IT systems tended to directly use specific implementation environments such as object orientation, procedure orientation, and message orientation to solve these business problems, resulting in systems that were often tied to the features and functions of a particular execution environment technology such as CICS, IMS, CORBA, J2EE, and COM/DCOM.

Competitive Value of SOA

Businesses that successfully implement an SOA using Web services are likely to have a competitive advantage over those who do not because those who have services aligned with strategic IT business goals can react more quickly to changing business requirements than those who have IT systems

continues

aligned to a particular execution environment. It's easier to combine Web services, easier to change Web services compositions, and cheaper to change the Web services and XML data than it is to change execution environments. The advantages and benefits of SOA with Web services include a better return on investment for IT spending on projects, a faster time to results for the projects, and an ability to more quickly respond to changing business and government requirements. Any business that can implement an IT infrastructure that allows it to change more rapidly has an advantage over a business that cannot do the same. Furthermore, the use of an SOA for integration, business process management, and multi-channel access should allow any enterprise to create a more strategic IT environment, one that more closely matches the operational characteristics of the business.

SOA is the best way to capitalize on the value of service-oriented development. Service orientation reduces project costs and improves project success rates by adapting technology more naturally to the people who need to use it, rather than focusing (as the previous generations of IT systems have) on the technology itself, which forces people to adapt to the technology. The major difference between service-oriented development and previous approaches is that service orientation lets you focus on the description of the business problem, whereas previous approaches require you to focus more on the use of a specific execution environment technology. The way in which services are developed better aligns them with solving business problems than was the case with previous generations of technology.

The concept of SOA isn't new—what is new is the ability to mix and match execution environments, clearly separating the service interface from the execution technology, allowing IT departments to choose the best execution environment for each job (whether it's a new or existing application) and tying them together using a consistent architectural approach. Previous implementations of SOA were based on a single execution environment technology.

SOA Isn't New, So What Is?

Everyone is talking about SOA, although the concepts behind it aren't new. The idea of separating an interface from its implementation to create a software service definition has been well proven in J2EE, CORBA, and COM, and even DCE before that. But the ability to more cleanly and completely separate—basically by interpreting a text file—a service description from its execution environment is new. This ability is part of what Web concepts and technologies bring to Web services. The traditional implementations of the interface concept might not have considered such a "loose" separation because the performance implications are negative. However, in many cases, the performance issue is less important than the ability to more easily achieve interoperability, something the industry has long strived for but only partially achieved until now. The success or failure of SOA, however, does not depend upon the advance in IT software brought about by Web services. Rather, it depends upon a change in approach. The greater separation of interface from execution environment in Web services facilitates the separation of work responsibilities as well. Separating the service description from its technology implementation means that businesses can think about and plan IT investments around the realization of operational business considerations, as represented by the description, more so than the capabilities of any individual product or software technology chosen to execute the description. In this case, the description becomes the definition of a kind of lowest common denominator—a set of features and functions that everything can support. But this is achievable only if businesses change their way of thinking about IT. A service is something that's just available—just there for the consumption. Of course, this is an exaggeration; plenty of services and applications still have to be developed to reach the ideals of automating a business operation so quickly and flexibly that it just becomes a given, like office-software automation. No single software solution can address every requirement any more than the same computer system can run a car and calculate the trajectory for the Mars Rover. The same type of computer system cannot, and should not, operate an insulin pump and process orders for Amazon.com and tracks Web links for Google. The world

continues

is by its very nature diverse, and SOA with Web services embraces this diversity and provides the ability to create IT systems that map better to business operations than anything previously. However, this will take a significant change in thinking, not just for IT departments, but also for the entire software industry. It's equally hard to imagine that a single software vendor would be an expert in all aspects of software as it is to imagine that a single hardware vendor is an expert in all aspects of computing. Specialization is what the industry needs, along with the ability to create reusable assemblies of those components. In this vision of a future environment, software vendors are likely to become even more specialized, perhaps shipping assemblies of services instead of complete products. In an SOA-enabled world, enterprises very likely will have to learn not only to think about services as distinct from execution environments, but also how to assemble applications out of components from a variety of vendors.

The real value of SOA comes from the later stages of deployment, when new applications can be developed entirely, or almost entirely, by composing existing services. When new applications can be assembled out of a collection of existing, reusable services, the best value for effort can be realized (that is, the lowest cost and fastest time to results and best ROI). But it takes some time to reach this point, and significant investment in service development may be required.

It's easy to understand the benefit of reusing common business services such as customer name lookup, ZIP Code validation, or credit checking. In a pre-service oriented development environment, these functions might be performed by reusable code libraries or class libraries that are loaded or linked into new applications. In SOA-based applications, common functions such as these, as well as typical system functions such as security checks, transaction coordination, and auditing are instead implemented using services. Using services not only reduces the amount of deployed code, but it also reduces the management, maintenance, and support burden by centralizing the deployed code and managing access to it. However, the performance implications of accessing services instead of using internal functions must be assessed because using a service typically consumes more computing resources than reusable code libraries.

The key to a successful SOA is determining the correct design and function of the services in the reusable service library, which should ultimately reflect the operational characteristics of the organization, such as how grants are applied for, how cash is managed overnight, or how containers are transferred from ships to trucks. The operational characteristics of the business are what need to be automated, and the successful SOA project will ensure that the reusable software services are properly aligned with the operational business processes. The successful alignment of business services and their implementation in software ensures that operational business processes can be changed quickly and easily as external environmental changes cause an organization to adapt and evolve.

CORBA vs. Web Services for SOA

People familiar with the CORBA standard often remark that Web services are simply CORBA implemented using XML and note the number of features Web services are missing compared to CORBA. Many CORBA deployments are SOAs, in fact, and the original goals of CORBA are very similar to the goals of Web services. Cynics say that CORBA didn't succeed widely because of vendor politics, and there's some truth to that. However, CORBA also hurt itself in its early days by not defining a standard for interoperability. When asked about this, OMG presenters used to say, "It's an exercise left up to the vendors and the customers to work out." The implication, and sometimes the direct statement, was that interoperability didn't matter if you had a standard interface. Web services actually started with SOAP, which is an interoperability standard. Many people still use SOAP without WSDL, which is perfectly possible, indicating another contrast between the two. In CORBA, it's impossible to use the interoperability transport without the interface definition language (IDL)—in fact, everything is generated from the IDL. Many Web services toolkits also generate proxies and stubs from WSDL and also generate the SOAP messages. But this is an implementation choice,

continues

not part of the SOAP standard. From a technical perspective, it is certainly true that you can use CORBA for almost everything you can use Web services for. And for many applications, CORBA remains a better choice. However, from a human perspective, which is what really counts in the end, if someone is unfamiliar with CORBA or new to distributed computing, Web services are much easier to learn and use, and the missing features don't matter as much as the interoperability.

Challenges to Adoption

The main challenges to adoption of SOA include ensuring adequate staff training and maintaining the level of discipline required to ensure the services that are developed are reusable. Any technology, no matter how promising, can be abused and improperly used. Services have to be developed not simply for immediate benefit, but also (and perhaps primarily) for long-term benefit. To put it another way, the existence of an individual service isn't of much value unless it fits into a larger collection of services that can be consumed by multiple applications, and out of which multiple new applications can be composed. In addition, the definition of a reusable service is very difficult to get right the first time.

Another challenge is managing short-term costs. Building an SOA isn't cheap; reengineering existing systems costs money, and the payback becomes larger over time. It requires business analysts to define the business processes, systems architects to turn processes into specifications, software engineers to develop the new code, and project managers to track it all.

Another challenge is that some applications may need to be modified in order to participate in the SOA. Some applications might not have a callable interface that can be service-enabled. Some applications are only accessible via file transfer or batch data input and output and may need additional programs for the purpose of service-enablement.

Of course, incrementally adopting SOA and leveraging SOA where it will have the greatest business impact can mitigate the challenges and amortize their costs, especially when services can be used to solve tactical problems along the way. Part of adopting Web services and SOA therefore is to identify those projects that provide immediate value by solving an immediate problem (such as integrating J2EE and .NET Framework applications) and at the same time lay the foundation for a departmental or enterprise SOA.

What Web Services Are Good For

Sometimes in the Web services literature, you will see a lot of discussion about things that Web services are not good for, such as developing and deploying mission-critical applications. It's a mistake, however, to assume that they never will be good for this. Other times, you'll see talk about identifying the "golden copy" or "single reference" data item instance for a particular data type, such as customer ID or customer name. This is indeed a problem that needs solving, but it also isn't part of the job of the Web services. This means it needs to be solved at the SOA level rather than at the Web services level. These discussions often indicate unfamiliarity with Web services and the problems they are trying to solve. The same people who would never imagine that a single tool in a workshop could be used for every purpose often make the mistake of thinking that Web services must be good for everything that all other technologies that preceded them are good for. This represents thinking that each new technology wave somehow obsoletes the previous wave or takes over everything that came before. Web services are not just adding more technology to the problems of IT; they are proposing a different approach to solving some of the problems of IT, especially around integration, because of new capabilities offered by the technology. Web services are not really a replacement technology; they are not the same thing as a new programming language like Java or C#, which you could reasonably assume must include all the major features of other successful programming languages. Web services are not really a new middleware system in the sense that J2EE, CORBA, and the .NET Framework are middleware systems. Web services are XML-based interface technologies; they are not executable; they do not have an execution environment—they depend upon other technologies for their execution environments. If you don't

continues

rethink your approach to IT based on the features, functions, and capabilities of Web services, of course you're not going to get the value out of them that you should. Using Web services successfully requires a change in thinking about technology, not simply learning a new grammar for the same old way of building and deploying systems. Web services currently and will always require a mix of technologies. Therefore, Web services need to be understood in terms of what they add to the picture, not only in the context of what they replace.

SOA and Web Services

The major advantages of implementing an SOA using Web services are that Web services are pervasive, simple, and platform-neutral.

As shown in Figure 1-6, the basic Web services architecture consists of specifications (SOAP, WSDL, and UDDI) that support the interaction of a Web service requester with a Web service provider and the potential discovery of the Web service description. The provider typically publishes a WSDL description of its Web service, and the requester accesses the description using a UDDI or other type of registry, and requests the execution of the provider's service by sending a SOAP message to it. The basic Web services standards are good for some SOA-based applications but are not adequate for many others.

Why UDDI Is Not a Core Web Services Specification

It's safe to say that the original vision of UDDI has not been realized. When UDDI was launched in late 2000, it was intended to become a public directory. Companies were supposed to register their Web services with UDDI, and other companies were to come along later and dynamically discover the services they needed to access over the Internet. The assumption, which has not proven true, was that companies would be interested in discovering and requesting services from providers with whom they had no prior relationship. Also UDDI was developed before WSDL, so initially

continues

WSDL was not well supported. The data structures proved to be problematic because they are so open-ended with very little required information and a structure based on categorization data that isn't universally recognized. UDDI was also positioned as an inside-the-enterprise technology, and here it has gained some measure of success; however, the standards remain incomplete for this purpose. Companies adopting UDDI for internal use have to define their own naming conventions and categorization structure and metadata, which inhibits adoption. While SOAP and WSDL have gone on to tremendous success and widespread adoption, UDDI still struggles to find its proper place in the Web services universe. It is clear that a service registry is a required part of the Web services platform, but it isn't clear that UDDI will ever truly become that solution.

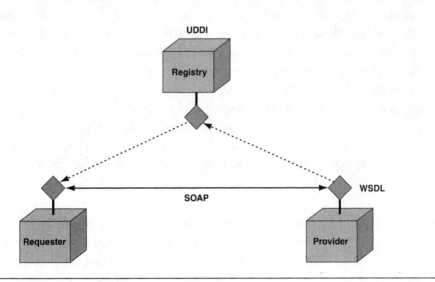

Figure 1-6   Basic Web services architecture.

Besides the core Web services specifications (SOAP and WSDL), a wide array of extended Web services specifications for security, reliability, transactions, metadata management, and orchestration are well on their way toward standardization, providing SOA-based solutions the necessary enterprise-level qualities of service to support a wide variety of mission-critical, corporate-wide projects.

Borrowing from the Web

Some of the important advantages of using Web services as the technology platform for an SOA are derived from the way in which the World Wide Web achieved its tremendous success; in particular, the fact that a simple document markup language approach such as HTML (or XML) can provide a powerful interoperability solution and the fact that a lightweight document transfer protocol such as HTTP can provide an effective, universal data transfer mechanism. On the Web, it doesn't matter whether the operating system is Linux, Windows, OS390, HP NonStop, or Solaris. It doesn't matter whether the Web server is Apache or IIS. It doesn't matter whether the business logic is coded in Java, C#, COBOL, Perl, or LISP. It doesn't matter whether the browser is Netscape, Internet Explorer, Mozilla, or the W3C's Amaya. All that matters is that the Web servers understand an HTTP request for an HTML file and that the browser understands how to render the HTML file into the display. Web services provide the same level of abstraction for IT systems. Similarly, all that matters for Web services is that they can understand and process an XML-formatted message received using a supported communications transport and return a reply if one is defined. Just as HTML and HTTP can be added to any computer system with a TCP connection, Web services can be added to any computer that understands XML and HTTP or XML and most other popular communications transports.

Figure 1-7 illustrates the features and capabilities of the complete Web services platform on which the broad range of SOA-based applications can be built. It includes the basic and extended Web services specifications. See Chapter 2, "Overview of Service-Oriented Architecture," for a complete description of the Web services platform.

The Web services platform contains the basic and extended features necessary to support an SOA, along with an enterprise service bus (ESB) to connect the services.

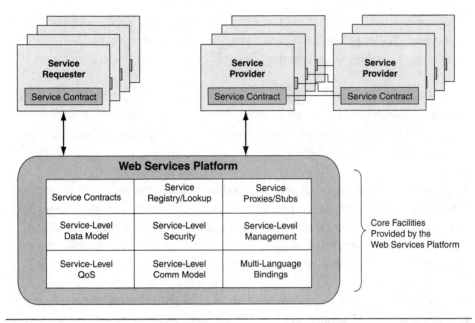

Figure 1-7   Web services platform.

Rapid Integration

A few years ago, businesses finding themselves in need of comprehensive integration solutions turned to products and practices developed specifically for that purpose. However, these enterprise application integration (EAI) products proved to be expensive, consumed considerable time and effort, and were subject to high project failure rates. Furthermore, because these various special purpose products are proprietary, many of the projects resulted in additional difficulties whenever a company invested in more than one of them.

Recent experience shows that a better answer is available by using Web services standards. Instead of dealing with the complexity of multiple incompatible applications on multiple computers, programming languages, and application packages by introducing an EAI product, it's possible to add a layer of abstraction that's open, standards-based, and easy to integrate with virtually any new and existing environment.

A new generation of integration products from BEA, IBM, IONA, Microsoft, SAP, SeeBeyond, Systinet, Tibco, WebMethods, and others, enabled by Web services technology, is emerging around the concepts of service-oriented integration.

The combination of Web services and SOA provides a rapid integration solution that more quickly and easily aligns IT investments and corporate strategies by focusing on shared data and reusable services rather than proprietary integration products.

To illustrate the benefits of service-oriented integration, consider the example of three fairly typical financial industry database applications, perhaps supporting retail banking, commercial banking, and mutual fund investment operations. The applications were developed using a classic three-tier architecture, separating presentation logic, business logic, and database logic.

As shown in Figure 1-8, it's possible to reuse a traditional three-tier application as a service-oriented application by creating services at the business logic layer and integrating that application with other applications using the service bus. Another benefit of service orientation is that it's easier to separate the presentation logic from the business logic when the business logic layer is service-enabled. It's easier to connect various types of GUIs and mobile devices to the application when the business logic layer is service-enabled than if a separate tightly coupled presentation logic layer has to be written for each. Instead of running the presentation logic tier as a tightly coupled interface on the same server, the presentation logic can be hosted on a separate device, and communication with the application can be performed using the service bus.

Applications can more easily exchange data by using a Web service defined at the business logic layer than by using a different integration technology because Web services represent a common standard across all types of software. XML can be used to independently define the data types and structures. And finally, the development of service-oriented entry points at the business logic tier allows a business process management engine to drive an automatic flow of execution across the multiple services.

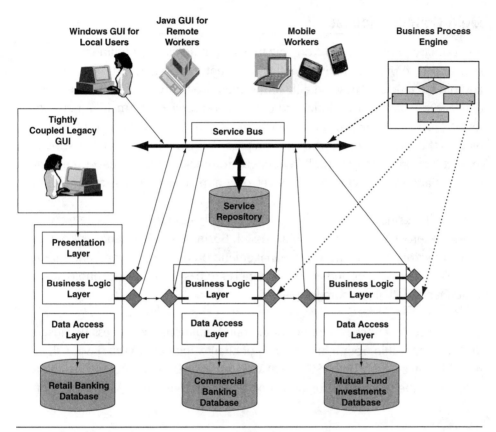

Figure 1-8   Designing for service-oriented integration.

Creating a common Web services layer or "overlay" of services into the business logic tiers of applications also allows you to use a common service repository in which to store and retrieve service descriptions. If a new application wishes to use an existing service into one of these applications, it can query the repository to obtain the service description and easily generate SOAP messages to interact with it.

Multi-Channel Access

The primary purpose of most organizations (commercial, government, non-profits, and so on) is to deliver services to clients, customers, partners, citizens, and other agencies. These organizations often use many channels for service delivery to reach their customers to ensure good service and maintain customer loyalty. Just as a bank prefers to offer services in a variety of ways for the convenience of their customers, whether using the Web, an ATM, or a teller window, many other organizations similarly benefit from being able to deliver a mixture of direct and indirect customer services over a mixture of access channels.

In general, business services change much less frequently than the delivery channels through which they are accessed. Business services represent operational functions such as account management, order management, and billing, whereas client devices and access channels are based on new technologies, which tend to change more frequently.

Web services interfaces are good for enabling multi-channel access because they are accessible from a broad range of clients, including Web, Java, C#, mobile devices, and so on. SOA with Web services is, therefore, well suited to simplifying the task for any organization to enable these multiple channels of access to their services.

Figure 1-9 illustrates an example of multi-channel access in which an organization's customer service application might expose various services for reporting a problem, tracking the status of a problem report, or finding new patches and error reports published to the user community. A customer account manager might want to access the services from his cell phone, to discover any updates to the customer's problem report list, for example, before going on a sales call. If the product was shipped through a reseller, the reseller might provide its own customer service, which would be tied to the supplier company's application to provide first- and second-level support, respectively. The customer service manager for a given major account might benefit from direct access to all of the features, functionality, and information stored in the organization's customer service application. The customers themselves might want to check the status of a trouble ticket from a mobile PDA device. And finally, the support center employees need access to the services in the application to perform their own jobs of interacting with the customers who have problems.

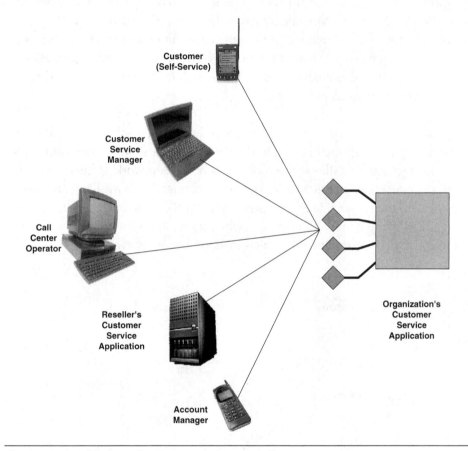

Customer
(Self-Service)

Customer
Service
Manager

Call
Center
Operator

Reseller's
Customer
Service
Application

Account
Manager

Organization's
Customer
Service
Application

Figure 1-9   Multi-channel access to customer service.

In the past, organizations often developed solutions like this as monolithic applications tied to a single access channel, such as a 3270 terminal, PC interface, or a browser. The proliferation of access channels, including new end-user devices, represents an opportunity for a service-oriented enterprise to better serve its customers, suppliers, and partners anytime and anywhere. However, it also represents a significant challenge to IT departments to convert existing monolithic applications to allow multi-channel access. The basic solution is, of course, to service-enable these applications using an SOA with Web services.

Occasionally Connected Computing

Integrating mobile devices into an SOA presents specific challenges because the mobile devices may not always be connected to a network. Mobile devices may also move through network connectivity zones, picking up new IP addresses when they reconnect. Most applications in production today are not designed to handle such variances in network connectivity. A new generation of "mobilized" software is emerging to integrate mobile devices quickly and easily into the service-oriented enterprise.

As shown in Figure 1-10, the SOAP messages in a mobile software solution are transported from the mobile client to the server using a store-and-forward asynchronous protocol that allows the mobile client to keep working even when a network connection isn't available. When the connection is available, transactions flow to the server-side SOA-based application directly using the messaging transport. When a connection isn't available, transactions are stored locally so that they can be transmitted when a connection becomes available.

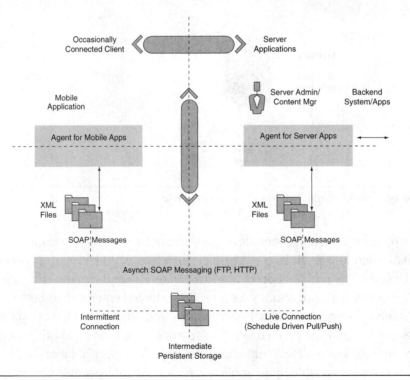

Figure 1-10   Occasionally connected architecture for mobile devices.

Business Process Management

A business process is a real-world activity consisting of a set of logically related tasks that, when performed in the appropriate sequence and according to the correct business rules, produce a business outcome, such as order-to-cash, purchase order fulfillment, or insurance claim processing.

Business process management (BPM) is the name for a set of software systems, tools, and methodologies that addresses how organizations identify, model, develop, deploy, and manage such business processes. A business process may include IT systems and human interaction or, when completely automated, simply the IT systems. Various BPM solutions have been in use for a long time, starting with early workflow systems and progressing up to modern Web services orchestration.

BPM techniques can exploit the foundation and the architectural work provided by an SOA to better automate business processes. This is among the important reasons for investing in a Web services-based SOA because Web services help achieve the goals of BPM more quickly and easily.

BPM systems are designed to help align business processes with desirable business outcomes and ensure that the IT systems support those business processes. BPM systems let business users model their business processes graphically, for example, in a way that the IT department can implement. All IT systems support and implement business processes in one form or another. What makes BPM unique is the explicit separation of business process logic from other application code (this contrasts with other forms of system development where the process logic is deeply embedded in the application code).

Separating business process logic from other application code helps increase productivity, reduce operational costs, and improve agility. When implemented correctly (for example, using BPM as a consumer of an SOA with Web services), organizations can more quickly respond to changing market conditions and seize opportunities for gaining a competitive advantage. Further efficiencies are gained when the graphical depiction of a business process can be used to generate an executable specification of the process.

Business Operational Changes

Most businesses have special operational characteristics derived from the reasons they got into business in the first place. One example is a pizza shop with a 30-minute delivery guarantee. To really make this happen without losing money, all kinds of operational characteristics have to be taken into account, such as pizza baking time, order-taking time, and delivery time within a defined area. Obviously, this is not the kind of operation that can be completely automated because it relies upon human drivers, but certainly many parts of the process could be automated, such as ordering from the Web, automatically triggering the delivery of new supplies to the restaurant, and using robots to prepare and cook the pizzas. Ideally, you'd like to be able to introduce as many operational efficiencies as possible with minimal cost to the IT systems involved. An SOA-based infrastructure can help.

BPM simplifies the problem of how to combine the execution of multiple Web services to solve a particular business problem. If we think about a service as the alignment of an IT system with a business function such as processing a purchase order, we can think about the BPM layer as something that ties multiple services together into a process flow of execution to complete the function, such as validating the order, performing a credit history check on the customer, calculating inventory to determine the ability to fill the order, and finally shipping the order and sending the customer an invoice. By taking the process flow out of the application-level code, the business process can be more easily changed and updated for new application features and functions such as a change in suppliers, inventory management, or the shipping process.

Figure 1-11 illustrates the kind of graph that a business analyst might produce for automating the flow of purchase order processing. The flow starts with the input of a purchase order document. The first processing step is responsible for accepting the document, checking security credentials and providing acknowledgment so that the sender knows the document was received.

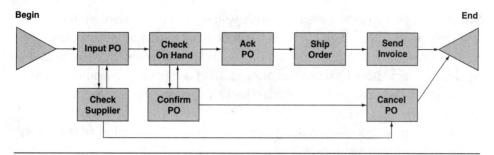

Figure 1-11   Example business process flow for a purchase order.

A typical process engine persists the input document so that the subsequent steps in the graph can access it. After the document is validated, a reference to the document's location in the database or file system is passed to the next step so that it can check whether on-hand inventory is sufficient to fill the required item quantities. If sufficient quantity is on hand, the next step in the flow acknowledges receipt of the purchase order and lets the purchaser know that the company can fill it. This acknowledgment can be sent using email or a Web service message.

At this point, the customer may have an opportunity to reconfirm the order, given the quoted price and delivery schedule. If the customer does not reconfirm, the process is cancelled and moves to the cancellation step (which basically erases the work of steps in the business process to that point, perhaps including one or more compensating transactions to release inventory that had been reserved for this customer and to remove the order from scheduled deliveries). If the customer reconfirms, the next step is activated to prepare the order for shipment. After the shipment confirmation has been received, the process moves to the final step, which sends an invoice to the customer.

Process flows are typically broken into individual tasks that call a Web service. Flows typically include tests that branch the flow based on the results of exectuting a task. Branches of the flow can handle errors. For example, when an item is out of stock from one supplier, the flow might branch to a task that invokes a Web service request to another supplier to find out whether that supplier has the item. Sometimes no one has the item, in which case, the flow might raise an error to the operator or submitter so they can decide what to do.

With a common services-based solution available to IT managers, architects, and developers, productivity increases will be much easier to achieve, and business systems will support the kind of flexibility demanded by the constant market and regulatory changes that are a fact of business and government life. In particular, laying an SOA foundation for business process management allows enterprises to concentrate on higher-level issues such as implementing the best business processes, rather than worrying about the technical details of application implementations.

Extended Web Services Specifications

Following the broad adoption and use of the basic Web services specifications— SOAP and WSDL—requirements have grown for the addition of extended technologies such as security, transactions, and reliability that are present in existing mission-critical applications. These extended features are sometimes also called *qualities of service* because they help implement some of the harder IT problems in the SOA environment and make Web services better suited for use in more kinds of SOA-enabled applications.

A class of applications will find the core specifications sufficient, while other applications will be blocked or hampered by the lack of one or more of the features in the extended specifications. For example, companies may not wish to publish their Web services without adequate security or may not wish to accept purchase orders without reliable messaging guarantees.

The core specifications were defined with built-in extensibility points such as SOAP headers in anticipation of the need to add the extended features.

Standardization

Web services specifications progress toward standardization through a variety of ways, including small groups of vendors and formally chartered technical committees. As a general rule of thumb, most specifications are started by a small group of vendors working together and are later submitted to a standards body for wider adoption. Specifications initially created by Microsoft and IBM, together with one or more of their collaborators (these vary by specification, but typically include BEA, Intel, SAP, Tibco, and Verisign), tend to gain the most market traction. Microsoft and IBM are the de facto leaders of the Web services specification movement and have defined or helped to define all the major specifications. Several of the WS-* specifications remain under private control at the time of writing, but we expect them to be submitted to a standards body in the near future.

Standards bodies currently active in Web services include:

- **World Wide Web Consortium (W3C)**—Making its initial name on progressing Web standards, notably HTTP, HTML, and XML, the W3C is home to SOAP, WSDL, WS-Choreography, WS-Addressing, WS-Policy, XML Encryption, and XML Signature.

- **Organization for the Advancement of Structured Information Standards (OASIS)**—Originally started to promote interoperability across Structured Generic Markup Language (SGML[1]) implementations, OASIS changed its name in 1998 to reflect its new emphasis on XML. OASIS is currently home to UDDI, WS-Security, WS-BPEL, WS-Composite Application Framework, WS-Notification, WS-Reliability, Web Services Policy Language (part of the Extensible Access Control Markup Language TC), and others such as Web Services for Remote Portlets, Web Services Distributed Management, and Web Services Resource Framework, which are not covered in this book.[2]

- **Web Services Interoperability (WS-I)**—Established in 2002 specifically to help ensure interoperability across Web services implementations, WS-I sponsors several working groups to try to resolve incompatibilities among Web services specifications. WS-I produces specifications called *profiles* that provide a common interpretation of other specifications and provides testing tools to help Web services vendors ensure conformance to WS-I specifications.

---

[1] Both HTML and XML are derived from SGML.

[2] These specifications are not all covered in this book because the book is focused on SOA.

- **Internet Engineering Task Force (IETF)**—The IETF is responsible for defining and maintaining basic Internet specifications such as TCP/IP and SSL/TLS. Their relationship to Web services is indirect in that TCP/IP is the most common communications protocol used for the HTTP transport, and basic IETF security mechanisms are used in Web services. The IETF collaborated with the W3C on XML Signature.

- **Java Community Process (JCP)**—Established by Sun to promote the adoption of Java and control its evolution, the JCP is home to several Java Specification Requests (JSRs) that define various Java APIs for Web services, including JAX-RPC for the Java language bindings for SOAP, JAX-B for XML data binding, and Java APIs for WSDL.

- **Object Management Group (OMG)**—Initially established to create and promote specifications for the Common Object Request Broker (CORBA), the OMG is home to specifications that define WSDL language mappings to C++ and CORBA to WSDL mappings.

Web services standardization started with the submission of the SOAP 1.1 specification to the W3C in mid-2000. After that, SOAP with Attachments, XKMS, and WSDL were submitted to W3C. At the same time, UDDI was launched in a private consortium and was later submitted to OASIS. Other major specifications submitted to OASIS include WS-Security, WS-BPEL, WS-CAF, and WS-Notification. More recently, WS-Addressing and WS-Policy were submitted to W3C, signaling a potential shift back toward W3C as the home of most of the major specifications.

Historically, OASIS is also the home of the ebXML set of specifications, which overlap to a large extent with the Web services stack. Web Services and ebXML share SOAP, but beyond that, the stacks diverge. ebXML has its own registry and its own orchestration (or choreography) language.

Standardization and Intellectual Property Rights

One of the difficulties with respect to Web services standardization is the fact that no single standards body is clearly in a leadership position.

continues

Specifications work is split across W3C, OASIS, WS-I, IETF, and OMG. How does a specification become an adopted standard? If anyone had a magic formula for this, they would be millionaires. In the end, it's market acceptance and adoption that makes the difference, and this means the economic factors become paramount, both in terms of vendor investment and customer procurement. Web services vendors often initiate work on specifications informally in small teams for the sake of rapid progress, publish the specifications themselves, and then submit the specifications to a standards body. Microsoft pioneered this approach with SOAP 1.1, and other vendors including BEA, HP, IBM, IONA, Oracle, SAP, Sun, Tibco, WebMethods, and others have significantly contributed to specifications this way. However, a major question with this approach often arises when it's time to submit the specification to an open standards body. In particular, it's necessary to resolve issues related to intellectual property (IP) rights, including copyrights and patents. It's an important step in a specification's lifetime, even if the standards body doesn't change it very much. Only when a specification is submitted to an open standards body and the IP issues resolved (or at least publicly declared) can that specification truly achieve widespread adoption. Without this step, software vendors not among the initial authoring community have no visibility into specification changes, which could invalidate their investments in products, and they might be faced with potential IP licensing fees, whether royalties or otherwise, that the specification owners might wish to charge.

Specification Composability

As mentioned previously, the SOAP and WSDL specifications are designed to be extended by other specifications. Two or more of the extended specifications can be combined within a single SOAP message header. For example:

```
<S:Header>

  <wsse:Security>
  ...
  </wsse:Security>

  <wsrm:Sequence>
```

```
   ...
   </wsrm:Sequence>

</S:Header>
```

This example illustrates the use of extended headers for security and reliability. The security header typically includes information such as the security token that can be used to ensure the message is from a trusted source. The reliability header typically includes information such as a message ID and sequence number to ensure the message (or set of messages) is reliably received.

Note the separate namespaces used for the security and reliability headers, wsse: and wsrm:, respectively. The headers use different namespaces so that they can be added incrementally to a SOAP message without concern over potential name clashes. Duplicate element and attribute names are not permitted in an XML document (and a SOAP message is an XML document, after all). Namespace prefixes provide a unique qualifier for XML element and attribute names, thus protecting names from duplication. This is one way in which SOAP header extensions work composably with each other.

Adding extended features may or may not require modification to existing Web services—that is, the extended features can be added into the SOAP headers without changing the SOAP body in many cases. But the execution environments and mapping layers may need to change in order to handle the extensions. Certainly at least adding SOAP headers for extended features must be done within the context of knowing whether the execution environment can support them and how; otherwise, the extended headers will not work.

Web service extensions are also added to the responsibility of the SOAP processors in the execution environment. Policy declarations associated with the WSDL contracts can be used during the generation of SOAP messages to determine what should go into the headers to help the execution environment negotiate the appropriate transport protocol or to agree on features such as transaction coordination.

As illustrated in Figure 1-12, each additional extended feature added to the Web service invocation results in additional processing before sending the message or after receiving it. Later chapters provide further detail on each of these extended features. The extended features may also be related to requirements from a business process engine and may need to be supported by the registry.

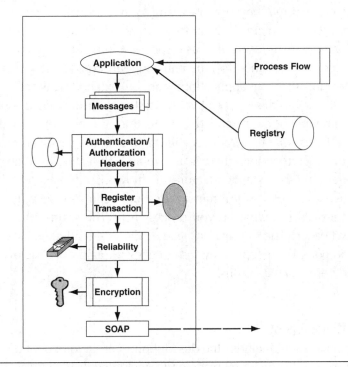

Figure 1-12   Adding extended features to SOAP.

Composability and Complexity

Supposedly, the composability of extended Web services specifications allows their incremental use or "progressive discovery" of new concepts and features. IBM and Microsoft, as the de facto leaders of the Web services specifications development, are obviously keen to avoid making them too complex. A large part—if not the largest part—of the value of Web services derives from their relative simplicity. CORBA, for example, is often criticized for being too complex and too hard to use. Of course, CORBA is

continues

easier than what preceded it, but CORBA is relatively complex compared to Web services. The issue with complexity is finding people well enough trained to use the technology productively, and because the highest IT cost is still labor, complexity typically means additional project expense. So for Web services to keep their promises, and to avoid having the whole effort fall apart, IBM and Microsoft want to preserve simplicity even as they start adding complex features to the basic specifications. One argument is that Web services are designed to inherently support composition of new features, meaning existing applications can be extended instead of being changed. However, this is a relatively untested assertion because products that fully implement the extended specifications are not yet available, and it isn't at all clear that the products will implement the extended features in the same way. Furthermore, there is no overall architecture for Web services that defines how the extended features really work with each other. When you receive a complex SOAP message full of headers for security, reliability, and transactions, what do you process first? The security header? The reliability header? The transaction header? No one really knows. If this all proves too complex, people may just go back to plain old XML over HTTP and hand code the extensions.

Metadata Management

Metadata management includes the description information about a Web service necessary to construct a message body (including its data types and structures) and message headers so that a service requester can invoke a service. The provider of the service publishes the metadata so that a requester can discover it and use it to construct messages that can be successfully processed by the provider.

When invoking a service, it's important to understand not only the data types and structures to send but also the additional qualities of service provided (if any), such as security, reliability, or transactions. If one or more of these features are missing from the message, it may prevent successful message processing.

Metadata specifications include:

- **XML Schema**—For message data typing and structuring and expressing policy information.

- **WSDL**—For associating messages and message exchange patterns with service names and network addresses.

- **WS-Addressing**—For including endpoint addressing and reference properties associated with endpoints. Many of the other extended specifications require WS-Addressing support for defining endpoints and reference properties in communication patterns.

- **WS-Policy**—For associating quality of service requirements with a WSDL definition. WS-Policy is a framework that includes policy declarations for various aspects of security, transactions, and reliability.

- **WS-MetadataExchange**—For querying and discovering metadata associated with a Web service, including the ability to fetch a WSDL file and associated WS-Policy definitions.

Service binding is different for an SOA based on Web services compared to an SOA based on J2EE or CORBA, for example. Instead of binding via reference pointers or names, Web services bind using discovery of services, which may be dynamic. If the service requester can understand the WSDL and associated policy files supplied by the provider, SOAP messages can be generated dynamically to execute the provider's service. The various metadata specifications are therefore critical to the correct operation of an SOA based on Web services.

Addressing
Addressing is an important requirement of extended Web services because no directory of Web services endpoint addresses exists on the Web. SOAP messages must include the endpoint address information within the message for all but the simplest MEP. WS-Addressing replaces earlier proposals called WS-Routing and WS-Referral.

Without an addressing solution, when you send a Web service request to a provider, typically the only address the provider has is the return address to the requester, and then only for the duration of the session. If anything goes wrong on the reply, there's no good way to retry it—basically the requester's address can be lost when there's a communication failure. Also there's no good way to specify a different return address than the requester's address. And finally, there's no way to define address schemes or to identify endpoint addresses for complicated message exchange patterns or multi-transport support.

Policy

Policy is necessary for expressing any extended Web services features of a service so that the requester can provide the necessary security, transaction, or reliability context in addition to the data requirements for the messages expressed in the WSDL file.

Policy provides a machine-readable expression of assertions that a service requester must adhere to in order to invoke upon a provider. Does the service require security or support transactions? The latter can be very important when trying to figure out whether or not a long running, complex interaction can involve a transaction, or whether a transaction can span across all the Web services identified for it.

WS-Policy is necessary for achieving interoperability for the extended features because the policy declarations are the only way in which a requester can discover whether a provider requires some or all of the extended features. In the case of security, for example, different providers may support different kinds of tokens, such as X.509 or Kerberos. WS-Security is designed as a kind of open framework that can carry any token type. However, if the token type the provider expects isn't declared, the requester can only guess at what it must be.

When making the decision to invoke the provider's service, it may also be important to discover whether it supports reliability or transactions. You might want to know, for example, whether the provider's service can accept retries if the original submission fails and whether it will let you know when it has successfully received a message. Finally, you may want to know whether or not to send a transaction context to the provider to enroll the provider Web service in the transaction.

Acquiring Metadata

It's possible that a requester will obtain the metadata it needs using WS-MetadataExchange or another similar mechanism that queries the WSDL and associated policy files directly. WS-MetadataExchange uses a feature of WS-Addressing called "actions" to access the metadata published by a service provider. WS-MetadataExchange is designed to provide any and all information about a Web service description—essentially replacing UDDI for most applications.

Developers may or may not use UDDI, despite its existence. It's fair to say that the public UDDI does not provide the metadata management facilities required to support interoperability requirements at the extended specification level and that WS-MetadataExchange may be needed for requesters to ensure they have the information they need to achieve interoperability with providers using extended features.

Security

Security concerns apply at every level of the Web services specification stack and require a variety of mechanisms to guard against the numerous challenges and threats that are a part of distributed computing. The mechanisms may have to be used in combination to guard against a particular threat or combination of threats. In the Web services and SOA world, it's particularly important to evaluate the need for protection at the network layer, the message layer, and for the data in the message.

Basic security protection mechanisms are built around encryption, authentication, and authorization mechanisms and typically include comprehensive logging for problem tracking. The industry has achieved consensus around a single specification framework, WS-Security, although ongoing work is necessary to complete the profiles and additional related specifications.

WS-Security was developed to provide message-level security on an end-to-end basis for Web services messages. Typical HTTP-based security mechanisms, such as SSL, provide only transport-level point-to-point protection. Sometimes additional security may be provided through the use of an alternative transport mapping, such as CORBA's IIOP or WebSphere MQ, but as with the rest of the extended features, the security specifications are written for HTTP as a kind of default or lowest common denominator transport and therefore can be applied to any transport.

WS-Security headers include the ability to carry strong authentication formats such as Kerberos tickets and X.509 certificates and can use XML Encryption and XML Signature technologies for further protecting the message contents. Although a WS-Security authorization profile for the Security Assertion Markup Language (SAML) is being developed, SAML can also be used on its own for exchanging authorization information.

Additional specifications from IBM, Microsoft, Verisign, and others further extend and complement WS-Security, including:

- **WS-SecurityPolicy**—Defines security assertions detailing a Web service's requirements so that the service requester can meet them.

- **WS-Trust**—Defines how to establish overall trust of the security system by acquiring any needed security tokens (such as Kerberos tickets) from trusted sources.

- **WS-SecureConversation**—Defines how to establish and maintain a persistent context for a secure session over which multiple Web service invocations might be sent without requiring expensive authentication each time.

- **WS-Federation**—Defines how to bridge multiple security domains into a federated session so that a Web service only has to be authenticated once to access Web services deployed in multiple security domains.

Because Web services are XML applications, and because XML has security challenges of its own (it is basically human-readable text sent over the Internet), XML-based security technologies are also often important for protecting the XML data before and after it's included in a SOAP message. These technologies include:

- **XML Encryption**—Designed to provide confidentiality, using a variety of supported encryption algorithms, of part or all of an XML document to ensure that the contents of a document cannot be intercepted and read by unauthorized persons.

- **XML Signature**—Designed to provide integrity, using a variety of encryption and signature mechanisms, to ensure that service providers can determine whether or not documents have been altered in transit and that they are received once and only once.

XML Encryption and XML Signature can be used to protect Web services metadata as well as data.

Reliability and Messaging

Messaging includes SOAP and its various message exchange patterns (MEP). The industry has not achieved consensus on a single, unified set of specifications for advanced messaging. However, competing specifications in the categories of reliability and notification work essentially the same way, and so an amalgam of the two is used here for the sake of introduction.

In general, reliable messaging is the mechanism that guarantees that one or more messages were received the appropriate number of times. Reliable messaging specifications include:

- WS-Reliability.

- WS-ReliableMessaging (from IBM and Microsoft).

Reliable messaging is designed to ensure reliable delivery of SOAP messages over potentially unreliable networks such as the HTTP-based Internet.

Reliable messaging is a protocol for exchanging SOAP messages with guaranteed delivery, no duplicates, and guaranteed message ordering. Reliable messaging works by grouping messages with the same ID, assembling messages into groups based on message number, and ordering them based on sequence number.

Reliable messaging automates recovery from certain transport-level error conditions that the application would otherwise have to deal with on its own. Reliable messaging also supports the concept of bridging two proprietary messaging protocols over the Internet.

Also in the general messaging area are specifications for extended MEPs such as event notification and publish/subscribe, which basically extend the asynchronous messaging capability of Web services. Specifications in this area include:

- WS-Eventing.

- WS-Notification.

Notification delivers messages through an intermediary often called a message broker or event broker. Subscribers identify the channels or topics for which they wish to receive messages. Publishers send messages to the channels or topics on which subscribers are listening. Notification is a messaging mechanism that can be used to set up broadcast and publish/subscribe messaging.

Transactions

Transactions allow multiple operations, usually on persistent data, to succeed or fail as a unit, such as processing an order or transferring funds. One of the most important aspects of transaction processing technologies is their ability to recover an application to a known state following an operating system or hardware failure. For example, if any failure occurs before a funds transfer operation is completed (that is, both the debit and credit operations), transactions ensure the bank account balances are what they were before the funds transfer operation started.

Many Web services applications may require only the transaction processing capabilities inherent in the underlying execution environment, such as those provided by application servers and databases. Others may require multiple Web service invocations to be grouped into a larger transactional unit, including a transactional context within SOAP headers so that the transaction can be coordinated across multiple execution environments.

Web services transaction specifications extend the concept of the transaction coordinator, adapt the familiar two-phase commit protocol for Web services, and define new extended transaction protocols for more loosely coupled Web services and orchestration flows. Transaction coordinators currently exist in most execution environments, including J2EE, the .NET Framework, and

CORBA. Web services specifications define extensions for these (and other) coordinators for compensation-based protocols and long-running coordinator-coordinator protocols that bridge software domains.

Coordination is a general mechanism for determining a consistent, predefined outcome for composite Web service applications. The coordinator model includes two major phases: the acquisition phase in which Web services that are participating in the composite are enrolled with the coordinator for a specific protocol (such as two-phase commit, compensation, or business process) and a second phase in which the coordinator drives the agreed-upon protocol to completion following the end of the execution of the set of services in the composite. When a failure occurs, the coordinator is responsible for driving the recovery protocol (if any).

The specifications in this area include:

- **WS-Transactions family** from BEA, IBM, and Microsoft:

  - **WS-AtomicTransactions**—Defines volatile and durable variations of a standard two-phase commit protocol for short-lived executions.

  - **WS-BusinessActivity**—Defines variations on the idea of tentative commit and compensation-based undo protocols for longer-lived executions.

  - **WS-Coordination**—Defines the coordinator for the two pluggable protocols (and their variations).

- **WS-Composite Application Framework (WS-CAF)** from OASIS:

  - **WS-Context**—Defines a standalone context management system for generic context (that is, for non-transaction protocol contexts such as security, device and network IDs, or database and file IDs).

  - **WS-CoordinationFramework**—Defines a coordinator for the basic context specification and the pluggable transaction protocols in the WS-TransactionManagement specification.

  - **WS-TransactionManagement**—Defines three transaction protocols for the pluggable coordinator: ACID, long-running actions (compensation), and business process management.

Both sets of specifications are centered on an extended coordinator with plug-gable transaction protocols. Both sets of specifications define atomic transactions (i.e., two-phase commit) and compensation-based transactions. WS-CAF breaks context management into a separate specification and adds a third transaction protocol specifically designed for business process management.

Orchestration

Web services can and eventually will be published for most software systems and applications within a given IT environment, and in fact across multiple organizations' IT environments. Rather than have Web services invoke each other using one or more of the message exchange patterns supported by SOAP and WSDL, an orchestration engine can be used to create more complex interaction patterns in long-running business process flows with exception handling, branching, and parallel execution. To accomplish this, the orchestration engine has to preserve context and provide correlation mechanisms across multiple services.

A Web service orchestration may also be published as a Web service, providing an interface that encapsulates a sequence of other Web services. Using the combination of MEPs and orchestration mechanisms, entire application suites can be built up out of Web services at multiple levels of encapsulation, from those that encapsulate a single software module to those that encapsulate a complex flow of other Web services.

The industry has reached a consensus around a single orchestration specification: the OASIS Web Services Business Process Execution Language (WS-BPEL). WS-BPEL assumes that Web services are defined using WSDL and policy assertions that identify any extended features.

Typically, a flow is initiated by the arrival of an XML document, and so the document-oriented Web services style tends to be used for modeling the entry point to a flow. Parts of the document are typically extracted and operated upon by the individual tasks in the flow, such as checking on the inventory availability for each line item from a different supplier, meaning the steps in the flow may be implemented using a combination of request/response and document-oriented Web services.

The WS-BPEL specification differs from other extended specifications in that it defines an executable language compatible with various software systems that drive business process automation. Whereas most other Web services specifications are XML representations of existing distributed computing features and capabilities that extend SOAP headers, orchestration represents the requirement for composing Web services in a declarative manner.

The W3C's Web Services Choreography Definition Language (WS-CDL) is another specification in the general area of orchestration. Choreography is defined as establishing the formal relationship between two or more external trading partners. One difference between WS-CDL and WS-BPEL is that WS-CDL does not require Web services infrastructure at all of the endpoints being integrated.

Strategic Value of Orchestration

Some people say orchestration is where Web services gain their strategic value. Web services have intrinsic value because of the relative ease with which they allow developers to solve interoperability problems across disparate types of software. Web services orchestration can be used in a variety of ways ranging from creating composite services in a declarative (non-programmatic) manner to full-blown business process management. Using Web services orchestration for BPM is clearly more difficult because it requires a deep understanding of an enterprise's business processes. In any case, it is true that the orchestration layer is where everyone expects the solution to be found to the hard problems of data type and structure incompatibilities, semantic data matching, and correlating the results of multiple Web services. It will take a while to prove whether or not these problems can really be solved at the orchestration layer and whether or not automated business process management is something companies really want or need at either the departmental or enterprise level.

Summary

So, we can see that the Web services standards, both the core and extended specifications, contribute significantly to the ability to create and maintain service-oriented architectures on which to build new enterprise applications. These applications are often called composite applications because they work through a combination of multiple services.

We've seen that SOA is not an end in itself but a preparation for a longer journey. It's a set of maps and directions to follow that lead to a better IT environment. It's a blueprint for an infrastructure that aligns IT with business, saves money through reuse of assets, rapid application development, and multi-channel access.

Web services have had an initial success with the core standards and are now on to the next step in the journey, which is to define extended features and functions that will support more and more kinds of applications.

Service orientation provides a different perspective and way of thinking than object orientation. It's as significant a change as going from procedure-oriented computing to object-oriented computing. Services tend toward complementary rather than replacement technology, and are best suited for interoperability across arbitrary execution environments, including object oriented, procedure oriented, and other systems.

Part I

SOA and Business Process Management Concepts

Part I introduces the major concepts of service, service-oriented architecture (SOA), and business process management (BPM). This part of the book describes how to develop and implement SOA and BPM solutions using Web services:

- Addressing the main reasons for investing in an SOA, including rapid integration, multi-channel access, and automated business process management.

- Focusing on the business and technical benefits of services and service orientation that underpin IT agility.

- Defining and detailing the features and capabilities of the Web services platform upon which SOA, BPM, and other solutions are built.

- Introducing Web services orchestration and choreography, including examples of the WS-BPEL and WS-CDL specifications.

■ Describing how SOA- and BPM-based solutions can be implemented using Web services specifications, including the extended specifications described in Part II.

Although Web services technologies provide the ideal platform for SOA-based solutions, including BPM, we also identify where and how the Web services platform does not yet provide a complete solution.

Chapter 2

Overview of Service-Oriented Architecture

The notion of services is deeply rooted in the business world. Service orientation is an organizational principle that applies to business and government as well as to software. The best place to start when trying to gain a better understanding of service-oriented architecture (SOA) is to review the types of services that businesses and governments provide to customers, clients, citizens, and partners, and how they provide them.

Service-Oriented Business and Government

Every business and government organization is engaged in delivering services. Here are some examples:

- **Bank**—Savings accounts, checking accounts, credit cards, safety deposit boxes, consumer loans, mortgages, credit verification.

- **Travel agency**—Holiday planning, business travel, travel insurance, annual summary of business travel expenditures.

- **Insurance agency**—Car insurance, home insurance, health insurance, accident asses

- **Retail store**—In-store shopping, online shopping, catalog shopping, credit cards, ext
  warranties, repair services.

- **Lawyer's office**—Legal advice, escrow services, will preparation, business incorporat
  bankruptcy proceedings.

- **Hospital**—Emergency medical care, in-patient services, out-patient services, chronic
  management.

- **Department of transportation**—Driver testing and licensing, vehicle licensing, licens
  administration, vehicle inspections and emissions testing.

- **Department of human services**—Benefits disbursement and administration, child sup
  services and case management.

- **Police department**—Law enforcement, community education.

These services are delivered in a variety of ways. The three most common approaches to se
delivery are:

- **Human-mediated delivery**—A human agent acting on behalf of the business or gove
  agency is involved in delivering some or all of the service to the customer, client, cit
  partner.

- **Self-service delivery**—The customer, client, citizen, or partner obtains the service on
  own, typically using an automated system provided by the business or government a

- **System-to-system service delivery**—The service is performed automatically for the c
  client, citizen, or partner by the business or government agency and usually involves
  mated interactions among two or more computer systems—examples include autom
  check deposit and business-to-business (B2B) exchanges.

Figure 2-1 illustrates the service-oriented business. A single service can be delivered using d
more service delivery approaches. For example, checking the status of an airline flight can
achieved as follows:

- **Human-mediated service delivery**—The traveler calls the airline's call center and asl
  call center agent about the status of the flight.

- **Self-service delivery**—The traveler goes to the airline's Web site and looks up the status of the flight using the flight number.

- **System-to-system service delivery**—The airline automatically notifies the traveler of changes in the status of the flight via an email or Web service (based on preferences previously defined by the traveler) and re-books her car rental based on the expected delay.

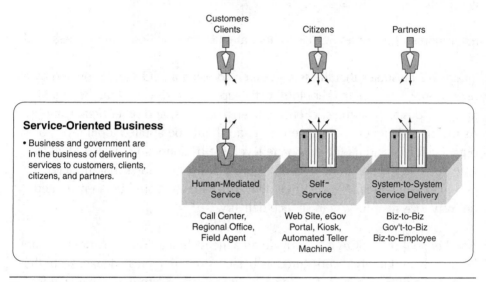

Figure 2-1   Service-oriented business.

The notion of a service-oriented business (or government) does not apply just at the boundary between the organization and its customers, clients, and partners; it also applies to the services that business units and departments within a single company supply to each other. For example:

- The legal department supplies contracting services to the sales department when a sale is being negotiated with a customer.

- The shipping department supplies order fulfillment services on behalf of the sales department to complete a sale.

- The information services department provides computer systems to the finance department so that the finance department can track accounts receivable and accounts payable.

Service-Oriented Architecture Concepts

A service-oriented architecture (SOA) is a style of design that guides all aspects of creating and using business services throughout their lifecycle (from conception to retirement), as well as defining and provisioning the IT infrastructure that allows different applications to exchange data and participate in business processes regardless of the operating systems or programming languages underlying those applications.

An important goal of an SOA is to help align IT capabilities with business goals.

Figure 2-2 illustrates that the services created using an SOA and provided by an organization's IT systems should directly support the services that the organization provides to customers, clients, citizens, partners, and other organizations. As mentioned earlier, this concept can and should be applied to all levels of the organization including the corporate level, the business unit level, and all the way down to the department level. Figure 2-2 also illustrates that the services provided using an SOA support all delivery channels, from human-mediated delivery to system-to-system service delivery.

Another goal of an SOA is to provide an agile technical infrastructure that can be quickly and easily reconfigured as business requirements change. Until the emergence of SOA-based IT systems, business and government organizations were faced with a difficult trade-off between the expense of a custom solution and the convenience of a packaged application. The promise of SOA is that it will break down the barriers in IT to implementing business process flows in a cost-effective and agile manner that combine the advantages of custom solutions and packaged applications while reducing lock-in to any single IT vendor.

Not surprisingly, the key organizing concept of an SOA is a service. The processes, principles, and methods defined by the SOA are oriented toward services (sometimes called service-oriented development). The development tools selected by an SOA are oriented toward creating and deploying services. The run-time infrastructure provided by an SOA is oriented to executing and managing services. In an SOA, services are the fundamental unit of the architecture for the following:

- Sharing business information across department and application boundaries.

- Updating business information across department and application boundaries.

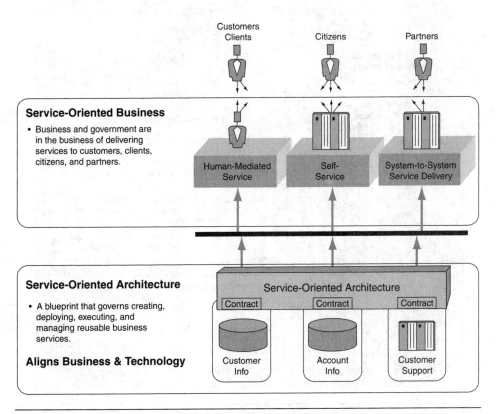

Figure 2-2   Using SOA to align business and information technology.

Any IT architecture must focus on certain things while deferring responsibility on other topics that are not the focus of the architecture. For example, a security architecture focuses on security from the GUI layer to the data layer, whereas a data architecture focuses on how data is modeled, secured, and managed across all application tiers.

Not surprisingly, an SOA focuses on all aspects of services while deferring responsibility on issues that fall into other areas of the enterprise architecture such as application architecture, integration architecture, information architecture, and so on.

Figure 2-3 illustrates the key elements of an SOA.

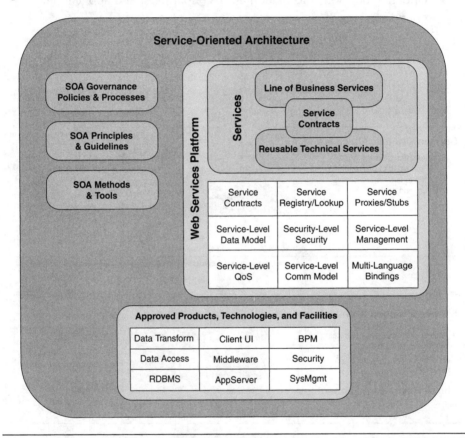

Figure 2-3   Key elements of a service-oriented architecture.

Is SOA Just Another Application Architecture?

Sometimes people wonder if SOA is just another form of application architecture. The short answer is "No, an SOA represents a different way of

continues

structuring systems and is a distinct element of an enterprise architecture, although it is true that an SOA must support the application architecture and the development of new applications."

Application architecture is concerned with delivering specific business functionality to specific user groups in a manner that allows them to do their job quickly and efficiently while meeting other organizational goals such as ROI, cost-effectiveness, and security. In many cases, the application architecture will offer guidelines and define the approved tools for delivering several types of applications, including "rich" client applications, Web applications, and mobile applications. In many cases, application architecture has included everything necessary for delivering the applications, including GUI design, business logic, and database design—this was true for 3270 applications, client/server applications, and many Web applications.

SOA focuses on defining and delivering business services and technical services (see the sections "Line of Business Services" and "Reusable Technical Services" later in this chapter) that provide business functionality and that are reusable across multiple user groups, multiple business processes, multiple application styles, and multiple delivery channels (including automated business-to-business delivery, something that application architecture is not concerned with) and is not concerned about how these services are combined into applications and presented to specific user groups.

For organizations using SOA, the application architecture will need to evolve away from a tightly coupled "GUI-to-DBMS" approach to a service-assembly approach that emphasizes building applications by assembling services from both internal and external sources.

The following sections describe the key elements shown in Figure 2-3.

SOA Processes, Principles, and Tools

An SOA is a living, breathing, growing, and evolving entity. Because an SOA changes over time, processes, principles, and tools need to be put in place to facilitate its evolution and growth.

The SOA Governance Policies & Processes box in Figure 2-3 represents the high-level processes for governing the SOA, including the SOA decision-making and issue-resolution processes, roles and responsibilities of teams, development processes, testing processes, quality assurance processes, registering services, versioning services, and so on.

The SOA Principles & Guidelines box in Figure 2-3 defines the principles that guide architects and developers when defining business and technical services, such as the principle of reusability that needs to be taken into account whenever designing or developing a service.

The SOA Methods & Tools box in Figure 2-3 defines the methods (analysis, design, testing, and so on) and tools (design tools, development tools, test tools, MDA, UML, and so on) that have been approved for use in this SOA. In general, the SOA should be based on Web services standards as much as possible so that it is independent of any single product and so that different products from different vendors can be used as part of the SOA as necessary.

Services

From a business perspective, services are IT assets that correspond to real-world business activities or recognizable business functions and that can be accessed according to the service policies that have been established for the services. The service policies define who or what is authorized to access the service, when the service is available, the cost of using the service, reliability levels for the service (e.g., mean time between failures), security levels for the service (e.g., privacy and integrity requirements), performance levels for the service (e.g., response time), and so on. The service policies should be captured in policy assertions where and when possible.

From a technical perspective, services are coarse-grained, reusable IT assets that have well-defined interfaces (a.k.a. service contracts) that clearly separate the services' externally accessible interface from the services' technical implementation. This separation of interface and implementation serves to decouple the service requesters from the service providers so that both can evolve independently as long as the service contract remains unchanged.

Each service consists of one or more operations. For example, a Customer-Management service could provide operations such as getContactInformation, registerLead, or updateCorporateAddress. These operations might be implemented using a variety of technologies including J2EE, .NET Framework, or CORBA objects, but none of the details of any of these technologies are visible to the service requesters because WSDL is used for the service description so that any service requester can read it.

The issues that the SOA focuses on are called *service-level abstractions* (see Figure 2-4) because they:

- Deal exclusively with services.

- Define all the important elements of the services.

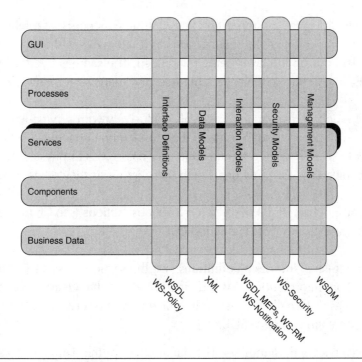

Figure 2-4   Service-level abstractions.

Figure 2-4 puts the service-level abstractions into context. The rows in the figure represent common layers in an enterprise architecture, including the following:

- GUI or end-user interface employed by business users.

- Business processes that coordinate the activities of the organization.

- Services that model and define individual activities in a reusable and technology-neutral manner using Web services.

- Components and objects that are used to implement and execute the services.

- Business data stored in systems-of-record, operational data stores, data warehouses, data marts, and reporting systems.

The columns in Figure 2-4 represent cross-cutting concerns that might apply to different layers. For example, security applies to all layers, although its exact meaning depends on the layer being referenced. The same is true for interface definitions, interaction models, data models, and management models.

Figure 2-4 emphasizes that an SOA deals exclusively with service-level abstractions. Therefore, even though some of the cross-cutting concerns like security might involve everything from managing user passwords to physical security of the data center, the SOA only deals with these issues as they relate to services.

Here is a description of the key service-level abstractions (see Chapter 3 for more information on the following topics):

- **Service-level interface definitions** (see the section "Service Contracts" for more information)—Well-defined interface that clearly separate the services' externally accessible interface from the services' technical implementation using WSDL.

- **Service-level data model**—The data model for the data that is defined in the service-level interfaces and exchanged among services. The service-level data model is defined using XML Schema referenced in the WSDL service contracts. The service-level data model for the SOA also defines which XML constructs are prescribed (if any) and which business-specific XML libraries should be used (if any).

- **Service-level interaction model**—Which interaction modes are available for interacting with services (e.g., request/reply, request/callback, one-way, publish/subscribe) defines the service-level interaction model.

- **Service-level security model**—The approach taken to securing services (such as how service requesters are authenticated, how and when service requesters are authorized, how SOAP messages are encrypted) defines the service-level security model.

- **Service-level management model**—The approach taken to managing services (such as deploying, starting, stopping, and monitoring services) defines the service-level management model.

These service-level abstractions can be applied to a single operation defined as part of a service, or a single service (which is made up of multiple operations), or a collection of services drawn from a specific line of business or business domain. For example, the service-level data model for a single service defines the data types used by all operations that make up that service. In contrast, the service-level data model for a set of line of business services will define the common vocabulary that those services will use to exchange data.

As an SOA scales up to deal with more and more services, then the notion of service-level abstractions becomes more and more important so that we can deal with collections of services, rather than individual services, when appropriate.

Line of Business Services
The Line of Business Services layer provides business services that automate (in whole or in part) the business services that the organization delivers to its customers, clients, citizens, and partners either directly (e.g., self-service) or indirectly (e.g., by providing information to an employee who performs a task on behalf of the customers, clients, citizens, and partners). For example, a bank teller might access an account creation service when opening an account for a new customer. The customer interacts with the teller, who interacts in turn with

the service provided by the IT system. The business services provided by the Line of Business Services layer includes services implemented by the organization's IT systems and services that it sources from third-party providers.

Granularity of Business Services

Clearly, the granularity of business services varies from organization to organization and process to process.

At one end of the spectrum, the business services map directly to the services that the organization offers to customers, clients, and partners. Google and Amazon are simple examples of organizations that have taken services they offer to customers via Web applications and made them directly available as business services.

At the other end of the spectrum are situations where business services simply automate specific business tasks that are part of larger services that the organization provides to customers, clients, and partners. For example, a bank that offers commercial loans as a business service may implement a credit check Web service that it uses as part of the loan origination process but that it doesn't offer to customers. (However, if the credit check Web service is properly designed and implemented, then the bank has the option of offering it to customers directly as a new service.)

Line of business services tend to be specific to a particular *service domain* such as finance, sales, marketing, manufacturing, shipping, engineering, case management, benefits management, or patient management (however, some line of business services are reusable across service domains). All services in a service domain should communicate using a common data vocabulary so that these services can be easily composed and used together.

Often services from different service domains will have inconsistent or even contradictory data vocabularies (e.g., "customer" means something different to the sales department and the shipping department) and therefore the Web services platform needs to provide facilities for data transformation when service requests cross service domain boundaries.

Reusable Technical Services

The Reusable Technical Services layer defines services that are not specific to a single line of business and that are reusable across multiple lines of business. For example, services that fall into this category include data transformation, data access, auditing, logging, and identity management.

Services in this category break from our emphasis on business services but are nevertheless extremely valuable to the business because they address a very serious business requirement: risk mitigation. One of the core benefits of an SOA is that it permits organizations to separate the business logic from a lot of the infrastructure functionality, thereby increasing the consistency and reliability of the infrastructure and enhancing business agility. Without a reliable, flexible infrastructure, the line of business services won't work.

Don't Let Reusable Technical Services Hijack Your SOA

Some IT organizations spend too much time building reusable technical services rather than delivering line of business services.

Sometimes this occurs because the IT organization has deep technical skills but only a cursory understanding of the business and the needs of its clients, customers, and partners. The deep technical skills drive the IT organization to build reusable technical services because they are closer to its "comfort zone."

Sometimes this occurs because the goals of the SOA are misunderstood. Ideally, an SOA is intended to help align the IT department with the business goals of the organization. However, if the success of the SOA is measured solely on service reuse, then the IT department may spend an inordinate amount of time building technical services such as logging services and auditing services that are reusable across all business projects, even though they may not contribute significantly to the organization's business goals.

Service Contracts

Every service (i.e., line of business services and reusable technical services) has a well-defined interface called its service contract that clearly separates the service's externally accessible interface from the service's technical implementation. The importance of the service contract in an SOA cannot be overstated. The formal contract is the mechanism that allows us to formalize system and scope boundaries, minimize dependencies, maximize adaptability, use black box testing, select among services, and more easily change service suppliers.

Web Services Platform

The Web services platform defines the standards and run-time facilities available to all services so that they can interact and interoperate in a consistent manner independent of the underlying technology. It is a "platform" in the sense that it provides the well-defined, ubiquitous service delivery infrastructure. It is a "service platform" because its primary purpose is facilitating the delivery of services (as opposed to, for example, an "application platform," which facilitates the creation of applications).

The key elements of the Web services platform are the Web services standards, including:

- Defining the business documents that are to be exchanged using XML and XML Schemas.

- Exchanging data using SOAP as the message format and HTTP as the transport protocol.

- Defining service contracts using WSDL for interface metadata and the WS-Policy family of standards for policy metadata.

- Registering and discovering services using UDDI.

- Securing services using WS-Security.

- Supporting multiple interaction patterns and providing additional qualities of service using WS-ReliableMessaging and WS-Eventing.

- Transaction management using the WS-Transactions family of specifications or the WS-CAF family of specifications.

- Managing services using WSDM.

Although the Web services platform is based on the Web services standards, it may be extended using other standards and technologies necessary for filling business-specific, industry-specific, or organization-specific requirements that are not covered by the extended Web services standards. For example:

- XBRL (Extensible Business Reporting Language) for filing reports with the SEC.

- FIXML (Financial Information eXchange Markup Language) for exchanging trading instructions among financial services organizations.

- LDAP (Lightweight Directory Access Protocol) for registering and finding resources.

- RDF (Resource Description Framework) for defining resources.

Care must be taken when extending the Web services platform to ensure that the features and functions exposed by services built on the platform do not contain vendor-specific features or break interoperability. In some cases, of course, this may also mean negotiating with a trading partner to ensure they conform to the same extended standards.

And finally (and this is really an SOA governance issue), every organization should explicitly define its own profile of the Web services platform and a roadmap for it (a statement of the standards and versions of those standards that an organization is going to adopt and when they are going to adopt them). Every business is different (e.g., the legacy systems and infrastructure it has in place, the types of services it offers, its tolerance for new technology, or its tolerance for risk) and will have different requirements. For example, you may not need transactions, or you may decide that you require Kerberos tickets rather than X.509 tickets for security, or you may not have a requirement for WS-SecureConversations, and so on.

Why Do We Call It the Web Services Platform?

Why do we call it the Web services platform when it is mostly defined by open, standards-based specifications? Isn't a "platform" associated with a specific piece of executable code, such as the Windows platform, or BEA's WebLogic platform, or SAP's NetWeaver platform?

Although it is true that some software platforms are tied to a specific piece of executable code, there is also a precedent for platforms that are based on APIs, specifications, and standards. For example:

- **J2EE (Java 2 Platform, Enterprise Edition)**—Web server, servlet engine, session beans, entity beans, message-driven beans, JDBC, JMS, JNDI, and many more APIs and services.

- **CORBA**—Distributed objects, CORBA IDL, portable object adapter, IIOP, Java language binding, and C++ language binding plus specifications for more than a dozen CORBA services.

- **Web application platform**—Browser, URLs, HTML, Cascading Style Sheets, and HTTP/S.

At the end of the day, a platform is simply a solid foundation on which you build something else (such as applications or services). If the platform is based on standards and specifications, then the important consideration is the extent to which they are open standards and how widely they are embraced and implemented by multiple vendors.

Heck, even the .NET platform is not tied to a single implementation because the Mono open-source project provides an implementation of the .NET platform that is not Windows-specific.

The Web services platform is the common infrastructure that all service consumers and all service providers can rely upon. Because of this, any service can locate and use any other service in a standardized manner, and new services can be added without affecting existing service domains, service consumers, or service providers. If you do create your own profile of the platform, you will have to find a good way to communicate this to developers inside and outside the company so that they clearly know which standards you support. The WS-PolicyFramework is a good way to accomplish this.

Defining Your Web Services Platform Profile

Deciding that you are going to use Web services as the cornerstone of your SOA is an important decision, but it is the beginning of a journey rather than the end of one. Defining your profile of the Web services platform involves synthesizing a solution that satisfies your organization's requirements by:

- Taking a pragmatic look at the existing and emerging Web services standards.

- Assessing the maturity of these standards and where there are competing standards.

- Assessing the interoperability of these standards across multiple vendor products and the vendors' roadmaps.

- Assessing whether or not the standards are being profiled by WS-I.

- Assessing where the Web services standards do not provide a complete solution and where there are gaps that need to be filled.

- Assessing the unique needs and assets of your organization—for example, if your organization has made a significant investment in building systems using WebSphere MQ, then you might want to take advantage of this investment rather than proposing a rip-and-replace strategy.

For example, WS-Security is a key Web services standard for securing services. However, in some areas, WS-Security simply provides an extensible framework that must mesh with other key architectural decisions such as authentication and authorization. WS-Security provides a mechanism for adding custom SOAP headers to a message for authentication information, but it does not prescribe any particular method of authentication. When you

continues

define your profile of the Web services platform, you need to decide on the particular authentication mechanism(s) that satisfy your organization's requirements (user name/password? X.509 certificates? SAML documents?). Furthermore, if you use security mechanisms at the edges of your organization that are different from what is used for internal business applications, then you'll need to decide how to bridge between these security domains—this is an area where Web services standards such as WS-Federation can assist, but ultimately each organization needs to define a solution that satisfies its own requirements.

Service Requesters and Service Providers

Figure 2-5 illustrates the relationship among service requesters, service providers, and the Web services platform.

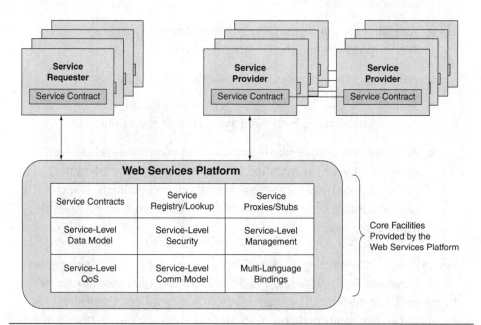

Figure 2-5   Relationships among service requesters and service providers.

A *service provider* is a software module that implements a service according to the service contract. There may be many different service providers for any particular service. A service instance is a run-time instantiation of a service provider. There may be many different service instances of a particular service provider.

A *service requester* is a software module that invokes a service implemented by a service provider to accomplish some task. The service requester uses the capabilities provided by the Web services platform to locate the service (e.g., UDDI) and communicate with it in a secure manner using SOAP, WS-Security, SAML, Kerberos, X.509, and so on.

A service provider may also be a service requester (that is, service requesters and service providers can be arranged into N-tier architectures).

Approved Products, Technologies, and Facilities

While the SOA is primarily concerned with providing an architecture for defining and using services, the SOA must be brought to fruition using products, technologies, and standards that have been approved for use as part of the SOA for modeling, developing, deploying, orchestrating, managing, and securing services. One of the responsibilities of the SOA governance policies and processes (see the next section) established by an organization is to define a list of products, technologies, and facilities that have been approved by that organization for realizing the SOA.

For instance, once an organization has defined a Web services platform based on Web services (e.g., SOAP, WSDL, UDDI, WS-Security, WS-Reliable-Messaging, and so on), it must also identify the internal facilities (such as Web server(s), application server(s), programming languages, email applications, GUI development tools, RDBMS(s), and so on) that are used to implement the service requesters, service providers, and Web services platform.

Although services provide the loosely coupled (see the section "Loosely Coupled Services") interfaces for accessing business functions, internal facilities almost always exhibit a relatively high degree of coupling. For example, assumptions can be made regarding the execution environment that is being used: Transactional and security functions are handled by the application server container. Language features can be fully used, which is fine within the confines of a single service.

Some capabilities (e.g., data transformation) may be available as both technical services and internal facilities. When this is the case, the service requesters and service providers can choose which version they want to use (i.e., they can choose between using the technical service or the internal facility) depending on factors such as performance and the degree of coupling they are willing to tolerate.

Service Governance, Processes, Guidelines, Principles, Methods, and Tools

Many organizations believe that they have adopted an SOA simply because they are using Web services technologies such as SOAP, WSDL, and/or UDDI. However, SOA is a discipline and mindset, not just an application of technology, and it touches almost every IT activity including the processes, methods, and tools that are used for designing, developing, deploying, managing, and maintaining IT assets.

SOA Governance Policies and Processes

The purpose of SOA governance is to align software governance and business governance including coordinating software development, acquisition, and (re)use across domains to achieve maximum agility and economies of scale/scope. SOA governance is really an extension of IT governance that focuses on managing services and the related service-level abstractions.

SOA governance recognizes that services are corporate assets that need to be managed throughout their service lifecycle. This is because services provide a common unit of management for requirements, service-level agreements, business and technical performance, and resource utilization.

The SOA governance policies and processes must answer basic questions such as:

1. **Why**—The goals of adopting an SOA and an SOA governance framework.

2. **Who**—The stakeholders and participants in the governance process.

3. **What**—Their roles, responsibilities, and activities.

4. **How**—The processes, structures, and meetings that must be in place for the SOA governance framework to operate effectively.

5. **When**—The timing around activities.

At a minimum, the SOA governance policies and processes should define and implement the following processes:

- Service lifecycle processes that govern proposing a new service, initial deployment of a new service, versioning a service, and retiring a service.

- SOA decision-making and issue-resolution process.

- SOA design and development process.

- Monitoring the business performance of services, including ROI.

- Monitoring the technical performance of services, including security.

- Ensuring that Web services standards are complied with and used appropriately.

The SOA governance policies and processes should establish a governing body within the enterprise that has representation from each service domain and the different business units and from subject matter experts who can speak to the key technological components of the solution. This governing body should define the policies and processes for identifying, implementing, deploying, and versioning services. This can range from a completely decentralized process (where each department or project is responsible for identifying, implementing, and deploying services that it wishes to make available to the rest of the organization) to a centralized process (where this governing body reviews addition and deletion of services, as well as changes to existing services, before authorizing their implementation and deployment). In either case, it is important that there is some level of standardization across departments and projects to promote service reuse.

The SOA governance policies and processes should identify mandatory and optional training that members of the SOA team and the larger project teams should complete to effectively implement the SOA processes and use the SOA tools.

The SOA governance policies and processes should identify the tools that the SOA will use for project management, business modeling, service modeling, data modeling, development, system management, and so on, and how these tools will exchange models/information.

SOA Principles and Guidelines

SOA principles and guidelines guide architects and developers when defining business and technical services.

The most important of these principles and guidelines are listed here. See the next section for a more in-depth discussion.

> **Principle #1**—Services are the central organizing concept of an SOA.
>
> **Principle #2**—Every service is defined by a formal contract that clearly separates the functionality being provided from the technical implementation.
>
> **Principle #3**—Services should only interact with other services through their well-defined public interfaces.
>
> **Principle #4**—Services should be accessible through standardized technologies that are available across a wide range of environments. This also implies that the invocation mechanisms (protocols, transports,

discovery mechanisms, and service descriptions) should comply with widely accepted industry standards. This means using SOAP, WSDL, XML, XML Schema, HTTP, JMS, and UDDI.

Principle #5—Services should be defined at a level of abstraction that corresponds to real world business activities and recognizable business functions so as to better align business needs and technical capabilities.

Principle #6—Services should be meaningful to service requester. Avoid letting legacy systems and implementation details dictate services and service contracts.

Principle #7—Services should be loosely coupled.

Principle #8—Collections of related services should use the same XML document types to facilitate information exchange among related services, and the structure and semantics of the documents must be agreed to and well understood.

Principle #9—Services should perform discrete tasks and provide simple interfaces to access their functionality to encourage reuse and loose coupling.

Principle #10—Services should provide metadata that defines their capabilities and constraints, and this metadata should be available in a repository, which itself can be accessed through services. This allows service definitions to be inspected without needing access to the service itself. This also allows service requesters to dynamically locate and invoke the service, and through indirection, it provides location transparency.

Key Service Characteristics

Services are touted as providing numerous technical and business benefits. This section presents the key characteristics that should go into the design, implementation, and management of services in order to deliver the touted technical and business benefits. The benefits derived from these characteristics are discussed in the next two sections.

The *primary characteristics* that should go into the design, implementation, and management of services are as follows:

- Loosely coupled.

- Well-defined service contracts.

- Meaningful to service requesters.

- Standards-based.

A service should also possess as many of the following *secondary characteristics* as possible in order to deliver the greatest business and technical benefits:

- Predictable service-level agreements.

- Dynamic, discoverable, metadata-driven.

- Design service contracts with related services in mind.

- Implementation independent of other services.

- Consider the need for compensating transactions.

- Design for multiple invocation styles.

- Stateless.

- Design services with performance in mind.

For maximum business agility and reuse, every service should possess all of these characteristics. However, this is not always possible, and sometimes the cost of adding a particular service characteristic (e.g., making the service stateless) is prohibitive when compared to your organization's goals. When faced with these types of trade-offs, focus on the primary characteristics listed above because they are the key to delivering the greatest business and technical benefits.

Primary Characteristics

Loosely Coupled Services

The notion of designing services to be loosely coupled is the most important, the most far reaching, and the least understood service characteristic. Loose coupling is a broad term that actually refers to several different elements of a service, its implementation, and its usage.

Interface coupling refers to the coupling between service requesters and service providers. Interface coupling measures the dependencies that the service provider imposes on the service requester—the fewer the dependencies, the looser the coupling. Ideally, the service requester should be able to use a service solely based on the published service contract and service-level agreement (see the next section), and under no circumstances should the service requester require information about the internal implementation of the service (for example, requiring that one of the input parameters be a SQL command because the service provider uses a RDBMS as a data store). Another way of saying this is that the interface should encapsulate all implementation details and make them opaque to service requesters.

Technology coupling measures the extent to which a service depends on a particular technology, product, or development platform (operating systems, application servers, packaged applications, and middleware platforms). For instance, if an organization standardizes on J2EE for implementing all services and requires all service requesters and service providers to use JNDI to look up user and role information, then the service is tightly coupled to the J2EE platform, which limits the extent to which diverse service requesters can access these services and the extent to which the service can be outsourced to a third-party provider. Even worse would be a situation where the service requesters and service providers are required to use a feature that is proprietary to a single vendor, which would increase vendor lock-in. This is one of the main reasons to implement your SOA with Web services.

Process coupling measures the extent to which a service is tied to a particular business process. Ideally, a service should not be tied to a single business process so that it can be reused across many different processes and applications. However, there are exceptions. For instance, sometimes it is important to define a service contract for a piece of business functionality (e.g., Photocopy-Check) that is only used in one business process so that you have the option of non-invasively substituting another implementation in the future. However, in this case, don't expect the service to be reusable across different processes and applications.

Well-Defined Service Contracts

Every service should have a well-defined interface called its service contract that clearly defines the service's capabilities and how to invoke the service in an interoperable fashion, and that clearly separates the service's externally accessible interface from the service's technical implementation (see also Chapter 3). In this context, WSDL provides the basis for service contracts; however, a service contract goes well beyond what can be defined in WSDL to include document metadata, security metadata, and policy metadata using the WS-Policy family of specifications.[1] It is important that the service contract is defined based on knowledge of the business domain and is not simply derived from the service's implementation. For example, suppose a service implementation uses an array to hold up to 10 customer orders. It would be a mistake to define the service contract to return a maximum of 10 customer orders (unless the upper limit of 10 customer orders is based on a business rule drawn from the business domain, and maybe not even then, given the volatility of business rules).

Although it is not widely recognized, service contracts are generally more valuable than the service implementations. This means that the service contract embodies significant business knowledge—the service contract is the basis for service sharing and reuse and is the primary mechanism for reducing interface coupling.

As a corollary, it is important to recognize that the service contract is independent of any single service implementation and that the service contract should be defined and managed as a separate artifact.

---

[1] Refer to [Bertrand Meyer, *Object-Oriented Software Construction*. Prentice Hall Professional Technical Reference, 1997, ISBN 0-13-629155-4] for an excellent discussion of design-by-contract as applied to object-oriented software construction—the parallels to defining service contracts are unmistakable.

Furthermore, changing a service contract is generally much more expensive than modifying the implementation of a service because changing a service contract might require changing hundreds or thousands of service requesters, while modifying the implementation of a service does not usually have such far reaching effects. As a corollary, it is important to have a formal mechanism for extending and versioning service contracts to manage these dependencies and costs.

Meaningful to the Service Requester

Services and service contracts must be defined at a level of abstraction that makes sense to service requesters. An appropriate level of abstraction will:

- Capture the essence of the business service being provided without unnecessarily restricting future uses or implementations of the service.

- Use a business-oriented vocabulary drawn from the business service domain to define the business service and the input and output documents of the business service.

- Avoid exposing technical details such as internal structures or conventions to service requesters.

An abstract interface promotes *substitutability*—that is, the interface captures a business theme and is independent of a specific implementation, which allows a new service provider to be substituted for an existing services provider as necessary without affecting any of the service requesters. In this way, defining abstract interfaces that are meaningful to service requesters promotes loose coupling.

In general, services should perform discrete tasks and provide simple interfaces to encourage reuse and loose coupling.

Open, Standards-Based

Services should be based on open standards as much as possible.

Using open standards provides a number of advantages, including:

- Minimizing vendor lock-in. The Web services platform is defined using open, standards-based technologies so that service requesters and service providers are isolated from proprietary, vendor-specific technologies and interfaces.

- Increasing the opportunities for the service requester to use alternative service providers.

- Increasing the opportunities for the service provider to support a wider base of service requesters.

- Increasing the opportunities to take advantage of open source implementations of the standards and the developer and users communities that have grown up around these open source implementations.

Besides complying with technology standards (such as SOAP, WSDL, UDDI, and the WS-* specifications), it is also important to base the service-level data model and the service-level process models on mature business domain standards and vertical industry standards as they become available (e.g., FIXML, UCCNet, and RosettaNet define vertical industry standards).

Secondary Characteristics
Predictable Service-Level Agreements
This service characteristic defines the extent to which a service's SLA can be relied upon. Typically, SLAs define metrics for services such as response time, throughput, availability, mean time between failure, and so on. Furthermore, SLAs are usually tied to a business model whereby service requesters pay[2] more for a higher SLA and service providers pay a penalty when they do not honor their SLAs.

Service requesters need SLAs to determine if a service satisfies their non-functional requirements (the service contracts allow them to determine if a service satisfies their functional requirements).

---

[2] For internal services, payment might not involve money, but it might involve some other incentive that the organization has established for internal accounting.

Service providers need SLAs to answer questions regarding how many service instances should be running, whether or not it is necessary to dynamically provision new services, whether services should be centralized at a single location or geographically distributed to multiple locations, what failover and recovery policies are needed, and so on.

The first rule for SLAs is to establish them and monitor them. SLAs should be established early because they affect service design, implementation, and management. Also make allowances to renegotiate the service objectives after the implementation is complete.

Ideally, your Web services platform should provide service-level management capabilities for defining SLAs, monitoring SLAs, logging SLA violations, and for metering service usage.

Dynamic, Discoverable, Metadata-Driven

Services should be published in a manner by which they can be discovered and consumed without intervention of the provider (depending on circumstance, some level of intervention by the provider may be necessary when the service is only intended for a well-defined group of authenticated service requesters, whereas in other cases, where the service provider is encouraging wide-spread reuse and has the infrastructure in place (such as Google and Amazon), the services may be consumed without any intervention by the provider). Service contracts should use metadata to define service capabilities and constraints. The service contracts should be machine-readable (i.e., XML Schema, WSDL, and the WS-Policy family of specifications) so that they can be dynamically registered and discovered. This lowers the cost of locating and using services, reduces errors associated with using services, and improves the management of services.

Design Service Contracts with Related Services in Mind

No service is an island. When designing service interfaces for a particular business domain, design the service-level data model and all of the related interfaces together. This is because all the services from this business domain will use elements from the same service-level data model. For example, all human resource services should have a consistent definition of "Employee."

By designing the service-level data model and the service interfaces together, you will be able ensure that data elements are defined and applied in a consistent manner and avoid situations where two services use similar but slightly different definitions of, say, "Customer."

Service-Level Data Model

By "service-level data model," we mean the XML Schema definition of the business documents that the services use to exchange information. Sometimes an organization will know the key business documents that need to be exchanged (e.g., PurchaseOrder or EmployeeRecord) prior to defining the services and the service interfaces, and other times, an organization will define the business documents and the service interface together.

In either case, it is important that all related services share the same service-level data model, including the structure and semantics of the business documents.

Implementation Independent of Other Services

Services should be implemented to minimize the dependencies among them. Most importantly, services should be self-sustaining so that they can interoperate with other services without unnecessary internal dependencies and without sharing state.

This is similar to the notion in object-oriented programming that each object should manage its own state. However, object classes often have dependencies such as inheritance relationships (e.g., most OOPLs) and "friend" relationships (e.g., C++), which are undesirable for services.

Consider the Need for Compensating Transactions

A business transaction is implemented by invoking a business service. If a business transaction needs to be corrected, then a compensating transaction should be executed by invoking a business service that implements the compensating transaction (see the section "Protocol Types" in Chapter 10, "Transaction

Processing," for an explanation of the differences between transaction rollback and transaction compensation).

Design the services for a business transaction and the corresponding compensating transactions together because this increases the likelihood that the business rules associated with the business transaction and the corresponding compensating transactions will be defined and applied consistently.

In addition, avoid using two-phase commit style transaction management across multiple independent services because this approach does not scale up efficiently, especially in situations involving geographically distributed services that are accessed over unreliable networks, such as the Internet. However, two-phase commit transactions are sometimes appropriate within the scope of a single service if all the resources being managed by the transaction are co-located and under the control of the same administrative unit (e.g., department).

Design for Multiple Invocation Styles

Design and implement service operations that support multiple invocation styles, including the following:

- Asynchronous queuing.

- Request/response.

- Request/callback.

- Request/polling.

- Batch processing.

- Event-driven, publish/subscribe.

The key insight is that in most cases, the business logic implemented by a service provider is completely independent of the invocation style. For instance, the business logic for debiting a bank account and returning the new account balance is independent of how the service is invoked and how the response is to be delivered. Implementing service operations that support multiple invocation styles makes them more reusable because they can be used in a wider range of situations and in a wider range of business processes.

Asynchronous Messaging

If forced to choose one invocation style to support, then choose asynchronous queuing (or publish/subscribe based on persistent queues) because:

- It scales better when services are geographically distributed.

- It scales better when services are accessed over unreliable networks.

- It decreases time-oriented dependencies and thus decreases coupling.

- It allows processes to continue even when systems can't respond and the process does not need an immediate response.

As Web services mature, support for asynchronous messaging is also maturing. One alternative for asynchronous messaging with Web services is WS-ReliableMessaging (see Chapter 9). The other alternative for asynchronous messaging with Web services is sending SOAP over JMS and WebSphere MQ (in Chapter 3, see the sections "Asynchronous Store-and-Forward Messaging," "Service-Level Communication and Alternative Transports," and "A Retrospective on Service-Oriented Architectures").

Design Stateless Services

Services should be stateless. In particular, they should be implemented so that each invocation is independent and does not depend on the service maintaining client-specific, conversational in-memory or persistent state between invocations.

Stateless interactions scale more efficiently because any service request can be routed to any service instance. In general, statefull interactions do not scale as efficiently because the server needs to remember which service is serving which client and cannot reuse a service until the conversation is finished or a timeout has expired (however, there are exceptions to this rule because it is sometime much more efficient to maintain state than to reconstruct state).

Design Services with Performance in Mind

Service invocations should not be treated like local function calls—location transparency means that a service can be on another machine on the same LAN or another machine on a different continent.

Also avoid fine-grained services. Instead of several short invocations, try to compose the services into one with a larger payload or with multiple business documents.

SOA Guidelines for Service Requesters

Whenever possible, service requesters should invoke service providers using a high-level service proxy:

- The service proxy should provide an easy-to-use interface that is specifically tailored to the service requester's programming model (e.g., for Java clients, the service proxy might provide a JAX-RPC interface).

- The service proxy should encapsulate the details of the SOAP binding (including data format and middleware transport such as HTTP, HTTPS, or JMS) so that these can be changed in the future as necessary.

- It should be possible to control the behavior of the service proxy using configuration data so that it can easily adapt to changes in data format and middleware transports without impacting the service requester.

The service requester should always have the option of bypassing the service proxy and manipulating the input and output XML messages directly.

Service Proxies

There are three common approaches for service requesters to invoke services that involve different levels of abstraction and different trade-offs.

The first approach, and the most primitive one, is for the service requester to create the entire SOAP message (including the SOAP envelope and SOAP

continues

body) using the XML-DOM (or string manipulation primitives) and call the transport-level API to send the message to the service endpoint.

The second approach is to use a documented-oriented service proxy. In Java, this type of service proxy is an object that represents the service and has one method for each service operation. The parameters to the Java methods are XML documents that correspond to the WSDL parts for that operation. When the service requester calls the proxy, it passes the appropriate XML documents as parameters, and the proxy (and/or the underlying run-time system) validates the XML documents against the corresponding XML Schema types, creates a SOAP message by building the SOAP envelope and using the XML documents to assemble the body of the SOAP message, and then calls the transport-level API to send the SOAP message to the service endpoint.

The third approach is to use an object-oriented service proxy. In Java, this type of service proxy is an object that represents the service and has one method for each service operation. The parameters to the Java methods are Java objects generated according to the WSDL parts for that operation. When the service requester calls the proxy, it passes the appropriate Java objects as parameters, and the proxy (and/or the underlying run time system) converts the Java objects to XML documents, creates a SOAP message by building the SOAP envelope and using the XML documents to assemble the body of the SOAP message, and then calls the transport-level API to send the SOAP message to the service endpoint.

In general, use service proxies (approach 2 and 3) instead of creating and manipulating the entire SOAP message directly (approach 1). This is because approach 1 is much more error-prone, requires detailed understanding of SOAP and WSDL, and does nothing to abstract away the underlying transport-level APIs.

The type of service proxy that you should use depends on the circumstances:

- Use document-oriented service proxies (approach 2) when (a) the data being exchanged represents business documents that can be easily mapped to XML Schema or (b) the data being exchanged

continues

represents business documents and XML applications, such as XPath, XSLT, and XQuery, which are well-suited to manipulating the documents and enforcing business rules associated with the business documents.

■ Use object-oriented service proxies (approach 3) when (a) the operation's parameters have been derived from a domain object model or (b) the operation's parameters are naturally represented as objects or (c) the application developers have little experience using XML directly or (d) the application is using other products/technology that produce/consume objects (such as a GUI framework, OODBMS, rules engine, or report generator).

Be aware that the decision of whether and when to use service proxies has nothing to do with the style (*rpc* versus *document*) or encoding (*soap-encoded* versus *literal*). In most cases, object-oriented service proxies (Java, C#, C++) accept programming language objects as parameters and serialize the objects as either rpc/document or soap-encoded/literal SOAP messages (and conversely the object-oriented service proxies take incoming SOAP messages and convert them to programming language objects). Similarly, document-oriented proxies serialize/de-serialize XML documents to and from SOAP messages using the necessary SOAP style and encoding.

SOA Guidelines for Legacy Systems and Legacy Services

Legacy services are services provided by existing production systems. Legacy services should be treated like other services, including being defined by a formal service contract (described using WSDL) and published in the service registry.

Legacy services that abstract existing applications should define contracts that:

■ Capture the essence of the services provided by the legacy system but that are independent of the current interface and current technology.

- Implement a wrapper for the legacy system that maps between the newly defined service contract and the legacy system.

- Do not expose the type system of the implementation language.

If the legacy service is accessed via middleware, then encapsulate the underlying middleware (e.g., JMS, WebSphere MQ, Tibco Rendezvous, or CORBA Notification) and:

- **Do not allow the underlying middleware to spoil your interfaces by exposing middleware specific APIs**—This may require using or creating a legacy gateway that acts as a SOAP endpoint and that is capable of receiving SOAP messages from service requesters before relaying them to the legacy service.

- **Hide protocol and encoding dependencies**—This may require using or creating a legacy gateway that translates between SOAP messages and the native message format of the middleware.

- **Do not expose middleware-specific data types or structures**—This may require using or creating a legacy gateway than translates between XML data types and the native data types of the middleware.

- **Do not expose middleware-specific error codes.**

- **Hide component models (Java, EJB, CORBA, DCOM).**

Technical Benefits of a Service-Oriented Architecture

Services that possess the characteristics discussed earlier deliver the following technical benefits:

- Efficient development.

- More reuse.

- Simplified maintenance.

- Incremental adoption.

- Graceful evolution.

In general, these are considered technical benefits because they deliver most of their benefits to the IT organization in terms of lower development costs, faster development cycles, and lower maintenance costs. Some of these benefits also contribute to the business benefits discussed in the next section.

Efficient Development

An SOA promotes modularity because services are loosely coupled. This modularity has positive implications for the development of composite applications because:

- After the service contracts have been defined (including the service-level data models), each service can be designed and implemented separately by the developers who best understand the particular functionality. In fact, the developers working on a service have no need to interact with or even know about the developers working on the other business services.

- Service requesters can be designed and implemented based solely on the published service contracts without any need to contact the developers who created the service provider and without access to the source code that implements the service provider (as long as the developers have access to information about the semantics of the service; for example, the service registry may provide a link to comprehensive documentation about the semantics of the service).

Independent Development

In many ways, SOA will redefine how business applications are developed. In the past, individual business applications were developed for a particular group of users to automate a particular business process. This high degree of specialization resulted in business logic that was tightly coupled to that particular business application and business process.

As SOAs mature, we'll begin to see organizations developing reusable business services independently of any single business application or business

continues

process, and application development will increasingly rely on creating composite applications by assembling pre-existing business services. The degree to which organizations will create reusable Web services will depend on the extent to which they are designed as reusable business services.

At the application level (i.e., when a developer wants to create a new composite application based on existing services), there are two distinct, well-defined tasks. The first task is to model the application in terms of the data it produces and consumes. After the model has been defined, the application can be created by composing or orchestrating the available services.

For simple applications, the services can be composed by simply calling them programmatically from the service requester.

For complex applications or applications where the service-composition-logic is likely to change, service composition or orchestration is best handled using a product designed for that purpose (such as one that supports WS-BPEL; see Chapter 6).

More Reuse

One of the great promises of an SOA is that service reuse will lower development costs and speed time to market. SOA pioneers such as Credit Suisse and AXA have demonstrated that service reuse can be achieved and can reduce development costs (see Chapter 3, in the section "A Retrospective on Service-Oriented Architectures").

The following service characteristics contribute to greater reuse:

■ **Meaningful to the service requester**—This characteristic makes it easier for the developer to find the right service.

- **Well-defined service contracts published in a service repository**—This characteristic makes it easier for the developer to find the right service. Proper registration policies and standardized taxonomies enable easy discovery.

- **Dynamic, discoverable, metadata-driven**—This characteristic makes it easier for development-time tools to find the right service and fully or partially generate artifacts for using the service and for run-time code to dynamically adapt to changing conditions.

- **Loose process coupling**—Services that are decoupled from a single business process are easier to reuse across different applications.

- **Loose technology coupling**—This characteristic is supported by the Web services platform and allows service requesters to reuse services even if they are implemented using different technology (e.g., J2EE or .NET Framework). The developer does not have to worry about compiler versions, platforms, and other incompatibilities that typically make code reuse difficult.

- **Open, standards-based**—This characteristic increases interoperability, so there is a better chance that you can interact with the service at run-time.

- **Predictable service-level agreements**—This characteristic makes it easier for the developer to verify that the service will satisfy any availability, reliability, and performance requirements.

- **Design for multiple invocation styles**—This characteristic makes it possible for a service provider to be reused in many different scenarios, including request/response, asynchronous messaging, and publish/subscribe interactions.

- **Design service contracts with related services in mind**—This characteristic makes it easier to share data among services so that it is easier to reuse them.

Object Reuse vs. Service Reuse

In general, object technology has been successful in achieving a high degree of reuse. Over the years, countless object libraries and object frameworks have been developed and reused for everything from GUI development (e.g., Microsoft Foundation Classes, Java Swing) to container and utility classes (e.g., C++ Standard Template Library) and data access frameworks. This work has been complemented and extended by the pioneering work done on design patterns. In a nutshell, here is the verdict:

- Building objects is easy.

- Building high-quality, reusable objects (including object libraries and object frameworks) is hard. And it is doubly hard when it comes to building business objects that can be reused across multiple applications in the same business domain.

- Reusing object libraries and object frameworks is moderately hard because it requires object-oriented programming skills and an understanding of inheritance, polymorphism, templates, and so on, but it is much easier than building the equivalent functionality from scratch.

Now let's look at the world of SOA and Web services:

- Building Web services is easy (including adding a Web services wrapper to a legacy system).

- Building high-quality, reusable business services is hard. It requires a combination of business domain expertise and technical design skills.

- Reusing business services is relatively easy because many BPM and WS-BPEL tools support service reuse (i.e., service composition and orchestration) without programming, and services can be reused from any platform independently of the technology in which the service is implemented.

Simplified Maintenance

SOA simplifies maintenance and reduces maintenance costs because SOA applications are modular and loosely coupled. This means that maintenance programmers can make changes to services (even major changes) as long as they adhere to the service contract that the service requesters depend upon without worrying if their changes will affect those who maintain other parts of the system.

Incremental Adoption

Because SOA applications are modular and loosely coupled, they can be developed and deployed in a series of small steps. Often, a reasonable subset of the full functionality can be developed and deployed quickly, which has obvious time-to-market advantages. Additional functionality can readily be added in planned stages until the full feature set has been realized.

Don't Sacrifice Too Much for Reuse

Although reuse is a valuable characteristic, you shouldn't sacrifice everything on the altar of reuse. For example, we've seen projects where a data access service is created that can be reused by every project, application, and department. However, the interface for the data access service accepts a SQL Query as input and returns an XML structure as the result. Although this is a highly reusable service, it violates SOA's loose-coupling principle because it forces the service requester to know about how the data is stored and the structure of data. Violating the loose-coupling principle results in expensive maintenance problems when the internal details of the data source are modified to expose vendor and technology lock-in.

Another benefit of SOA is the ability to start small and grow big. Normally, a software implementation is an all-or-nothing scenario. SOA allows an organization to move at the pace it can afford.

As shown in Figure 2-6, when an organization moves from monolithic applications to SOA, it usually starts with an application portfolio made up of monolithic applications that the IT department focused on for the automation of previously manual business processes. It then moves to an intermediate stage where some of the key business functions are packaged as standalone services that can be reused across multiple applications. Over time, as more and more reusable services are built, applications can be constructed using more and more of them. Furthermore, new functionality should be implemented as services so that services replace code that would otherwise have to be developed from scratch, improving productivity through reuse.

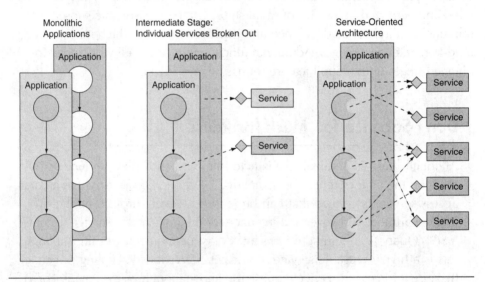

Figure 2-6   Moving toward an SOA.

Graceful Evolution

A service and its associated service contract encapsulate business logic in such a way that other services do not need to know anything about how it provides the service, only about what the service takes as input and returns as a response.

This encapsulation allows service requesters and service providers to evolve gracefully over time. For instance, the service provider can be rewritten and hosted on a lower-cost platform without having any impact on the service requesters.

Service-Oriented Architecture—Business Benefits

Services that possess the characteristics discussed in the section "Key Service Characteristics" deliver the following business benefits:

- Increased business agility.

- Better business alignment.

- Improved customer satisfaction.

- Improved ROI of existing IT assets.

- Reduced integration costs.

- Reduced vendor lock-in and switching costs.

Evaluating the Range of SOA Benefits

The benefits that an organization reaps from using services depend on the goals it sets and the approach it takes:

- Some will adopt a tactical approach by simply building point-to-point connections between systems using SOAP and will be satisfied with those results.

- Others will invest a little more to achieve a little more reuse or a little more business agility.

- Some will make a significant investment, hoping to dramatically improve business agility and achieve significant cost savings.

Of course, these represent only three points on the spectrum.

This is a familiar pattern that we've seen many times for earlier technologies. Consider, for example, the early days of object-oriented computing. At one end of the spectrum were organizations that simply converted to an object-oriented programming language but did not adopt any other object-

continues

oriented techniques. At the other end of the spectrum were organizations that adopted the "complete OO lifestyle," including the following:

- Object-oriented analysis (including UML, use cases, and domain-object models).

- Object-oriented design (including design-by-contract and object-oriented patterns).

- Object-oriented programming languages and tools.

- Object-oriented testing.

- Formally incorporated object-oriented techniques in their project planning approaches, applications architectures, and project management techniques.

And of course, there were as many points on the spectrum between these extremes as there were organizations. It is not surprising that those organizations adopting the complete OO lifestyle reaped the biggest benefits from OO technology. Similar patterns can be seen in the adoption of EAI and BPM.

The message here is that an organization must assess what its goals are in moving to SOA and services. If the goals are ambitious, such as achieving 70% reuse and 70% reduction in development costs, then be prepared to make a significant investment in people, processes, and tools.

Increased Business Agility

By far, the most important business benefit of services and SOA is increased business agility. For many organizations, business agility in the form of quickly responding to new business requirements and opportunities is now more important than development productivity. Two key elements of business agility are velocity and flexibility.

Velocity means moving quickly along a selected path, and in this context, it is means faster time-to-market. SOA improves velocity by dramatically reducing the amount of time required to assemble new business applications from existing services and IT assets.

In this context, flexibility is the ability to adapt IT systems when necessary. We all know that continual change is a fact of life in business and software, and it's also a major source of expense. SOA makes it significantly easier and less expensive to reconfigure and adapt services and IT assets to meet new and unanticipated requirements. Thus, the business adapts quickly to new opportunities and competitive threats, while IT quickly changes existing systems.

Let's look at business agility in terms of specific scenarios:

- **Agility in terms of finding the right service**—Every business relies on business services that it obtains from other organizations. Whether the service is located by word of mouth or by looking in the Yellow Pages, finding the right service quickly and efficiently is vital. This same principle applies to IT services created using an SOA and Web services—it is vital to be able to quickly and efficiently locate the right service, whether it is provided by another department or a partner.

- **Agility in terms of changing service providers**—Sometimes it is necessary to change service providers. Maybe the incumbent service provider goes out of business, is acquired, or discontinues offering the service. Once again, it is vital to quickly and efficiently locate an alternative service provider that provides similar or equivalent capabilities that suits our needs, including our budget.

- **Agility in terms of quickly assembling services into applications**—An agile business can respond to new business opportunities and threats quickly. Services designed with abstract interfaces that are not tied to a single business process are ideal for assembling quickly into new applications. Furthermore, BPM and Web services standards such as WS-BPEL enhance this capability by providing facilities for composing services quickly and easily.

- **Agility in terms of supporting new service requesters and new delivery channels**—Businesses often grow by offering existing services to new customers that are often served by new or alternative delivery channels (call center, Web self-serve, kiosk, ATM, point-of-sale, mobile device, and so on). Services that are loosely coupled and platform-independent can be quickly adapted to support new and alternative delivery channels.

- **Agility in terms of dynamically adjusting capacity to meet increased (or decreased) business demands**—All businesses see demand for services change. Whether it is a spike due to a unique event (e.g., the Super Bowl) or a long-term trend (e.g., due to demographic changes), the agile business must be able to add or shed capacity as necessary. Dynamic provisioning of services is possible because services represent discrete business functions, are dynamically discovered, and are location-independent. Ideally, your Web services platform should directly support dynamic service provisioning so that it can isolate service requesters and service providers from these issues.

- **Agility in terms of using an existing service to support new and unforeseen business requirements**—Services designed with abstract interfaces that are not tied to a single business process can be easily adapted to support new and unforeseen business requirements.

In general, what makes services agile is a combination of factors, including:

- Being loosely coupled.

- Standards-based interfaces.

- Well-defined service contracts.

- Services that are meaningful to service requesters.

- Dynamic, discoverable, metadata-driven services.

Better Business Alignment

Alignment is when all business functions (including IT) support common goals and outcomes. As we already mentioned, the services provided by an organization's IT systems using an SOA approach can and should be defined so that they directly support the services that the organization provides to customers, clients, citizens, and partners.

Using services and an SOA to align business and IT leads to improved service design and development. It does this by streamlining communication of needs and requirements from business users to IT technologists because it helps elevate the discussion to the business level.

Better Business Alignment with Technology

This is a claim that we have all heard before from proponents of object technology, CASE (computer-aided software engineering), 4GLs (fourth generation languages), and business process management, to name a few. One common thread in all of these earlier approaches is that it has only been possible to elevate the discussion to the business level during the earliest phases of analysis and design:

- For instance, object-oriented analysis and design did elevate the discussion to the business level by developing domain object models that better reflected the user's business domain, but object-oriented programming languages, steeped in inheritance and polymorphism, never achieved the same level of success in elevating the discussion to the business level.

- Early BPM efforts were successful in helping organizations to define their "as-is" business processes and even map out "to-be" business processes (but successful implementation was often derailed by people issues and immature BPM products).

These lessons suggest that if we expect to elevate the discussion to the business level using services, then we need to make a concerted effort to engage business users as early and as frequently as possible:

- The SOA should be part of a larger enterprise architecture that includes a business architecture that explicitly models the business and links services to business requirements and needs.

- The SOA needs to define and model the services that the organization provides to customers, clients, citizens, partners, government,

continues

and other departments and that the organization expects these other organizations to provide to it.

■ The SOA needs to define and model the information shared by these services in the most abstract, least technically oriented fashion as possible. Modeling information exchanges based on business documents (real and virtual business documents) is one good way of doing this.

As you can see, creating business-friendly services has more to do with the SOA and less to do with Web services technologies. Furthermore, there is no silver bullet, and an organization can easily create services that are not business-friendly if it does not take the time to understand the business domain or if it concentrates on reusable technical services rather than business services.

Using services and an SOA to align business and IT leads to better management of IT assets because:

■ Metrics about service usage and utilization are easier to understand and more relevant to business users than metrics based on underlying implementation technology layer, such as the databases or message queues.

■ Service-level agreements that ensure a contract's quality of service are easier to understand and more relevant to business users than technical measures, such as server utilization and network capacity.

By using services and an SOA to align business and IT, monitoring the software service can provide feedback that is meaningful to the business.

Improved Customer Satisfaction

Many organizations struggle to provide a consistent customer experience across all customer touch points (face-to-face interaction, web self-service, call center support, ATMs, kiosks, and so on). For example, consider a scenario where an airline's Web site reports that a flight has been delayed but the customer service representative in the call center is unaware of any changes in the flight's status. Customer satisfaction drops when a customer gets contradictory answers to the same request depending on the access mechanism they use.

Customer-centric SOA strives to ensure a consistent customer experience, regardless of the access mechanism the customer is using. It does this by creating services that are independent of any particular technology or end user device, thus allowing one service to be readily reused across all customer touch points.

Furthermore, creating services that are generic enough that they can work with an array of customer-facing systems reduces development time and frees developers to spend more time on creating business solutions.

Reduced Vendor Lock-In and Reduced Switching Costs

In traditional IT systems, vendor or technology lock-in can occur at any number of levels:

- Application platform (e.g., J2EE, .NET Framework, Oracle, CICS, or IMS).

- Packaged application (e.g., SAP, PeopleSoft, or Siebel).

- Middleware technology (e.g., WebSphere MQ, Tibco, or CORBA).

- Specific product feature (stored procedures or cluster caching).

As any CIO can attest, it can be very expensive to break long-established ties to an entrenched packaged application, development platform, or middleware platform.

SOA "future-proofs" an organization and dramatically reduces vendor and technology lock-in. This is because an SOA-centric organization bases its fundamental IT architecture on service contracts, which are aligned to business-level services and which are technology-neutral, application-independent, and middleware-agnostic.

This level of decoupling between the service contracts and the underlying technology makes it much easier to replace applications, technologies, and middleware with new in-house or external service providers when the time comes to make these changes.

Reduced Integration Costs

Integration costs continue to rank among the top CIO concerns.

SOA significantly reduces integration costs for the same reasons that it reduces vendor lock-in: because it is based on loosely coupled services with well-defined, platform-neutral service contracts. The use of Web services within an SOA provides a reusable services layer that not only joins applications together more easily but that also lays the foundation for further improvements to business process automation.

Service-oriented integration projects can focus on developing, publishing, and composing Web services independently of their execution environments instead of dealing with the complexity of multiple incompatible APIs, custom applications, packaged applications, programming languages, operating systems, and middleware. Web services and XML simplify integration because they focus on the data being exchanged instead of the underlying programs and execution environments. SOA provides the architecture and project methodology, and Web services provide the unifying glue.

These cost reductions are particularly dramatic in heterogeneous environments that employ multiple packaged applications and application platforms because Web services provide a uniform and consistent technology infrastructure that eliminates the need to write custom integration code and deploy and configure dozens of special-purpose application adapters.

Improved ROI of Existing IT Assets

An SOA dramatically improves the ROI of existing IT assets by reusing them as services in the SOA. Identifying the key business capabilities of existing systems and using them as the basis for new services as part of the SOA can do this. In this way, an SOA helps to maximize the value of existing IT investments while minimizing risk.

At the same time, not all IT assets can be reused in this way, so an assessment and triage process is required. This process must pay special attention to defining abstract interfaces that capture the essence of the business functionality while encapsulating technical details.

Qualifying the SOA Promise

The promised business and technical benefits of using services must be taken with a grain of salt. Usually, the business and technical benefits touted by analysts and vendors assume an idealized view of the world, including assuming that:

- You put an SOA in place immediately, tailor it to the needs of your organization, everyone adopts it right away, and everyone attends the SOA governance meetings on a regular basis.

- You define services that ideally suit your business and that are reusable across multiple lines of business without any subsequent rework or revision.

- You define services that achieve the perfect balance of granularity, loose-coupling, reuse, and technology-neutrality while also being high-performing, scalable, secure, and reliable.

On one hand, this idealized view of the world is a fantasy. This is a classic "good-news-bad-news" scenario:

- Some companies have achieved business and technical benefits by using SOA and services (see the section "A Retrospective on Service-Oriented Architectures," in Chapter 3 for brief case studies about the SOA developed by Credit Suisse and AXA).

- These companies only achieved these results after investing in an SOA and years of hard work. The industry can leverage the pioneering work of these early customers and vendors and benefit from the lessons they have learned.

continues

- You can achieve some short-term, tactical cost savings from using simple technologies like SOAP to build point-to-point connections between systems.

- However tactical, opportunistic approaches like building point-to-point connections between systems using SOAP do not scale up to support enterprise-wide business requirements and do not deliver the ultimate value of services and SOA that is being promised by analysts and vendors. This is because tactical, opportunistic approaches are by definition "tactical" and "opportunistic," meaning that little thought is given to how a new Web service created to tactically link a CICS billing management system with a SAS reporting system can be reused by the customer management system or the order management system or the customer service system.

- It is easier to achieve the strategic benefits of using services today than at anytime in the past. The key ingredients of an SOA are better understood due to the pioneering work of early customers and vendors. Vendors are providing better tools. Analysts are helping to clarify concepts and identify trends. And XML and Web services are here!

Summary

The notion of services is deeply rooted in the business world. In this chapter, we defined what a service is, the key concepts of an SOA, the characteristics that a service should possess, and the business and technical benefits of using an SOA with Web services.

Chapter 3

SOA and Web Services

In Chapter 2, we focused on defining the core concepts and principles of SOA in a technology-neutral manner. In this chapter, we consider the relationship between SOA and Web services.

Web services (SOAP, WSDL, UDDI, and the extended Web services specifications) are a set of open standards that will lead to widespread adoption of SOAs and serve as the basis for a new generation of service oriented development.

An SOA based on Web services has the following advantages:

- It is standards-based, meaning that the organization no longer needs to invest in proprietary solutions, which create vendor lock-in.

- It provides interoperability of solutions and allows you to mix and match best-of-breed products from several vendors, which can reduce costs significantly.

- It supports intra-organization integration and can be extended to provide cross-organization and inter-organization integration.

The Web Services Platform

The Web services platform provides all the facilities necessary to do the following:

1. Allow service requesters and service providers (both line of business services and reusable technical services) to interact in a consistent manner independent of the underlying software domains (i.e., programming languages, application servers, TP monitors, communication middleware, directory services, operating systems, and so on).

2. Enforce business rules and policies such as data validation rules, service-level security, service-level management, and service-level agreements.

3. Allow an SOA to scale up to handle enterprise-wide, mission-critical business requirements.

The Web services platform to the greatest extent possible is based on open standards that are product-neutral, technology-neutral, and middleware-neutral so that it can support and integrate services created using a wide variety of products, technologies, platforms, and middleware.

Figure 3-1 is a high-level diagram showing the role of the Web services platform.

The Web services platform provides the core facilities so that service requesters and service providers can interact in a consistent manner independent of the underlying technology platforms.

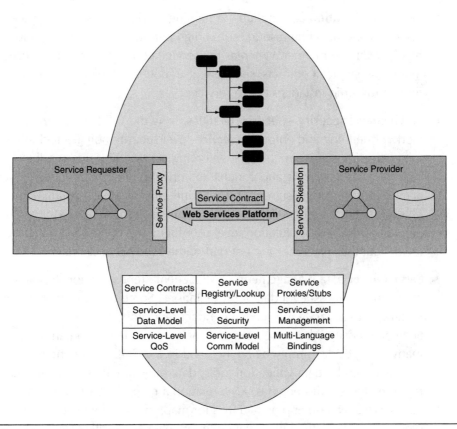

Figure 3-1   Web services platform.

Elements of the Web Services Platform

Here are some of the key elements of a Web services platform:

- **Service contract**—Unambiguous, well-defined service interface using WSDL. Ideally, it should be human-readable and machine-readable.

- **Service contract repository**—A repository for storing, looking up, and versioning service contracts. This might include using taxonomies in UDDI or another registry to categorize services and then using these taxonomies to search for services—taxonomies give you much better searching capabilities than just searching based on the WSDL documents. Ideally, it should be highly available and replicated.

■ **Service registration and lookup**—A naming service for locating service instances and run-time resources in a high performance, scalable, and highly available manner. Whereas the service contract repository is used to look up service contracts, service registration and lookup is used for finding run-time instances of the services.

■ **Service-level security**—Security facilities using the WS-Security framework for defining and enforcing service-level security policies including authenticating service requesters, enforcing access control to service providers based on role and context authorization (e.g., role-based access control), single-sign-on, privacy, integrity, and non-repudiation. Of course, there will be other security facilities in the system—for example, for controlling application-level user login and controlling database login—but these facilities are not part of the Web services platform.

■ **Service-level data management**—XML Schema repository for storing and managing business-level data representations. Some organizations find it preferable to separate the service contract repository and the XML Schema repository because a single XML Schema definition can have many uses besides simply being included in a WSDL document, such as being used by data validation tools, data transformation tools, BPMS, reporting tools, rules engines, XML-relational mapping tools, and XML data servers. Data-mapping facilities for mapping data between different message structures including data filtering, data aggregation, and simple translation functions. Semantic-level data transform facilities define information taxonomies and perform semantic transformations across service domain boundaries.

■ **Service-level communication**—Support for multiple interaction patterns and communication styles using SOAP. Ideally, the communication infrastructure should support multiple interaction patterns and communication styles so that business requirements can be easily mapped onto the Web services platform.

■ **Multiple protocol and transport support**—Ideally, the messaging infrastructure should support multiple transports/protocols to support the wide range of clients, servers, and platforms.

- **Service-level qualities of service**—Support for reliable messaging technologies and various qualities of service including message-ordering, guaranteed delivery, at-most-once delivery, and best-effort delivery. Transaction management capabilities for defining and supporting transaction execution and control including two-phase commit and/or compensating transactions. High-availability capabilities include clustering, failover, automatic-restart, load balancing, and hot-deployment of services.

- **Service-level management**—Support for deploying, starting, stopping, and monitoring services. Of course, there will be other system management facilities in the system—for example, for managing hardware servers—but these facilities are not part of the Web services platform. Support for versioning services. Support for auditing service usage. Support for metering and billing for service usage. Service-level support for business activity monitoring (BAM) including service monitoring, service status, service responsiveness, and compliance or deviations from service-level agreements.

- **Support for multiple programming languages**—Bindings for multiple programming languages—To fully support a wide range of applications and execution platforms, the Web services platform needs to support multiple programming languages, including generating service proxies and service skeletons for all supported programming languages.

- **Service programming interfaces**—Typically, the Web services platform will provide service programming interfaces so that developers can access the facilities of the Web services platform from their favorite programming language(s) and so that developers can be isolated from the complexity of the underlying technical infrastructure.

The Web services standards (SOAP, WSDL, UDDI, WS-*) are the best bet for defining a service platform, but it may be several years before the complete set of standards is approved, implemented, and interoperable across most vendor products. Because the Web services specifications are composable, however, it's possible to start with what's available now and add the rest later. In most cases, the platform will be composed of a wide assortment of products from a number of vendors—almost by definition, it can't come from a single vendor.

Web Services Platform Principles

One principle that applies to the Web services platform is that it should (a) only provide the facilities necessary for allowing service requesters and service providers to interact in a consistent manner independent of the underlying technology platforms, (b) enforce service-level business rules (sometimes called policy enforcement points or PEPs), and (c) scale up to handle enterprise-wide, mission-critical business requirements.

In particular, the Web services platform should avoid trying to include all reusable technical services because each reusable technical service that is embedded in the Web services platform makes it more complicated, harder to maintain, and harder to evolve as requirements change. Instead, reusable technical services should be built on top of the Web services platform using the core facilities provided by the Web services platform so that changes can be made to the reusable technical services without changing the Web services platform. For example, policy enforcement points can be implemented as SOAP interceptors or WSM agents. See Chapter 4, in the section "Applying SOA and Web Services for Integration—Enterprise Service Bus Pattern" for an example of a reusable technical service that can and should be built *on* the Web services platform rather than being built *into* the Web services platform.

A second principle that applies to the Web services platform is that it should incorporate common facilities, especially when they can be used to automatically enforce business rules or move complexity out of the application layer and into the Web services platform. This principle explains why facilities such as single sign-on, role-based access control, audit logging, reliable messaging, and transaction management are included in the Web services platform. Even though each and every one of these facilities could be implemented at the application layer by the service requesters and service providers, this approach would make the application layer significantly more complex, would be error-prone, and would make it very difficult to automatically enforce service-level policies. For example, role-based access control rules should be built into the Web services platform so that it can automatically enforce these rules.

Tension Between Big and Small

As you can see, there is some tension between these two principles because the first one suggests making the Web services platform as small, simple, and minimal as possible while the second principle suggests expanding the scope of the Web services platform to include any and all facilities that could conceivably move complexity out of the applications and into the Web services platform. We therefore define the Web services platform primarily in terms of adopted and proposed standards.

Service Contracts

Every service (i.e., line of business service or reusable technical service) has a well-defined, formal interface called its service contract that (a) clearly defines what the service does and (b) clearly separates the service's externally accessible interface from the service's technical implementation.

Service Contract Elements

Some elements of the service contract apply to the entire service, while other elements apply to the operations that make up the service. The elements of the service contract should be machine-readable so that tools can be used to automate development, run-time, and management activities. The service contract for a service should include all of the following elements.

Elements of Service Contract

- **Service names**—Human-friendly name (plus aliases) as well as a unique machine-readable name.

- **Version number**—Supports the service lifecycle.

- **Pre-conditions**—Conditions that must be satisfied prior to using the service—for example, an operation may not be accessible between midnight and 2 am.

- **Service classification**—Notes and keywords that identify the business domain(s) that the service supports—"yellow page" entries for the service.

For Each Operation

- **Operation name**—Human-understandable name, plus aliases.

- **Pre-conditions**—Conditions that must be satisfied prior to invoking the operation.

- **Post-conditions**—State changes that occur when the operation completes successfully.

- **Input data profile** (i.e., documents/messages)—Name, type, structure, constraints, and meaning of each input document. Also indicate required fields, optional fields, cardinality of fields, dependencies among fields, and data validation rules.

- **Output data profile** (i.e., documents/messages)—Name, type, structure, constraints, and meaning of each output document. Also indicate required fields, optional fields, cardinality of fields, dependencies among fields, and data validation rules.

- **Interaction profile**—What invocation modes does the operation support—request/reply, request/poll for results, request with callback, one-way asynchronous invocations? How are correlation identifiers handled for matching requests and responses? Is the operation conversational in nature, and how is session management handled? Is the operation id-empotent?

- **Exception conditions and error handling**—Error codes and mappings to error messages. State changes that occur under error conditions. Which output fields, if any, contain useful data under error conditions?

- **Security profile**—Security policies that apply to this operation including authentication/authorization techniques, access control list, and requirements for privacy, data integrity, non-repudiation, and so on.

- **Transactional profile and recovery semantics**—Transactional policies, if any. Does it support two-phase commit style transactions? Or does it require compensating transactions if the operation fails?

- **Service-level management agreement**—For example, availability guarantees, time-to-respond, time-to-live, audit logging requirements.

Documenting and Defining Service Contracts

Whether or not you formally define it, every service has a service contract. The service contract can be explicit and well-defined using WSDL, XML Schema, and the WS-Policy framework, or it can be implicitly defined based on the input messages the service accepts, the output messages it responds with, and the business activities that it implements. It is always better to explicitly document service contracts because it makes it easier to build service requesters and service providers and allows them to evolve in an orderly manner.

For Web services-based SOA implementations, WSDL is used to define key elements of the service contracts, while other elements that cannot be expressed in WSDL are defined using the WS-Policy framework or documented in a Microsoft Word document or Microsoft Excel spreadsheet.

Importance of Well-Defined Contracts

The importance of having well-defined service contracts is a timeless SOA principle. For older, homegrown SOA implementations, service contracts were usually defined in a Microsoft Word document or Microsoft Excel spreadsheet. For newer, CORBA-based SOA implementations, CORBA IDL was used to define some elements, while other elements were documented in a Microsoft Word document or Microsoft Excel spreadsheet. For an SOA based on Web services, WSDL provides the extensible framework on which a well-defined contract is based.

Service Contract Principles

In any case, certain principles apply to defining service contracts:

Principle #1—Clear and complete separation of the interface from the implementation. This is different from some object-oriented techniques where developers need to have access to the object's implementation so they can create derived classes.

Principle #2—SOAs should strive for making service contracts as abstract and general as possible so that alternative implementations can be provided or swapped in when necessary. This is particularly important in B2B integration when it may become necessary to replace one supply chain partner with another one.

Principle #3—Because SOA is intended to allow many service requesters to look up and use the same service provider, the service contracts must be defined in a manner that imposes the fewest restrictions and assumptions on the service requesters that use it and on the service providers that are intended to implement it. For example, you should not impose arbitrary restrictions on customer names just because your current database schema defines customer names to be a maximum of 35 characters in length.

Service Contracts Focus on Service-Level Abstractions

Although it may be obvious, it is worth noting that the elements of a service contract only deal with service-level information and do not deal with internal implementation details. For instance:

- The input data profile for an operation is typically defined using XML Schema, but this does not explicitly say anything about how the XML data should be mapped to an underlying RDBMS being used by the service provider.

- The security profile for an operation may specify that X.509 certificates must be used for authentication, but this does not affect how the service provider connects to a RDBMS.

- The interaction profile for an operation may specify that the operation is invoked as a one-way operation (i.e., does not return any results), but this does not affect how the service provider accesses an internal data transformation engine and a local RDBMS.

- The transactional profile for an operation may define that a compensating transaction is required when the operation fails, but this may not affect how the service provider commits a transaction involving two or more RDBMSs.

WSDL and Service Contracts

Services contracts are the means by which interoperability and integration are achieved. Basically, both sides to an interaction need to be able to understand the same definition of the service, including the service name, the messages, the SOAP message exchange patterns, the data types, and any associated policy information.

WSDL[1] is the ideal choice as a service definition language because it is standards-based, extensible, built on XML Schema, and clearly separates the logical contract from the physical contract:

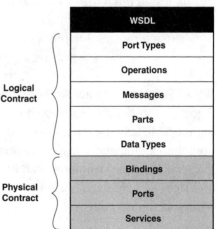

- The logical contract defines the public interface that is independent of transports, on-the-wire data formats, and programming languages.

- The physical contract defines bindings to transports and wire-level data formats, and multiple physical contracts can be defined for each logical contract.

---

[1] WSDL 1.1 is used here. See Chapter 7, "Metadata Management," for information on WSDL 2.0.

The normal pattern for Web services interoperability is that one side creates an initial service, defining the messages, service names, and network address, and publishes the information within a WSDL file for external consumption. The requester of a Web service typically downloads or otherwise obtains a copy of the WSDL file and parses it to find out what kind of messages are required by the service provider, including the service name and associated data types and structures, and then it generates the message.

Interoperability Problems

Interoperability problems, if any, typically occur at the stage when the WSDL is parsed and a compatible SOAP message is generated. WS-I and SOAP Builders have been attacking the problem of interoperability across Web services implementations, but incompatibilities across products remains a problem. Not all products support the same collection of data types and structures, and sometimes one vendor's Web services toolkit cannot recognize all of the data types and structures in a WSDL file generated by another vendor. However, efforts are underway to resolve this issue. The simplest approach to minimizing data interoperability problems is to use simple XML data types and structures because the more complex ones are where interoperability breaks down.

WSDL Service Contract Architecture

Figure 3-2 shows the major components of the WSDL service contract, including the XML Schema data types and structures for the messages, the specification of encoding and transport options, and the physical endpoint address for the service. These definitions can be used to dynamically generate the SOAP messages that are exchanged to execute the service, illustrated here using the request/response pattern.

The WSDL service contract defines the information necessary for interoperability (e.g., message format and transport details, such as HTTP, JMS, and WebSphere MQ) while at the same time defining the service in a manner that abstracts away (i.e., encapsulates) the execution environment (e.g., J2EE, .NET Framework, CORBA, CICS). Because J2EE, the .NET Framework, CORBA, and SAP NetWeaver (and virtually any other software system) all are capable of understanding Web services, achieving interoperability is a matter of defining and executing the appropriate Web services contract(s) upon which the disparate systems and applications can agree.

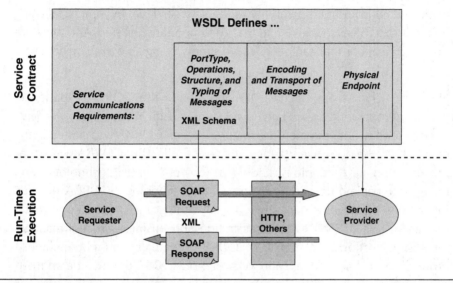

Figure 3-2   WSDL service contract architecture.

Web services contracts vary in complexity, including the following:

- Point-to-point agreements for solving specific interoperability problems, such as connecting J2EE to .NET.

- Complex messaging interactions such as publish and subscribe.

- Enterprise-wide patterns such as those designed for use in comprehensive integration architectures such as SOA.

The basic Web services specifications provide interoperability solutions for sharing data across existing and new applications, while the extended Web services specifications provide integration solutions that include reliability, transactions, and security. WSDL service contracts can be easily extended to include these additional enterprise qualities of service typically present in existing applications.

Achieving Interoperable Qualities of Service

The trick with Web services is achieving enterprise qualities of service that are interoperable across vendor implementations. It's relatively easy to achieve data-level interoperability at the services level by simply focusing on the data to be exchanged, and that's an important first step. And there are many applications that can benefit from simply being able to share data very easily.

The Web services approach is the opposite of the CORBA experience, where interoperability wasn't achieved at first—with Web services, we have interoperability but not enterprise features. When CORBA was started in the early 1990s, the objective was actually very similar. But CORBA was based on an emerging technology known as object-oriented technology, and rather than remaining purely an integration technology, CORBA evolved into a full-scale development environment with security, transactions, meta-data management, and even orchestration and business process management specifications. Version 1 of CORBA ironically did not include a protocol for interoperability, and Version 2 of CORBA did include an interoperability protocol, IIOP. The original Version 1 focus was on the interface definition language, or IDL, which is a central concept of CORBA. The IDL was created using advanced concepts, but originally it was meant to bridge languages such as COBOL to C. It ended up becoming most popular when used with C++ and Java, even though IDL mappings exist also for PL/I, COBOL, and several other languages. If the trick was accomplished for CORBA, however, it can also be accomplished for Web services.

Example WSDL Service Contract—Calendar Service

An example of basic WSDL in Listing 3-1 shows a portType for the calendar service that can be used by both service requesters and service providers.[2]

<hr />

[2] Reference: http://rzm-hamy-wsx.rz.uni-karlsruhe.de/Training/SOAP-1/html-generated/instances/axis-wsdl-2/wsdl/CalendarService.wsdl.txt.

Listing 3-1   `portType` for the Calendar Service

```
<portType name="CalendarComputation">
<operation name="computeFinalTimestamp">
    <documentation>This operation computes the final
    ➡...</documentation>
    <input message="tns:ComputeFinalTimestampRequest" />
    <output message="tns:ComputeFinalTimestampResponse" />
</operation>
<operation name="computeInitialTimestamp">
        <documentation>This operation computes the ...
        ➡</documentation>
        <input message="tns:ComputeInitialTimestampRequest" />
        <output message="tns:ComputeInitialTimestamp
        ➡Response" />
</operation>
<operation name="computeDuration">
        <documentation>This operation computes the duration
        ➡...</documentation>
        <input message="tns:ComputeDurationRequest" />
        <output message="tns:ComputeDurationResponse" />
</operation>
<operation name="millisToDuration">
        <documentation>This operation converts a given
        ➡...</documentation>
        <input message="tns:MillisToDurationRequest" />
        <output message="tns:MillisToDurationResponse" />
</operation>
<operation name="durationToMillis">
        <documentation>This operation converts a duration
        ➡...</documentation>
        <input message="tns:DurationToMillisRequest" />
        <output message="tns:DurationToMillisResponse" />
</operation>
<operation name="millisToTimestamp">
        <documentation>This operation converts a given
        ➡...</documentation>
        <input message="tns:MillisToTimestampRequest" />
        <output message="tns:MillisToTimestampResponse" />
</operation>
<operation name="timestampToMillis">
        <documentation>This operation converts a
        ➡timestamp...</documentation>
        <input message="tns:TimestampToMillisRequest" />
        <output message="tns:TimestampToMillisResponse" />
</operation>
</portType>
```

Service-Level Data Model

A service contract defines a data model. This data model is made up of all the XML data types of all the input documents/messages and output documents/messages of the operations that make up that service, which are defined in the WSDL document. This data model is independent of the data types that the service requesters and service providers use internally.

The service-level data model (see Figure 3-3) is also shared by the service requesters and the service providers and provides the mechanism by which they exchange data in a format and structure that they both can interpret (i.e., XML):

- The service provider knows the service-level data model because it must be capable of accepting and generating data values according to the data typing information specified by the service contract.

- The service requester also knows this data model because it must be capable of sending and receiving data values according to the data typing information specified by the service contract.

Relationship Between Service-Level Data Models and Internal Data Models

The service requester has its own internal data model (e.g., a business object model or a database schema) that it uses internally for implementing internal business logic. When the service requester wishes to invoke a service, it must compose a service request that conforms to the service contract—to do this, it may have to perform a data transformation to translate data elements from its internal data model to the service-level data model in XML. Similarly, when the service requester receives a response from the service provider, it may have to perform a data transformation to translate data elements from the service-level data model in XML to its internal data model. These transformations are a purely internal implementation matter encapsulated within the service requester, and they are completely hidden from the service provider and the Web services platform.

Similarly, the service provider has its own internal data model and it may have to perform data transformations to translate data elements from the service-level data model to its own internal data model.

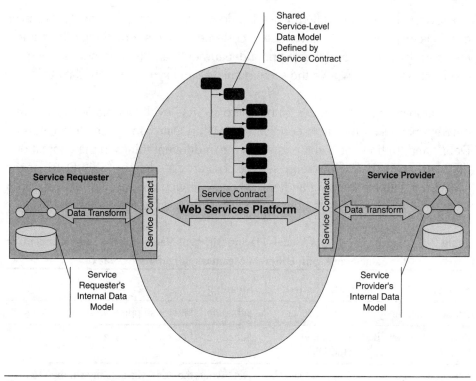

Figure 3-3   Service-level data model.

The SOA may facilitate converting data between service-level data models and internal data models in any number of ways, including:

1. Providing a transformation facility that can be called directly from the service requester and/or the service provider.

2. Providing a transformation service that can be invoked by the service requester and/or the service provider using the service platform.

Reconciling Disparate Data Models Across Different Service Domains

A service domain is a collection of services related to a specific line of business such as finance, sales, marketing, manufacturing, shipping, or patient management. All services in a service domain should communicate using a common data model so that these services can be easily composed and used together.

However, services from different service domains may have inconsistent or even contradictory data vocabularies (e.g., "customer" means something different to the sales department and the shipping department), and two or more service-level data models may give the same name to similar but different data types.

For example, Table 3-1 shows (a) how two service-level data models can have different names for the same concept (e.g., "Ship Date" and "Scheduled Ship Date") and (b) how the same name can mean different things in the context of different service definitions (e.g., service contract "A" defines "Ship Date" as the scheduled date for shipping an item, whereas service contract "B" defines "Ship Date" as the date when the item was actually shipped to the customer).

Table 3-1   **Service-Level Data Models Having Different Names for the Same Concept, or the Same Name with Different Meanings in Different Contexts**

Service	Data Element	Meaning
Service Contract "A"	Ship Date	Scheduled date for shipping an item
Service Contract "B"	Scheduled Ship Date	Scheduled date for shipping an item
Service Contract "A"	Shipped Date	Date when the item was actually shipped to the customer
Service Contract "B"	Ship Date	Date when the item was actually shipped to the customer

Therefore, when using services from two or more service domains, it is vital that you understand the semantic and structural differences between service-level data models so that you apply the appropriate semantic and structural data transformations as information flows between the service domains.

Figure 3-4 illustrates a situation where a service requester uses two services from two different service domains (Service "A" and Service "B") that both define "Ship Date," but each service assigns a different meaning to "Ship Date."

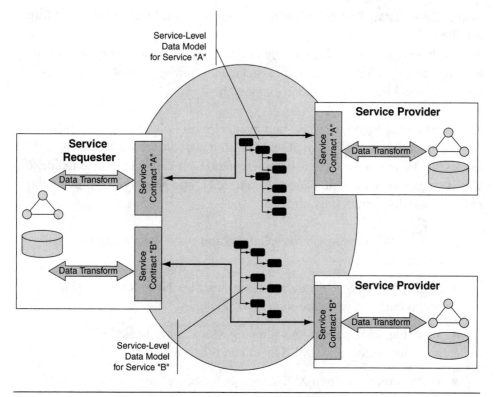

Figure 3-4   Reconciling disparate service-level data models.

Ideally, this situation would never occur because it would be identified and resolved during system analysis and design. However, this is not always possible, especially when services developed for different purposes and by different teams are being reused on a new project. In these cases, it is necessary to identify these types of data model conflicts, resolve the conflicts by properly categorizing the similar but different data elements, and then provide data transformation facilities for mapping data elements among service domains and data models. Once again, the SOA may facilitate converting data between two service-level data models by providing a transformation service that can be invoked by the service requester and/or the service provider using the Web services platform.

Using XML-Related Technologies for the Service-Level Data Model and Data Handling

An SOA needs to provide facilities for defining, parsing, validating, and transforming messages. Taken together, these facilities provide the SOA's service-level data model and data-handling capabilities.

XML Schema has emerged as the best available technology for representing the service-level data model for an SOA because it is open, standards-based, and extensible. Furthermore, XML is complemented by a family of related technologies such as validating XML parsers, XPath, XSLT, and XQuery that provide the rich functionality required by an SOA:

- **XML**—XML provides a cross-platform approach to data encoding and formatting.

- **XML Schema**—Specification used to describe the structure of XML documents and to define shared vocabularies.

- **Validating XML parser**—A validating XML parser checks an XML document against an XML Schema and reports errors.

- **XPath**—XPath is a non-XML language for addressing parts of an XML document.

- **XSL transformation** (XSLT)—XSLT is a language for transforming XML documents into other XML documents or native formats.

- **XQuery**—XQuery is the W3C's query language for XML and is designed to be broadly applicable across all types of XML data sources. Think "SQL for XML."

In addition, the wide availability of commercial and open-source implementations of these technologies makes them easy to adopt and saves countless hours of development time. And, of course, SOAP and WSDL are themselves XML technologies.

SOA Message Syntax Prior to XML

Prior to XML, most SOAs, especially homegrown SOAs, defined their own custom message syntax. In fact, hundreds of these custom message syntaxes were invented over time. Each time a custom message syntax was defined, someone had to write a custom parser for it, a tool for validating messages, and a tool for serializing and deserializing these messages, and so on. Furthermore, these tools had to be enhanced and maintained. All of this activity imposed an enormous cost on SOAs with custom message syntaxes and reduced the amount of time that could be spent applying the SOA to solving business problems.

XML and its family of related technologies have freed us from custom message syntax hell.

Service Discovery—Registration and Lookup

One of the core capabilities of an SOA's service platform is service registration and lookup.

The Universal Description, Discovery, and Integration (UDDI) specifications define a way to publish and discover information about Web services. UDDI creates a platform-independent, open framework for describing services, discovering businesses, and integrating business services using the Internet. UDDI takes an approach that relies upon a distributed registry of businesses and their service descriptions implemented in a common XML format. UDDI defines a SOAP-based programming protocol for registering and discovering Web services. However, UDDI has not been as widely adopted as SOAP and WSDL, and other solutions are often used for service registration and lookup.

Broadly speaking, there are two types of UDDI registries: public registries and private registries. The public registries are a logically centralized, physically distributed service that replicate data with each other on a regular basis. When a business registers with a single instance of the public UDDI registry, the data is automatically shared with other public UDDI registries and becomes freely available to anyone who needs to discover which Web services are exposed by a given business. A private registry is a UDDI that is not publicly accessible and is only accessible within a single organization or shared by a well-defined set of business partners.

Service-Level Security

Security is an important yet complicated topic. An SOA is primarily concerned with service-level security, although transport-level security mechanisms (such as HTTPS) are still widely used because of their ubiquity. Listed in Table 3-2 are the key factors in providing service-level security. WS-Security is the key Web services standard for security because it incorporates existing standards for XML encryption and signing while also providing an extensible framework for authentication.

Table 3-2   Service-Level Security

	Description	Web Services Support
Authentication	Establishing that whoever is sending and/or receiving SOAP messages is who they say they are.	**HTTP**—Basic authentication (user name and password), .NET supports HTTP Digest rather than HTTP Basic Authentication. **HTTPS**—Authenticates through the use of certificates, which can be used on the server side, the client side, or both sides. **WS-Security**—SOAP security headers capable of handling user name tokens, X.509 certificates, Kerberos tickets, SAML tokens, and other tokens. **SAML**—Supports exchanging authentication and authorization information between security domains.

	Description	Web Services Support
Authorization	Controlling access to resources including individual Web services based on user identity or role.	**SAML**—Supports exchanging authentication and authorization information between security domains. **XACML**—Provides an access-control policy language for specifying the rules about who can do what and when, and a protocol for making access requests.
Data privacy and encryption	Ensures that the data in the SOAP message is only viewable by the intended parties.	**HTTPS**—Provides transport-level encryption; encrypts the entire document. **WS-Security**—XML Encryption provides SOAP message privacy; element-level encryption.
Data integrity and digital signature	Detects when data in the SOAP message is modified during transmission.	**HTTPS**—Provides transport-level digital signature; signs the entire document. **WS-Security**—XML Signature provides SOAP message integrity; element-level signing.
Non-repudiation	Allows a party to prove that a SOAP message was sent or received or that a transaction occurred. Used by a third party to resolve disagreements.	**WS-Security**—Message non-repudiation is provided by leveraging XML Signature.
Single sign-on	Allows a service requester to be authenticated once and then have access to authorized resources across security domains.	**SAML**—Standard for exchanging authentication and authorization information between systems and supports single sign-on for both automatic and manual interactions between systems.
Service-level security audit log	Maintain a record of all service invocations so that security problems can be reviewed after the fact.	Custom.

In general, WS-Security is not a complete security solution. There are other issues—such as exchange of security tokens, key management, authorization, trust, federation, and privacy—that are not answered by WS-Security, although it is the foundation for these advanced requirements. Work in these areas is under way within several other related specifications.

Of course, a complete SOA security solution would need to be integrated with other security infrastructure, including:

- **Public Key Infrastructure (PKI)**—PKI deals with distribution and lifecycle management of certificates. Also, PKI integration in the Web services space is being worked on by OASIS, and standards are not finalized.

- **Key management**—XKMS (XML Key Management System) specifies key management protocols for key generation and key distribution and is intended to interface with public key infrastructure such as PKI.

- **Identity management systems**—These include access management, identity administration, and directory services.

- **Directory services (LDAP [Lightweight Directory Access Protocol], ADS [Microsoft Active Directory System])**—Used for supporting identity management systems and registering and discovering resources.

As you can see, a complete solution for service-level security for Web services is a patchwork of standards, and this is no better or worse than previous SOA technologies.

See Chapter 8, "Web Services Security," for a more in-depth review of Web services security.

Service-Level Interaction Patterns

Organizations exchange information in a variety of ways. To accommodate this, an SOA needs to support a variety of service interaction patterns.

The most common interaction patterns are the following:

- Request/reply interactions.

- Request/callback interactions.

- One-way, store-and-forward messaging.

- Publish/subscribe interactions.

In this section, we look at how Web services support these interaction patterns.

A Quick Look at SOAP and HTTP

As illustrated in Figure 3-5, a typical HTTP operation either gets an HTML file from a remote Web server and downloads it to the local machine, or posts an HTML file from the local machine to the remote server.

To work well over the tremendous scale of the Web, HTTP deliberately omits a very key and essential aspect of typical RPC implementations—persistent sessions. There is no way (in the standards at least) to correlate requests with replies, no way for the client to know for sure whether or not the request was processed, and no mechanism to associate transaction, security, or any other context with the transport for multiple related interactions.

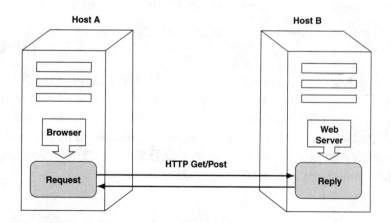

Figure 3-5   Browser/HTTP interaction paradigm.

SOAP over HTTP is inherently synchronous, request/response messaging:

- Synchronous because it requires the sender and the receiver to be online simultaneously for data to be exchanged. (Unlike asynchronous, store-and-forward techniques that do not require the sender and receiver to be online simultaneously.)

- Request/response because it allows for data to be exchanged in both directions.

WSDL defines several operation-level message exchange patterns based on the rules imposed by SOAP messaging. The most commonly used ones are request/response (an input message and an output message are defined for the operation):

```
<operation name="computeFinalTimestamp">
    <documentation>This operation computes the final
    ➡...</documentation>
    <input message="tns:ComputeFinalTimestampRequest" />
    <output message="tns:ComputeFinalTimestampResponse" />
</operation>
```

and one-way (a single input or output message is defined for the operation):

```
<operation name="sendPurchaseOrder">
    <documentation>This operation sends a Purchase Order
    ➡...</documentation>
    <input message="tns: sendPurchaseOrderRequest" />
</operation>
```

Because the default transport binding for SOAP is HTTP, it is not possible for SOAP to rely upon features in transports other than HTTP for extended functions such as security or transactions (since they might not be compatible with HTTP). However, SOAP is extensible, so it is possible to extend SOAP to include additional qualities of service not provided by HTTP and then implement these extensions over HTTP or any other protocol.

Request/Response Interactions

When using the request/response interaction paradigm, the service requester sends a request to the service provider and then waits for a response (see Figure 3-6).

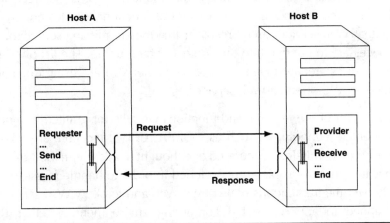

Figure 3-6   Request/response interaction paradigm.

In WSDL, a request/response operation is defined by specifying both an input message (i.e., request message) and an output message (i.e., response message) as follows:

```
<operation name="computeFinalTimestamp">
      <documentation>This operation computes the final
      ➡...</documentation>
      <input message="tns:ComputeFinalTimestampRequest" />
      <output message="tns:ComputeFinalTimestampResponse" />
</operation>
```

Although WSDL and SOAP both support a request/response interaction style, it is important to understand that the SOAP and WSDL definitions are not executable and that any business logic needs to be implemented by a run-time environment such as J2EE, .NET Framework, or CORBA.

Web Services Are Not Well Suited for RPCs

The misconception that Web services are well suited for RPCs leads to a lot of confusion and to a lot of industry talk about how "Web services aren't ready" or "Web services are missing a lot of functionality." It's not enough to say that Web services aren't ready or that they're missing something; it's also necessary to put that into the context of their usage. The list of missing features varies greatly depending upon whether you are using document-oriented or RPC-oriented Web services.

In short, a lot of the features and functions we take for granted in modern RPC-oriented technologies such as CORBA, COM, and J2EE are missing. But they are not missing because no one thought to add them; they are missing because they were explicitly excluded in order to handle messages efficiently over the tremendous scale of the Web and to allow Web services to be mapped to any distributed computing environment, whether RPC-oriented or asynchronous message-oriented.

Request/Callback Interaction Paradigm

The request/callback interaction paradigm is usually employed when the service requester cannot be blocked while waiting for a synchronous response, so instead it sets up a callback agent to handle the response. Figure 3-7 illustrates the request/callback interaction paradigm.

The typical sequence of actions is:

1. The service requester sends a request message to the service provider using a one-way request message. The request message includes a correlation ID and a callback address. After the service requester sends the request message, it continues executing and does *not* block while waiting for the response.

2. The service provider receives the request message, composes a response, and sends an asynchronous callback[3] message to the callback service by sending a one-way response message to the callback address that was included in the service requester's original request, including the correlation ID.

3. The callback service receives the response message and processes it as appropriate (which may include notifying the service requester of the response).

The service requester and the callback service can be running on the same machine but do not have to be.

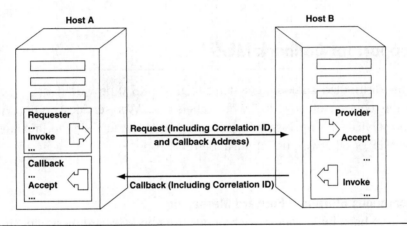

Figure 3-7   Request/callback interaction paradigm.

WSDL and SOAP do not provide formal support for request/callback interactions, and it is up to the application layer to manage the various elements of the request/callback interaction, including defining callback addresses and generating correlation IDs. WS-Addressing can also be used, however, to implement the callback MEP.

---

[3] The callback is sometimes referred to as an asynchronous callback because it can happen at any time (i.e., not synchronized with the original request).

In WSDL, a request/callback interaction can be defined by specifying two one-way operations to model the request and the callback:

```
<!-- Request Message -->
<operation name="computeFinalTimestampRequest">
    <input message="tns:ComputeFinalTimestampRequest" />
</operation>

<!-- Callback Message -->
<operation name="computeFinalTimestampResponse">
    <output message="tns:ComputeFinalTimestampResponse" />
</operation>
```

WS-BPEL also defines correlation IDs based on the application data in the messages being exchanged (see Chapter 6).

Support for Callback MEP

Some distributed computing systems (e.g., CORBA) provide direct support for the request/callback MEP, while others (e.g., Web services) do not. With Web services, it's necessary to explicitly use WS-Addressing to implement this MEP or otherwise use application-level code.

Asynchronous Store-and-Forward Messaging

SOAs have been built using asynchronous store-and-forward messaging architectures, and asynchronous messaging has proven to be ideal for document-centric enterprise integration because it allows for a loosely coupled solution that overcomes the limitations of remote communication, such as latency and unreliability.

As illustrated in Figure 3-8, communication between services using asynchronous messaging is accomplished via the use of persistent queues. The service on Host A places a request message in a request queue, and the messaging technology reliably delivers the message to Host B where the receiving service dequeues it and processes it.

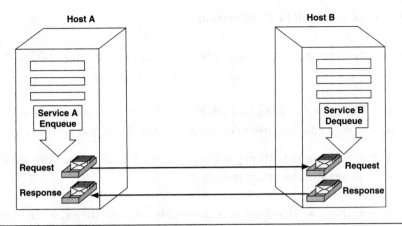

Figure 3-8   Asynchronous store-and-forward interaction paradigm.

One of the advantages of the asynchronous messaging paradigm is that a request queue can be *persistent,* allowing the application to continue working whether or not a connection to the remote machine is available. Whether or not the queue is persistent, the service on Host B receives the request by dequeuing the request from the request queue. Asynchronous message queuing does not depend upon the format of a remote procedure call, which typically ties the request name to an object method name and the data to input and output arguments of the method named.

After dequeueing the request and processing it, the service on Host B enqueues the reply message on to the reply queue, and the messaging technology reliably delivers the message to Host A, where the receiving service dequeues it and processes it. Just like the request queue, the reply queue can either be remote or local.

In WSDL, it is possible to specify a one-way message by only specifying an input message without an output message:

```
<operation name="sendPurchaseOrder">
     <documentation>This operation sends a Purchase Order
     ➡...</documentation>
     <input message="tns: sendPurchaseOrderRequest" />
</operation>
```

And this maps very well to SOAP messaging.

Communication using asynchronous messaging can be accomplished in two ways:

- By using service proxies that abstract the communication layer and policy metadata that are enforced automatically by the service platform.

- By having the programs explicitly perform all data marshalling required to enqueue and dequeue messages.

In most cases, using service proxies is preferable because they can abstract the communication layer and perform data marshalling and un-marshalling—such as converting objects to messages and parsing message buffers.

It should be noted that, by default, one-way SOAP messages do not provide guaranteed message delivery in the same way that asynchronous messaging systems do, and therefore the service requester calling the operation shown previously would have to implement its own quality of service by retrying the operation invocation until it succeeded.

The following two standards have been proposed to provide guaranteed message delivery on top of the core Web services standards and within the Web services framework:

- WS-Reliability.
- WS-ReliableMessaging.

See Chapter 9, "Advanced Messaging," for more details on these specifications.

It is also possible to achieve guaranteed message delivery using SOAP and messaging middleware such as WebSphere MQ and JMS (see the section "WSDL Extensibility" for more information on using SOAP with non-HTTP transports).

Example Business Scenario Using Request/Response and Asynchronous Messaging

Here is a business scenario that demonstrates both request/response and asynchronous messaging types of interactions being used side-by-side for different purposes. Consider a telecommunications company call center where customers place orders for products and services. Typically, this interaction consists of the customer selecting the products and services and the customer service representative (CSR) validating that the products and services can be provided and then provisioning the service (i.e., turning on the service, which may take minutes, hours, or days).

What is required is an architecture that decouples the product and service selections from the actual provisioning. In other words, we want to complete the service selection and validation while the customer is waiting on the phone so that we can ensure that he gets what he wants. This may involve using request/response interactions with several backend systems to ensure data validity and integrity. Indeed, the selection of one product or service might make the customer eligible for other products and services, which could change the information on the CSR's screen. Request/response communication is ideal for this type of real-time interaction.

After the customer has selected all of the products and services and all validation is performed, the customer call can be wrapped up, and then the order or orders can be placed using an asynchronous service invocation. This request, which may be made up of multiple product and service requests, can then be sent asynchronously through a workflow process that performs the actual provisioning.

Publish/Subscribe Interaction Paradigm

With publish/subscribe interactions, event subscribers indicate which event types they are interested in, and then they receive event notifications when event publishers generate events in which they are interested.

As Figure 3-9 illustrates:

■ Event subscribers are responsible for registering interest in events.

■ Events are delivered to all interested event subscribers (sometimes called event sinks) when an event publisher (sometimes called an event source) publishes an event.

An event may be delivered to any number of subscribers based on the number of subscriptions that are active when the event is published.

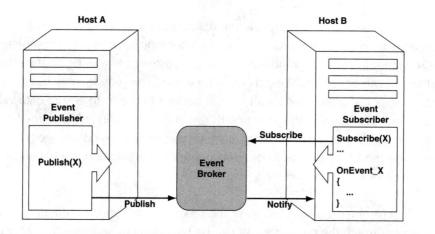

Figure 3-9   Publish/subscribe interaction paradigm.

Publish/subscribe is the most loosely coupled interaction paradigm because there is a dynamic, many-to-many relationship between event publishers and event subscribers:

■ There can be any number of publishers for any type of event.

■ There can be any number of subscribers for any type of event.

■ The number of publishers and subscribers can change at any time.

This is different than request/response interactions where a service requester sends a single request to a single, well-defined service provider.

Publish/subscribe technology typically provides a variety of options, including the following:

- Subscription termination, which is the ability for a subscriber to delete an existing subscription.

- Timed subscriptions that expire after a specified time unless renewed by the subscriber.

- Various message delivery options including best effort, at-least-once delivery, at-most-once delivery, once-and-only-once-delivery, and so on.

- Event filtering to specify business rules that better define which events should be delivered to which subscribers.

- Brokered subscriptions where an intermediate subscription manager manages the subscriptions and the distribution of events to subscribers.

- Persistent subscriptions that survive system failures.

The following standards provide publish/subscribe-style communication on top of the core Web services standards and within the Web services platform:

- WS-Eventing.

- WS-Notification.

SOAP and HTTP Provide a Simple but Extensible Mechanism

SOAP and HTTP provide exactly what they were designed for—a simple, lightweight mechanism for interoperability and distributed communication. However, SOAP and HTTP do not provide the traditional enterprise qualities of service typically needed for an enterprise SOA (such as guaranteed message delivery, transaction management, and publish/subscribe). However, SOAP was designed to be extensible, and it can be extended to support any desired QoS feature by adding SOAP headers to the SOAP messages and adding QoS features to the basic SOAP run-time facilities.

continues

You can use features and modules that allow you to transparently add additional QoS features to the basic SOAP run-time facilities, such as WS-ReliableMessaging, WS-Reliability, WS-AT/C, WS-CAF, and more. These are SOAP extensions that conform to the SOAP extension model.

The extended Web services standards listed here are SOAP extensions that conform to the SOAP extension model:

- WS-Reliability.

- WS-ReliableMessaging (WS-RM).

- WS-AtomicTransaction/Coordination (WS-AT/C).

- WS-Composite Application Framework (WS-CAF).

- WS-Eventing.

- WS-Notification.

These extensions can help make up for missing functionality.

In the meantime, creating an SOA based on the Web services platform may require mixing the best of the new (i.e., WSDL and SOAP) with the best of the old (e.g., JMS, WebSphere MQ, Tibco Rendezvous, and CORBA Notification) and some "glue" code. (Ideally, this "glue" code should be isolated so that it can be replaced by features in the Web services platform when they are ready.)

Atomic Services and Composite Services

Sometimes it is useful to categorize services into atomic services and composite services (see Figure 3-10).

Atomic services do not rely on other services and are usually associated with straightforward business transactions or with executing data queries and data updates.

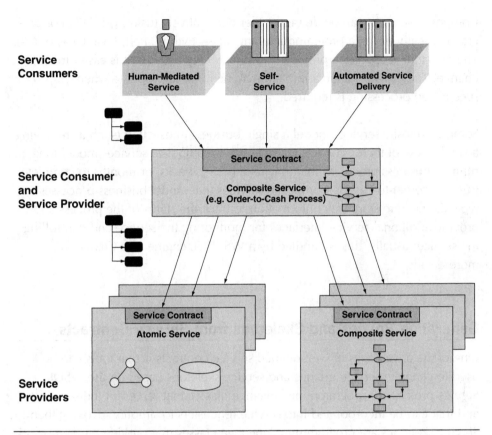

Figure 3-10   Atomic services and composite services.

Composite services use other services. In all other respects, composite services are just like any other service, in that they:

- Have a well-defined service contract.

- Are registered in the service registry, can be looked up via the service registry, and can be invoked like any other service provider.

- Are deployed, managed, and secured like other services.

- Can look up and use other services, including other composite services.

Composite services can be defined either declaratively (using WS-BPEL) or programmatically (using a programming language—Python, Perl, Java, C++, or C#). The declarative approach provides more flexibility because it is easier to change. The programmatic approach may be more appropriate when specialized processing is required.

Some composite services model a single business transaction (such as retrieving a single view of the customer), whereas other composite services model long running business processes that may take hours, weeks, or months to complete (such as "order-to-cash"). Composite services that model business processes typically need to store state information to track the status of the process and provide additional service interfaces for monitoring the service and controlling the service; usually, this is handled by a WS-BPEL engine (see Chapter 6 for more details).

Generating Proxies and Skeletons from Service Contracts

One of the advantages of well-defined service contracts is that tools can be used to generate service proxies and service skeletons based on the WSDL. Service proxies are programming language classes that represent the service and that can be incorporated into service requesters to simplify invoking them. Service skeletons are programming language classes that provide the framework for implementing new services.

The main advantages of generating and using service proxies and service skeletons is that developers can work with familiar programming language constructs when invoking and implementing services without having to deal with low-level WSDL and SOAP details. Most Web services products and IDEs provide this capability.

Generating Java Classes from Service Contracts

Here is an example of a Java service proxy class generated from the
`CalendarService` WSDL (refer to Listing 3-1):

```
public interface CalendarComputation extends java.rmi.Remote {
    public Timestamp computeFinalTimestamp(
            Timestamp initialTimestamp,Duration duration);
    public Timestamp computeInitialTimestamp(
            Timestamp finalTimestamp,Duration duration);
    public Duration computeDuration(
            Timestamp initialTimestamp,Timestamp finalTimestamp);
    public Duration millisToDuration(long millis);
    public long durationToMillis(Duration duration);
    public Timestamp millisToTimestamp(long millis,TimeZoneId
    ➡timeZoneId);
    public long timestampToMillis(Timestamp timestamp);
}
```

As you can see, `CalendarComputation` is a Java service proxy class that models
the calendar service and provides methods that model the operations of the
calendar service.

Here is an example of a Java service skeleton class generated from the
`CalendarService` WSDL (refer to Listing 3-1):

```
public class CalendarComputationImpl {
    public Timestamp computeFinalTimestamp(
        Timestamp initialTimestamp,Duration duration) {
        // User code goes in here.
        return new com.iona.CalendarService.Timestamp();
    }

    public Timestamp computeInitialTimestamp(
        Timestamp finalTimestamp,Duration duration) {
        // User code goes in here.
        return new com.iona.CalendarService.Timestamp();
    }

    public Duration computeDuration(
        Timestamp initialTimestamp,Timestamp finalTimestamp) {
        // User code goes in here.
        return new com.iona.CalendarService.Duration();
    }

...
}
```

As you can see, `CalendarComputationImpl` is a Java service skeleton class that provides the framework for implementing the `CalendarService`.

Generating C# Classes from Service Contracts

Here is a fragment of a C# service proxy class generated from the `CalendarService` WSDL (refer to Listing 3-1). Notice how the code generator places source code annotations inside of square brackets ("[" and "]") before the class definition and the method definitions. These annotations indicate, among other things, the protocol to use and how the return value should be serialized:

```
using System;
using System.Diagnostics;
using System.Xml.Serialization;
using System.Web.Services.Protocols;
using System.ComponentModel;
using System.Web.Services;

[System.Diagnostics.DebuggerStepThroughAttribute()]
[System.ComponentModel.DesignerCategoryAttribute("code")]
[System.Web.Services.WebServiceBindingAttribute(Name=
➥"CalendarComputationBinding",

Namespace="urn:calsv")]
public class CalendarService : System.Web.Services.Protocols.
➥SoapHttpClientProtocol {

    public CalendarService() {
        this.Url = "http://rynt02.rz.uni-karlsruhe.de:8080/axis/
        ➥services/CalendarService";
    }

    [System.Web.Services.Protocols.SoapRpcMethodAttribute
    ➥("computeFinalTimestamp",
                    RequestNamespace="urn:calsv",
                    ➥ResponseNamespace="urn:calsv")]
    [return: System.Xml.Serialization.SoapElementAttribute
    ➥("finalTimestamp")]
    public timestamp computeFinalTimestamp(timestamp
    ➥initialTimestamp,
                                        duration duration) {
        object[] results = this.Invoke("computeFinalTimestamp",
        ➥new object[] {
                    initialTimestamp,
                    duration});
        return ((timestamp)(results[0]));
    }
```

```
[System.Web.Services.Protocols.SoapRpcMethodAttribute
➥("computeInitialTimestamp",
                        RequestNamespace="urn:calsv",
                        ➥ResponseNamespace="urn:calsv")]
[return: System.Xml.Serialization.SoapElementAttribute
➥("initialTimestamp")]
public timestamp computeInitialTimestamp(timestamp
➥finalTimestamp,
                                        duration duration) {
    object[] results = this.Invoke("computeInitialTimestamp",
    ➥new object[] {
                finalTimestamp,
                duration});
    return ((timestamp)(results[0]));
}
...
}
```

And here are the C# data types generated from the `CalendarService` WSDL
(refer to Listing 3-1):

```
[System.Xml.Serialization.SoapTypeAttribute("timestamp",
➥"urn:calsv")]
public class timestamp {
    public int year;
    public int month;
    public int day;
    public int hour;
    public int minute;
    public int second;
    public timeZoneId timeZoneId;
}

 [System.Xml.Serialization.SoapTypeAttribute("timeZoneId",
 ➥"urn:calsv")]
public enum timeZoneId {
    ECT,
    GMT,
    PST,
}

/// <remarks/>
[System.Xml.Serialization.SoapTypeAttribute("duration",
➥"urn:calsv")]
public class duration {
    public int day;
    public int hour;
    public int minute;
    public int second;
    public bool forward;
}
```

As you can see, the XML types `timestamp` and `duration` are modeled as C# classes, and the XML type `timeZoneId` is modeled as a C# enumeration.

Generating C++ Classes from Service Contracts

Here is an example of a C++ service proxy class generated from the calendar service WSDL (refer to Listing 3-1):

```cpp
class CalendarComputationClient : public CalendarComputation
{
public:
    CalendarComputationClient();
    CalendarComputationClient(const String & wsdl);
    CalendarComputationClient(const String & wsdl,
            const QName & service_name,  const String &
            ➥port_name);
    CalendarComputationClient();

    virtual void
        computeFinalTimestamp(
            const timestamp &initialTimestamp,
            const duration &duration,
            timestamp &finalTimestamp);

    virtual void
        computeInitialTimestamp(
            const timestamp &finalTimestamp,
            const duration &duration,
            timestamp &initialTimestamp);

    virtual void
        computeDuration(
            const timestamp &initialTimestamp,
            const timestamp &finalTimestamp,
            duration &duration);
    . . .
};
```

As you can see, `CalendarComputationClient` is a C++ service proxy class that models the calendar service and that provides constructors for creating instances of the proxy class and methods that model the operations of the calendar service.

Service-Level Communication and Alternative Transports

Web services are based on SOAP, and SOAP is transport-neutral. Although SOAP defines only one mandatory transport binding (HTTP) and the WS-I basic profile only requires SOAP over HTTP, other bindings can be defined for other transports. For many applications, HTTP is perfectly acceptable; however, HTTP deliberately omits certain features (such as persistent sessions) so that it can scale up and work well over the Web. However, many organizations want to use Web services on their internal networks where (a) the scalability issues of the World Wide Web are not present and (b) they have already invested heavily in designing and deploying an enterprise messaging infrastructure that is based on JMS, WebSphere MQ, CORBA Notification, or Tibco Rendezvous. These organizations want to take advantage of SOAP and WSDL while also taking advantage of their existing enterprise messaging infrastructure.

One of the advantages of a well-defined service contracts is that the logical contract can be defined in a manner that is independent of the underlying communication transport or middleware. This allows the service requesters and service providers to be developed without being tied to a particular transport. WSDL supports this approach by providing extension mechanisms so that alternative (non-HTTP) communication transports can be specified (refer to the figure on page 113). This makes it possible to isolate the application-level code from the underlying communication transports:

1. The application can take advantage of the qualities of service provided by the enterprise messaging infrastructure (such as guaranteed message delivery and security) without being tightly bound to any particular protocol or middleware.

2. The underlying communication transport or middleware can be changed at any time by simply modifying the WSDL without affecting the application code at all.

3. A service provider can be available over multiple communication transports (such as HTTP, HTTPS, JMS, SMTP, and FTP) simultaneously, and service requesters can choose which one to use depending on the qualities of service they require (see Figure 3-11).

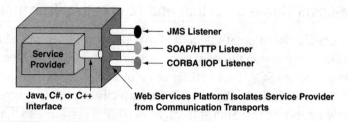

Figure 3-11   Defining multiple transports for a service.

WSDL Extensibility

Although WSDL defines a SOAP binding and an HTTP binding, WSDL is also designed to be extensible and includes binding and port extensibility elements so that additional bindings can be added. For instance, the port definitions can be extended to specify address information for alternative transports. A port defines an individual endpoint by specifying a single address for a binding. Here is the syntax for a port:

```
<wsdl:definitions .... >
    <wsdl:service .... > *
        <wsdl:port name="nmtoken" binding="qname"> *
            <-- extensibility element (1) -->
        </wsdl:port>
    </wsdl:service>
</wsdl:definitions>
```

The binding attribute refers to the binding using the linking rules defined by WSDL.

The name attribute provides a unique name among all ports defined within the enclosing WSDL document.

The binding extensibility elements identified using the number (1) in the listing are used to specify the address information for the port.

The only stipulations are that:

- A port cannot specify more than one address.

- A port cannot specify any binding information other than address information.

SOAP over IBM WebSphere MQ

IBM WebSphere MQ is the granddaddy of commercial message-oriented middleware. It is a proprietary product from IBM, but it is widely used in Global 2000 organizations, and it runs on most operating system platforms in use today.

Here is what a port definition for IBM WebSphere MQ might look like:

```
<service name="CalendarService">
    <port binding="tns:CalendarComputationBinding"
    ➥name="CalendarService">
        <mq:client
                    QueueManager="QManager"
                    QueueName="CalendarRequest"
                    ReplyQueueManager="QManager"
                    ReplyQueueName="CalendarReply"
                    AccessMode="send"
                    CorrelationStyle="correlationId"
                    Delivery="persistent"/>

        <mq:server
                    QueueManager="QManager"
                    QueueName="CalendarRequest"
                    ReplyQueueManager="QManager"
                    ReplyQueueName="CalendarReply"
                    AccessMode="receive"
                    CorrelationStyle="correlationId"
                    Delivery="persistent"/>

    </port>
</service>
```

As you can see, the WSDL port extensors allow WebSphere MQ-related config-uration parameters to be defined in the WSDL, which the service platform can use when sending and receiving SOAP messages over this port.

SOAP over JMS

JMS is the standard Java API for message queuing. It is part of the J2EE specification and a J2EE application server must implement it to be certified. JMS is available anywhere that you find a J2EE application server, and standalone implementations are also available.

Here is what a port definition for JMS might look like:

```
<service name="CalendarService">
    <port binding="tns:CalendarComputationBinding"
    ➥name="jmsPort">
        <jms:address destinationStyle="queue"
            initialContextFactory="com.iona.jbus.jms.naming"
            jndiConnectionFactoryName="sonic:jms/queue/
            ➥connectionFactory"
            jndiDestinationName="sonic:jms/queue/SampleQ1"
            jndiProviderURL="tcp://localhost:2506" messageType=
            ➥"text"/>
    </port>
</service>
```

Unfortunately, interoperability among JMS implementations is limited because the JMS specification only defines the message API and does not specify the on-the-wire format.

SOAP over CORBA IIOP

CORBA is an open standard from the Object Management Group (OMG), and it has been around as long as IBM WebSphere MQ. Over the years, CORBA has evolved to include asynchronous callbacks, guaranteed messaging delivery, publish/subscribe, and message prioritization. CORBA is well known for supporting mission-critical applications, especially in the telecommunications industry, where it serves as the backbone for many telephone communications systems.

Here is what a port definition for CORBA might look like:

```
<service name="CalendarService">
    <port binding="tns:CalendarComputationBinding" name=
    ➥"IIOPPort">
        <iiop:address location="file:../../CalendarService.ior"/>
        <iiop:policy persistent="true"/>
        <iiop:payload type="string"/>
    </port>
</service>
```

Interoperability among CORBA implementations is very good because the CORBA specification not only defines the CORBA APIs but also specifies the on-the-wire format.

SOAP over Tibco Rendezvous

Tibco Rendezvous has been around as long as IBM WebSphere MQ. It is a highly specialized message-oriented middleware primarily known for its publish/subscribe capabilities.

Here is what a port definition for Tibco Rendezvous might look like:

```
<service name="CalendarService">
    <port binding="tns:CalendarComputationBinding" name=
    ➥"TibRvPort">
        <tibrv:port
            serverSubject="CalendarSubject"
            bindingType="string"
            callbackLevel="INFO"/>
    </port>
</service>
```

Tibco Rendezvous is a proprietary product, and it is a favorite in the brokerage and investment management vertical markets.

A Retrospective on Service-Oriented Architectures

In this section, we take a retrospective look at the technologies that have been used in the past to implement SOAs to identify guideposts that can assist in developing SOAs based on Web services technology.

Some people are surprised to learn that service-oriented architectures have been in use for more than 20 years. This is because SOAs are based upon a design philosophy and a broad set of design principles that are technology-independent (see Chapter 2 in the section "Key Service Characteristics").

Although SOAs have been in use for years and adhere to some common principles, each IT department historically has had to create its own SOA and develop most of the practices and infrastructure required to support the SOA itself. Because of the "roll your own nature" of historical SOAs, the implementation of SOAs across organization has been very uneven:

- Some organizations have been able to invest heavily in their SOAs and have established company-wide practices, global infrastructure, and comprehensive tool sets to support the creation, deployment, management, and revision of their SOAs and the accompanying business services—these companies have been enjoying the fruits of their labor (see the "CORBA" section for a case study on Credit Suisse).

- Other organizations with more limited goals and budgets have only rolled out SOAs on a limited basis: for example, one region, one department, less tool support, no central SOA organization, and so on.

- Still other companies never took the "SOA plunge," even on a limited basis.

Even today, as organizations begin rolling out SOAs based on Web services technology, they are finding that they still need to define the appropriate SOA governance framework, development processes, principles, and guidelines. They are also finding that they need to figure out how to piece together the various Web services technologies and fill in any gaps themselves.

Overview of Selected Technologies That Have Been Used to Implement SOAs
Over the years, SOAs have been implemented using a wide variety of technologies:

- **Distributed objects**—CORBA, J2EE, COM/DCOM.

- **Message-oriented middleware (MOM)**—WebSphere MQ, Tibco Rendezvous.

- **TP monitors**—CICS, IMS, Encinia, Tuxedo.

- **Homegrown middleware** developed in house.

- **B2B platforms**—ebXML, RosettaNet.

Of course, some of these technologies are better suited for SOAs than others. The more capabilities a technology provides that match the Web services platform, the better that technology is suited to implement an SOA.

WebSphere MQ

Many large organizations have created SOAs using WebSphere MQ, such as AXA Financial.

Because WebSphere MQ is simply message-oriented middleware, the IT customer is required to provide most of the service platform, including the following:

- Specifying how contracts will be defined (usually a Word or Excel document).

- Defining message formats (e.g., comma-delimited strings, fixed format messages, and more recently, XML).

- Defining how services will be registered and discovered (usually a custom registry).

- Providing service-level security mechanisms (including authentication, authorization, encryption, audit logs).

- Providing service-level management facilities.

Given the amount of work required, why would anyone use WebSphere MQ as the basis for an SOA?

- **IT vendor affinity**—Most organizations using WebSphere MQ for their SOA are long-time IBM customers.

- **Mainframe affinity**—Most organizations using WebSphere MQ for their SOA are using it in whole or in part to access mainframe transactions implemented in CICS or IMS.

- **Wide platform availability**—WebSphere MQ is available across a wide range of platforms.

- **Promotes loose-coupling**—WebSphere MQ imposes very few requirements on service requesters or service providers. For example, the WebSphere MQ APIs can be invoked from nearly any programming language. Also, the service requesters or service providers can compose messages using simple string concatenation without having to adopt more sophisticated techniques such as those provided/imposed by distributed object technologies (J2EE, CORBA, DCOM/COM).

- **Simple programming model**—WebSphere MQ has a very simple API that application developers can quickly learn.

- **Reliable messaging**—WebSphere MQ provides guaranteed message delivery, which is one of the core requirements of many mission-critical applications using an SOA.

- **Availability of third-party products to secure and manage WebSphere MQ.**

Here is a case study of an SOA being implemented using WebSphere MQ. AXA Financial, a $US 7.5 billion insurance and financial services company, achieved a 300 percent return on this SOA investment using IBM's WebSphere MQ as a messaging and integration layer to connect legacy systems with front-end applications.

AXA created an SOA that sits in front of all of the legacy systems and provides all of the communications between the legacy and front-end systems. AXA began developing the architecture in 1989. The SOA integration architecture currently handles more than 600,000 transactions a day.[4]

Although WebSphere MQ can be used to implement an SOA, this does not mean that all WebSphere MQ systems are service-oriented, and in fact, it is probably safe to say that only a small fraction of WebSphere MQ systems are service-oriented.

---

[4] References: *CIO* magazine, 10/03/2004, http://www.cio.com.au/index.php?id=1878902006
FinanceTech, Oct 29, 2003, http://www.financetech.com/utils/printableArticle.jhtml?
articleID=15800042.

CORBA

Many large organizations have created SOAs using CORBA, such as Credit Suisse. Using CORBA to implement an SOA requires looking beyond CORBA's traditional role in distributed object technology and realizing that it provides many of the key ingredients of a service platform, including the following:

- CORBA is an open standard.

- CORBA supports remote method invocation (i.e., RPC calls), asynchronous messaging, and publish/subscribe communications.

- CORBA provides integrated security, naming services, transaction management, and reliable messaging.

- CORBA supports multiple programming languages.

- CORBA provides CORBA IDL, which can be used as a service definition language.

- CORBA objects can be exposed as Web services because the OMG has defined a CORBA IDL to WSDL mapping.

Of course, CORBA also has some limitations for implementing an SOA:

- CORBA is perceived as being complex.

- CORBA requires both the service requester and the service provider to be using CORBA.

- CORBA does not provide explicit support for XML and does not support loosely coupled, asynchronous exchange of business documents over the Internet.

Here is a case study of an SOA being implemented using CORBA. Credit Suisse Group is a leading global financial services company headquartered in Zurich, Switzerland. Like many other financial institutions, Credit Suisse is the result of mergers among several companies. Its information systems have been evolving since the mid-1990s to support the restructuring of the company along the lines of its business units.

In 1997, Credit Suisse started the implementation of an SOA called the Credit Suisse Information Bus (CSIB), an integration infrastructure meant to enable service-oriented access to the back-end core application systems. The goal of the CSIB was to enable reliable, secure, and scalable real-time request/reply interoperability between back-end systems and a variety of front-end applications based on different platforms (J2EE, C++, SmallTalk, HTML, COM, and Visual Basic). CSIB is built using CORBA, specifically, IONA's Orbix product, and it replaced an integration infrastructure based on IBM WebSphere MQ that was becoming expensive and difficult to maintain because Credit Suisse had to develop a number of layers on top of WebSphere MQ to support the request/ reply paradigm and to provide error handling, data conversion, a naming service, and other services.

Credit Suisse's SOA supports more than 100,000 users, including 600 business services in production. Credit Suisse's SOA has resulted in a 70 percent reuse of business services, a 73 percent cost reduction for systems development and integration, and time to market of new solutions has dramatically improved.

As with WebSphere MQ, although CORBA can be used to implement an SOA, this does not mean that all CORBA systems are service-oriented, and in fact, it is probably safe to say that only a small percentage of CORBA systems are service-oriented.

Java and J2EE
Java and J2EE technologies have many of the same advantages and disadvantages as CORBA when it comes to implementing an SOA. Here are some of the similarities related to SOA:

- Both are open standards.
- Both are distributed object technologies that provide excellent support for remote method invocation (i.e., RMI-IIOP and IIOP).
- Both require the service requester and the service provider to be using the same technology stack (i.e., J2EE and CORBA).

- Both provide integrated security, naming services (JNDI and CORBA Naming Service), transaction management (JTA/JTS and Object Transaction Service), and reliable messaging (JMS and CORBA Notification).

- Both J2EE EJBs and CORBA objects can be exposed as Web services. J2EE provides explicit support for Web services starting with J2EE 1.4, and the OMG has defined a CORBA IDL to WSDL mapping.

Here are some of the differences related to SOA:

- CORBA supports multiple programming languages.

- CORBA provides CORBA IDL as an explicit interface definition language.

- J2EE Web services communicate natively using XML and SOAP, whereas the CORBA WSDL mapping still communicates using CDL and IIOP.

- The Java Community Process has defined a series of APIs for manipulating XML (e.g., JAX-RPC, JAAS, JAX-B, and so on).

- J2EE has a much larger and more robust developer community.

- J2EE implementations are available from most of the major IT vendors.

As with WebSphere and CORBA, although J2EE can be used to implement an SOA, this does not mean that all J2EE systems are service-oriented, and in fact, it is probably safe to say that most J2EE applications are tightly coupled, stove-pipe applications.

B2B Platforms

Although often overlooked when discussing SOA, B2B platforms such as ebXML and RosettaNet are ideal Web services platforms because:

- They are open standards.

- They are loosely coupled.

- They are based on XML.

- They are based on the asynchronous exchange of business documents (i.e., XML documents).

- They provide integrated mechanisms for service registration, service security, service monitoring and management, business process management, compensating transactions, and reliable messaging.

Detailed Comparison of SOA Technologies

To assess the current maturity of XML Web Services for SOAs, they can be compared to earlier technologies that were successfully used to build SOAs. Table 3-3 presents a side-by-side comparison of three approaches to SOAs:

- WebSphere MQ with Custom Extensions.

- CORBA.

- XML Web Services.

Table 3-3   Three Approaches to SOAs

Element of the Service Platform	WebSphere MQ with Custom Extensions	CORBA	XML Web Services
Open standards	No—proprietary	Yes—OMG	Yes—standards in place but fragmented across multiple organizations
Support for multiple programming languages	Yes	Yes	Yes
Loosely coupled	Yes	Mediocre	Yes
XML-based	Can be	Can be	Yes
Service Contracts			
Technology neutral service contract definition	Ad hoc—text file, Word, Excel, Access	CORBA IDL	WSDL and XML Schema Proposed standards—WS-Policy family
Message/parameter definition	Usually COBOL Copybook	CORBA IDL	WSDL and XML Schema

Element of the Service Platform	WebSphere MQ with Custom Extensions	CORBA	XML Web Services
Message/parameter validation	Custom built	CORBA IDL enforces interface compiler	XML Schema and validating XML parsers
Message/parameter parsing	Custom built	Automatic and built-in via language bindings	Automatic via a wide variety of tools DOM, SAX, JAAS, JAX-RPC, and so on
Service-Level Data Management			
Data typing	None	CORBA IDL	XML Schema and WSDL
Data validation	None	Methods parameter validation	XML Schema and validating XML parsers
Data query	None	None	XPath and XQuery
Data transformation	None	None	XSLT
Service Registration and Discovery			
Interface repository	None	CORBA interface repository	UDDI—public or private
Naming service	None	CORBA naming service	UDDI—public or private
Trading service	None	CORBA trading service	UDDI—public or private
Service-Level Security			
Authentication	User id / password	IIOP/TLS	HTTP/S, WS-Security
Authorization	None	IIOP/TLS	SAML, XACML
Data privacy	None	IIOP/TLS	HTTP/S, WS-Security
Data integrity	None	IIOP/TLS	HTTP/S, WS-Security
Service-Level Interaction Patterns			
One-way, synchronous	Yes	Yes	Yes

continues

Table 3-3   Three Approaches to SOAs (continued)

Element of the Service Platform	WebSphere MQ with Custom Extensions	CORBA	XML Web Services
Request/response	Yes—weak support, application level management of correlated message pairs	Yes	Yes
One-way, asynchronous	Yes—strong support	Yes—weak support	Multiple proposed standards ■ WS-Reliability ■ WS-ReliableMessaging
Publish/subscribe	Yes—weak support	Yes	Multiple proposed standards ■ WS-Eventing ■ WS-Notification
Service-Level Communication			
Data conversion between platforms and programming languages	Rudimentary ASCII ←→ EDCIDIC	Yes	Text-based messages do not require translation
Service-Level Qualities of Service			
Session management	Yes	Yes	WS-SecureConversation, WS-Context
Load balancing	Yes	Yes	Not addressed by standards; support depends on vendor products
Guaranteed message delivery	Yes	Yes	Multiple proposed standards ■ WS-Reliability ■ WS-ReliableMessaging

Element of the Service Platform	WebSphere MQ with Custom Extensions	CORBA	XML Web Services
Transaction management	WebSphere MQ's as XA-compliant transaction manager	OTS (including XA support)	Multiple proposed standards ■ WS-AT, BA, C ■ WS-CAF ■ Support for both two-phase commit and compensating transactions
Service-level management	None—third-party products	None—third-party products	Web services distributed management (WSDM) and WS-Management

From this chart, you can see that XML Web Services have many of the building blocks for creating an SOA, but the extended Web services standards are required to deliver enterprise qualities of service.

Summary

In this chapter, we continued discussing SOA by explaining in greater detail the core elements of defining a SOA using Web services, including defining service contracts using WSDL, defining service-level data models using XML Schema, connecting service requesters and service providers using different service level interaction patterns, providing service-level security using WS-Security and related security specifications, and using alternative transports for Web services. Finally, we presented a retrospective on SOA and looked at how SOAs have been implemented in the past using non-Web services technologies such as WebSphere MQ and CORBA.

Chapter 4

SOA and Web Services for Integration

This chapter discusses using SOA and Web services for integration. It begins by presenting an overview of integration, including business drivers, common business and technical goals, and recurring technical challenges. Next, it discusses why XML and Web services are ideal technologies for solving integration problems. It then presents Web services integration (WSI) and service-oriented integration (SOI), which represent two alternative views about how to use Web services technology for integration.

Organizations can choose between WSI and SOI, depending on business and technical requirements and goals and the level of formality that they wish to incorporate into the integration process. In reality, most organizations will fall somewhere in between these two views.

Finally, the chapter illustrates using Web services for integration by demonstrating the integration of .NET Framework and J2EE applications.

Overview of Integration

There was a brief instance in the early days of management information systems when IT departments did not have any integration problems…then somebody wrote the *second* business application, and integration has been IT's dirty little secret ever since. Actually, it isn't that little anymore (IDC estimates that by 2005, companies will spend more than $15 billion for enterprise integration software[1]), and it isn't that secret (system integration consistently ranks as one of the top three priorities for IT executives[2]).

Before we can fully appreciate how and why Web services will change integration, we need to review some of the business drivers and technical factors that make integration such a hard problem in the first place. In general, it boils down to the fact that integration techniques and products have the unenviable job of reconciling the differences between multiple IT systems whenever those systems need to interact. Of course, if all of these differences happened to lie along one dimension (such as reconciling data between systems), then the problem wouldn't be so tough to solve. However, integration is required to resolve multiple layers of business and technical requirements among systems that, more often than not, were developed by different development teams using different technology and solving different business problems.

Common Business Drivers for Integration

First, let's review a list of common business drivers for integration and why organizations need to invest in SOA with Web services:

- **Mergers and acquisitions**—M&A activity typically results in multiple IT systems that handle similar transactions and that need to be consolidated before the business value of the M&A can be fully realized.

- **Internal reorganization**—Although not as dramatic as M&As, internal reorganizations pose many of the same problems, and they occur more frequently.

---

[1] Stephen D. Hendrick, IDC, EIS Review and Forecast, December 2001.

[2] Stephen D. Hendrick, IDC, SW Strategies & Investment Survey, Final, Users, Fall 2001.

- **Application/system consolidation**—In this scenario, multiple IT systems handle similar transactions, so they need to be consolidated or replaced to save money, reduce head count, and streamline business operations. For example, consider a telecommunications company that has a dozen different billing systems.

- **Inconsistent/duplicated/fragmented data**—Sometimes important business data is spread across many systems and must be consolidated and "cleansed" to facilitate better decision-making. For example, you might want to give all employees a single view of the customer.

- **New business strategies**—Innovative companies frequently implement new business strategies that redefine the business environment but also requires IT systems to work together in novel ways. Eventually, other companies in the same industry have to adopt the same changes to stay competitive. Examples include relationship banking, billing on behalf of others in telecommunications, and just-in-time manufacturing.

- **Comply with new government regulations**—New government regulations may require redefining business processes to protect consumers and/or meet new information reporting requirements. Examples include HIPPA (insurance), T+1 trade settlement (securities), and local number portability (telecommunications).

- **Streamlining business processes**—Old business process that required data to be manually entered into multiple systems often need to be replaced with newer systems where transactions flow among systems without human intervention. For example, a company might previously have received orders via fax and manually entered them into the order management system and manufacturing control system. Now, the company receives orders via the Web site and automatically enters them into the order management system and manufacturing control system.

Common Technical Challenges Faced During Integration

Here is a partial list of the problems that often fall under the integration umbrella:

1. Reconcile incompatible business processes implemented by different systems.

2. Reconcile the differences between the data used by different systems (including both data syntax and information semantics).

3. Reconcile incompatible technologies used to implement the different systems.

4. Reconcile the different time scales in which different systems operate (e.g., OLTP systems operate at the granularity of sub-seconds, whereas batch systems operate at the granularity of days or weeks).

5. Reconcile the different interaction patterns used by different systems (e.g., synchronous communication versus asynchronous communication versus event-driven processing).

Requirements That the "Ideal" Integration Solution Must Satisfy

Besides the technical challenges listed previously, the "ideal" integration solution must satisfy the following requirements, too:

1. Inexpensive, with a fast ROI.

2. Easy to learn and easy to administer.

3. Non-invasive—existing systems should remain untouched.

4. Scalable, reliable, highly available, fault-tolerant, secure, and so on.

5. Flexible and easily customized so that it can be adapted to each project's requirements.

To complicate matters further, there is no single set of business goals that everyone agrees upon that any particular integration project should strive to achieve. Sometimes a tactical/opportunistic approach is best, while in other cases, a strategic/systematic approach is appropriate—it all depends on the business requirements. Here is a list of goals that typically apply at either end of the strategic versus tactical spectrum:

Strategic	Tactical
Systematic.	Opportunistic.
Invest for the future.	Quick and dirty.
Enterprise-solution ("Integrate our systems worldwide!")	Point-solution ("Solve this problem now!")
Fastest time-to-market across multiple projects.	Fastest time-to-market for this project.
Lowest cost across multiple projects.	Lowest cost for this project.
Define and use an enterprise data model, which can facilitate many diverse integration projects but requires getting "buy in" from many departments.	Rely on ad hoc data models that can be quickly created for the needs of a single project.
Create an enterprise integration backbone or "enterprise nervous system," which can provide a foundation for many diverse integration projects but requires getting "buy in" from many departments.	Rely on point-to-point integrations that can be quickly created for the needs of a single project.
Strive for loosely coupled integration because it provides more flexibility across multiple projects and administrative boundaries.	Rely on tightly coupled integrations on a project-by-project basis, which are less flexible but usually easier to define.
Insist on standards-based integration techniques that are vendor-neutral and technology-neutral so that they can evolve as vendors and technology change.	Integrate the systems in the quickest manner, even if it means using proprietary, vendor-specific features and technology.
Provide enterprise qualities of service (QoS) that support global requirements for transaction volume and security.	"Just get it up and running ASAP—we'll worry about scaling up later."

Often, business and technical people wonder, "Which is better: a strategic approach to integration or a tactical one?." There is no hard and fast rule. For instance, it is hard to avoid tactical solutions when you are paying $5 million a month in fines because you can't deliver the information and reports required by a regulatory agency. At the same time, the costs associated with the "care and feeding" of dozens of ad hoc tactical integrations quickly outweigh the costs associated with a more strategic approach. A pragmatic motto is:

Be strategic when you can, and be tactical when you have to.

Integration Can Be Performed at Different Layers of the Technology Stack
Furthermore, integration can be accomplished at many different layers of the IT technology stack:

- **Data integration**—Focus on integrating at the data level, often by synchronizing the contents of various databases, data marts, and data warehouses. The key problems encountered involve reconciling the database schema across databases and reconciling the meaning of the data elements.

- **Message integration**—Focus on creating integrations by exchanging messages between applications; the messages usually represent transactions that occurred in one application and need to be reliably propagated to other applications. The key problems encountered involve converting application data to and from messages and transforming messages between the different formats understood by the different applications.

- **Component integration**—Focus on wrapping legacy systems using component technology (CORBA, .NET, or J2EE) and linking components using their component interfaces. The key problems encountered are integration across component models (i.e., it can be a challenge to integrate CORBA and .NET or J2EE and .NET).

- **Application integration**—Focus on integrating applications using their published APIs, object models, message formats, database schema, and whatever techniques the resourceful programmer can come up with. The key problems encountered involve reconciling the data models of different applications and the fact that most packaged applications only provided rudimentary integration facilities until recently. This form of integration usually refers to integrating packaged applications.

- **Service integration**—Focus on creating abstract business services that are not tied to a single database, component model, or packaged application and using these services as the building blocks for integrating systems.

The key problems encountered with this form of integration usually require a mature integration architecture (i.e., an SOA) so that the service interfaces can be cleanly separated from the underlying implementations.

■ **Process integration**—Focus on creating new business processes by integrating existing IT assets (such as data, components, applications, and services). This form of integration explicitly defines and manages the business processes separately from any specific application. The key problems encountered with this form of integration usually require cross-organizational agreement on the business processes and a mature integration infrastructure so that the existing IT assets can be cleanly integrated.

■ **User interface integration**—Often has two different meanings: 1. Using the UI of a legacy application as the interface for extracting data from the application or executing transactions against the application (a.k.a. screen-scraping); 2. Integration is done at the desktop or the presentation layer (as in a portal). The key problem encountered with screen-scraping is that it can be very brittle, especially when the user interface of the target application changes; the key problem encountered with portals is that they only solve the user-facing piece of the integration puzzle.

■ **B2B integration**—Focus on automating key business processes and business services across two or more organizations. This can be as simple as two organizations linking their systems on an ad hoc basis using a VPN and file transfer. This process becomes exponentially more complicated when dozens of companies want to automate their processes across a complex supply chain using the insecure Internet.

Integration and Interoperability Using XML and Web Services

Recent experience shows that a better answer to the myriad challenges of integration is the introduction of an additional layer of abstraction for existing and new IT systems—the XML layer represented by Web services standards. Instead of dealing with the complexity of multiple incompatible applications on multiple computers, programming languages, and application packages by introducing yet another programming environment, it turns out that it's possible to add a layer of abstraction or system of extensions to virtually any new or existing environment.

Defining Web Services

Most people, when they refer to Web services, mean the formal definition of XML applications contained within the SOAP, WSDL, and other related specifications. However, it is entirely possible, and often done in practice, to define a Web service as a free form or special form of XML document exchanged by private agreement. In other words, it's possible to create a Web service that follows no standard other than XML and HTTP. In practice, using the standards provides the basis for interoperability and integration because they provide more structure and commonality than simply using XML and HTTP. Web services also support the clean separation of application from infrastructure functionality—the SOAP engine can automatically manage infrastructure functionality, such as security, reliability, and transactions. With straight XML over HTTP, the application itself must implement these advanced functions.

Common approaches to using Web services for integration include:

- **Legacy data-driven**—Deciding on the legacy data to be shared (database tables, file formats, legacy message formats), developing XML Schema for the legacy data, and then using SOAP as the message format.

- **API/method-driven**—Deciding on the remote methods or program APIs to be exposed as Web services, defining XML data types for the methods or program arguments, and then using SOAP for the message format.

- **Contract-driven**—Defining the contracts for the Web services first and then providing wrappers for the legacy systems that map between the interface defined by the contract and the legacy data/messages/APIs. In these cases, the contract is typically derived from the business data that needs to be shared, rather than the format of the legacy data or the program APIs of the underlying software systems.

After the Web services are defined, it is necessary for them to be categorized and stored in a UDDI or other service registry so that service requestors can locate them.

In particular, Web services technologies:

- Provide a new way for allowing existing and new applications to interoperate.

- Support the ability to create composite applications by quickly and easily combining interfaces to individual applications.

- Make it easier to combine and analyze data from various sources, using XML as the standard data format.

- Introduce new and cheaper mechanisms for interaction with applications on PCs, laptops, and portable devices.

- Allow less highly trained workers to interact with IT systems for generating reports, automating business processes, and updating important documents.

Figure 4-1 illustrates the problem when multiple systems with disparate application environments interoperate. Once again, we can see the pivotal role that WSDL service contracts play in defining the services provided by each system.

When using Web services technologies as the basis for an integration architecture, as shown in Figure 4-1, data is converted into a canonical format understood by everyone (in this case, XML), and messages are passed in a standard format from one endpoint to another. Each endpoint is responsible for transforming its native data types and formats into XML when sending a message and for translating XML data types into its native data types and formats when receiving a message.

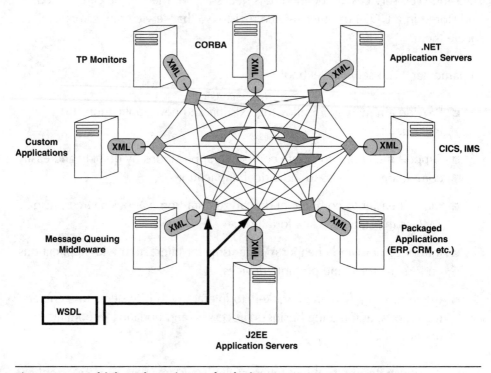

Figure 4-1   Multiple Web services technologies.

However, there are clearly cases in which the canonical message approach does not make sense. This is when the technologies on both sides of the communication link are the same. There's no sense in converting a CORBA data structure to XML and then back again when the sender and receiver are both implemented using CORBA and are running inside the firewall. In this case, and any other case of pair-wise communication, it's important to have the flexibility to use the native data types and protocols for performance and ease of integration when it's possible to do so.

Two Approaches for Using XML and Web Services for Integration and Interoperability

Two approaches have emerged for using XML and Web services for integration and interoperability:

- **Web services integration (WSI[3])**—The tactical and opportunistic application of Web services to solving integration and interoperability problems.

- **Service-oriented integration (SOI)**—Integration using Web services in the context of an SOA—that is, the strategic and systematic application of Web services to solving integration and interoperability problems.

Both approaches are built on the bedrock of XML, SOAP, and WSDL. Both approaches use the same technology defined by the Web services platform, but only SOI applies them in a strategic and systematic manner based on the principles of an SOA, including defining an SOA governance framework and defining SOA processes and best practices that are implemented on a department-wide or organization-wide basis. For instance, both approaches might use UDDI as a service registry, but SOI will define a consistent service taxonomy that satisfies the organization's requirements across multiple projects, while WSI has each integration team catalog services in the UDDI registry with little or no regard for consistency across multiple projects.

Neither approach is inherently better, although they lead to different outcomes and are better (or worse) depending on your goals.

In the next two sub-sections, we take a closer look at WSI and SOI.

Web Services Integration (WSI)

WSI tends to work best for opportunistic, tactical integration projects when immediate results and short-term ROI are required and when longer-term costs are less important.

---

[3] Not to be confused with WS-I, the abbreviation for the Web Services Interoperability Organization.

A typical WSI project involves a small number of systems (two to four) that need to exchange data. The project team defines SOAP messages based on the following:

- Data the systems need to exchange.

- Legacy message formats that the systems already understand.

- Legacy APIs/methods that are available for accessing the systems.

The team then defines WSDL contracts, which include interfaces, operations, and message exchange patterns that fulfill the immediate project requirements. Enterprise qualities of service (such as security, reliable messaging, transaction management, and failover) are implemented on an as-needed basis and defined using associated policy information.

Here are some of the advantages of WSI:

- Faster time-to-market, especially for the first couple of WSI projects and especially when the number of systems is small.

- Lower integration costs, especially for the first couple of WSI projects and when the number of systems is small.

Here are some of the limitations of WSI:

- Minimal consideration is given to creating data, service, and process models that are broadly reusable in this service domain or across service domains. For instance, the `Customer` type might mean one thing on the first WSI project and something else on the next one.

- Applications send SOAP messages by using the transport-level or middle-ware APIs directly, thus making it difficult to migrate to alternative transports or middleware when necessary.

- Security is handled in a tactical, ad hoc manner, and typically no allowance is made for using the same security architecture across multiple WSI projects. This greatly complicates implementing facilities such as single sign-on in the future.

- No consideration is given for applying the Web services platform in a consistent fashion across multiple projects—for instance, one project uses UDDI as the service registry, the next one allows service requesters to retrieve WSDL documents using simple HTTP GET messages, while the third one uses WS-MetadataExchange.

- No provisions are made for versioning the Web services in a consistent fashion across multiple projects, so the organization ends up with multiple versioning schemes, which reduces long-term service reuse.

After a series of WSI projects have been completed, the organization essentially has created a series of point-to-point integrations (see Figure 4-2). Of course, the integrations aren't point-to-point in the old-fashioned sense, where one uses file transfer, another uses TCP/IP, and yet another uses database synchronization. However, they are point-to-point in the sense that they don't share the same data model, they don't share the same security architecture, and they don't provide a high degree of reusability.

Figure 4-2 illustrates the situation after three WSI projects are completed:

1. Project #1 (solid lines) integrated applications based upon J2EE, message queuing, a TP monitor, and legacy custom applications using one set of XML Schema and one set of service contracts.

2. Project #2 (lines with long dashes) integrated legacy custom applications and applications based upon CORBA, .NET, and a TP monitor using a second set of XML Schema and service contracts.

3. Project #3 (lines with small squares) integrated legacy packaged applications and applications based upon J2EE, .NET, and CICS using a third set of XML Schema and service contracts.

In this example, each project developed different data and service models and employed different security techniques. Needless to say, each project was completed relatively quickly due to its narrow scope. However, imagine the problems that will be encountered when the results of these projects need to be integrated and there are three different definitions of a customer, three different definitions of an account, and three different ways of enforcing role-based access control.

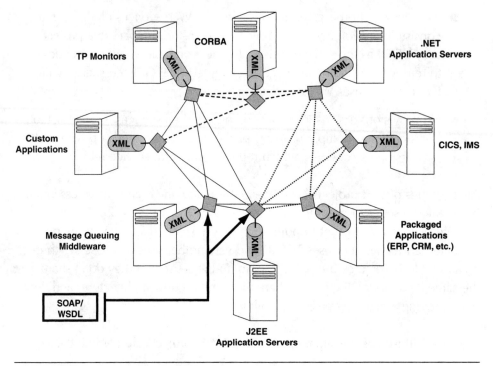

Figure 4-2   WSI creates a series of point-to-point integrations.

Service-Oriented Integration (SOI)

SOI is integration using Web services in the context of an SOA. SOI is the strategic and systematic application of Web services to solving integration and interoperability problems. SOI tends to work best for organizations that are trying to maximize the long-term results of an integration architecture by heavily investing in one.

Unlike WSI, implementing SOI starts before the first project begins. During the start-up phase:

■ The SOA governance framework, processes, guidelines, models, and tools are defined.

■ Formal modeling of the service domain is used—these models do not have to be exhaustive, but they should identify key data types, service contracts, and processes that are used within the organization and are visible to other organizations. Ideally, some of the data, service, and processes models can be reused from established vertical industry standards.

■ A service taxonomy is defined so services can be consistently categorized and cataloged across multiple projects to promote future service reuse.

■ Where the Web services platform offers multiple options for accomplishing similar tasks, a single consistent approach is selected and applied across multiple projects. For example, distribution of WSDL service contracts is standardized.

Within this framework, a typical SOI project involves:

■ Refining existing data models to accommodate this integration project.

■ Defining formal service contracts beyond what can be defined in WSDL to include business rules, security policies, management policies, versioning policies, and recovery policies. Where possible, WS-Policy is used to define and communicate these policy decisions.

■ Configuring legacy system wrappers that comply with the service contract (while encapsulating implementation details of the legacy systems), or creating new services that are required for this integration project.

■ Defining data transformations that map data between different data models when the data cross service domain boundaries.

■ Configuring the execution environment(s) for the Web services platform to provide and enforce enterprise qualities of service such as transactional requirements, guaranteed message delivery, and recovering policies.

Figure 4-3 illustrates how an SOI would evolve over time. Modeling tools are used to create initial data, service, and process models for the service domain, and these are stored in a metadata repository. Each integration project begins by using and refining the same models—therefore, consistent definitions of Customer and Account are used when information is exchanged between systems in this service domain (although internally each legacy system might represent Customer differently). At run-time, IT systems use the service registry (possibly UDDI) to look up services but then invoke the services directly.

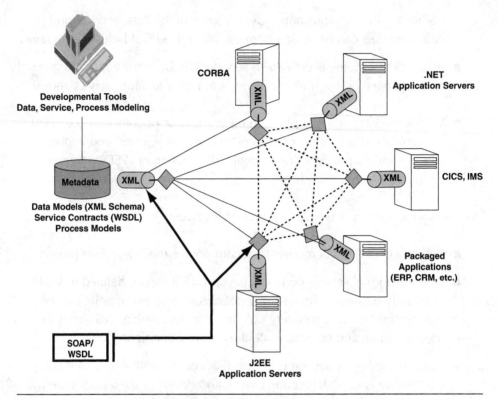

Figure 4-3   SOI maximizes the long-term value of an integration architecture.

This leads to the centralized/decentralized SOI architecture shown in Figure 4-3.

■ It is centralized in the sense that all projects and all IT systems have access to the same metadata repository[4] of data, service, and process models and can use these as the basis for exchanging information and executing transactions.

---

[4] Figure 4-3 shows a single metadata repository, but in fact, there might be separate metadata repositories for different departments, or there could be separate development-time, pre-production, and production versions of the metadata repository. (It could also be a single metadata repository that stores development-time, pre-production, and production versions of the metadata in different partitions of the repository.)

- It is decentralized in the sense that any system can directly utilize the services provided by any other system and there isn't a centralized EAI hub connecting them.

The centralized/decentralized SOI architecture allows each integration team to independently implement and register the service providers for which it is responsible (either by writing greenfield services or creating SOI wrappers for legacy systems), while ensuring that any other integration team can access and use these services.

Here are some of the advantages of SOI:

- The SOI creates formal and reusable data, service, and process models that are broadly applicable in this service domain or across service domains.

- A Web services platform is established that creates an abstraction layer that reduces vendor lock-in and simplifies application migration and consolidation in the future.

- The Web services platform provides enterprise qualities of service (such as security, reliable messaging, transaction management, and failover) so that they can be applied in a consistent fashion across all integration projects.

- Application code does not need to implement enterprise qualities of service (such as security, reliable messaging, transaction management, and failover) because the Web services platform provides them.

- The SOI also creates a formally defined security architecture capable of supporting a wide range of integration projects that is better able to support cross-application, cross-project, and cross-organization security requirements, such as ensuring that role-based access control and single sign-on can be implemented in a consistent manner across all integration projects.

Here are some of the limitations of SOI:

■ Incurs relatively high start-up costs (and slower time-to-market) as the SOI is established, but marginal costs of successive projects drop dramatically (and time-to-market accelerates) as reusable data models, service models, and process models are created and validated, which in turn streamline successive integration projects.

■ Requires a skilled and dedicated cadre of enterprise architects.

■ Requires the commitment of business managers and technical managers.

■ Requires a culture that values strategic and systematic IT projects (or a willingness to create such a culture).

Applying SOA and Web Services for Integration—.NET and J2EE Interoperability

Web services are typically created for the purpose of exchanging data between applications or services, or for exposing an object method for access by another software program.[5] A Web service contract defines how the Web services messages are mapped between various applications, technologies, and software systems.

In an ideal world, a Java bean could seamlessly invoke any .NET Framework object developed using Visual Basic, C#, or Visual C++, but because of platform and language differences, this is not possible. In a nutshell, the .NET platform is designed for close compatibility with the Windows operating system, and it takes full advantage of native Windows features such as multithreading, memory management, file system access, and other system-level APIs. On the other hand, the J2EE platform takes advantage of the Java virtual machine's

---

[5] It must be noted that using Web services for remote object invocation is an inappropriate use of Web services. If you want to implement distributed objects, then you should use a distributed object technology, like Java RMI or CORBA. Web services is a document-oriented technology, not an object-oriented technology. Nevertheless, it is a fact of life that some analysts and vendors recommend that the best way for, say, a C# requestor to communicate with, say, a Java provider is using RPC-oriented Web services.

portability layer to provide the same features and functionality across all operating systems on which it runs.

Web services can be used to provide interoperability across applications developed using .NET and J2EE, but there are limitations because of the level of functionality currently available in Web services and because of significant differences between the .NET architecture and the J2EE architecture.

Figure 4-4 places the .NET and J2EE environments side by side, highlighting the fundamental difference in their designs with respect to operating system integration. .NET is designed to integrate very closely with the Windows operating system, while J2EE is designed to work on any operating system, including Windows.

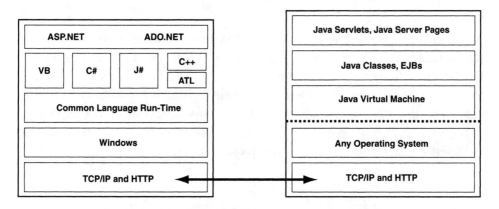

Figure 4-4   Comparing J2EE and .NET architectures.

Because of key differences, interoperability between the .NET platform and the J2EE platform is limited and can only be achieved at a fairly high level of abstraction. The best approach is to define service contracts (i.e., WSDL interfaces) that either exchange coarse-grained data objects or encapsulate multiple method invocations into a single WSDL service. For example, if both applications need to share customer data, then you should define an XML Schema for the customer record, use it to define the appropriate WSDL operations, and generate SOAP messages based upon it. The WSDL file and the associated XML Schema are crucial because they define the shared data model.

Different Approaches to Web Services

It's interesting to note that the .NET platform was completely redesigned for Web services, thereby introducing a discontinuity for Microsoft developers. Applications written using VB6, for example, have to be rewritten to take advantage of .NET features, including Web services. The J2EE approach, on the other hand, did not involve a fundamental rewrite or redesign of the platform but instead viewed Web services as being similar to any other external technology (such as directories, databases, or security servers) for which a new J2EE API had to be developed. It's very interesting to consider which approach is better—a revolutionary re-architecting of the platform or a more evolutionary embrace-and-extend approach.

As Figure 4-5 illustrates, when both a .NET system and a J2EE system, for example, are able to share and understand the same WSDL file, they can interoperate. Because Web services do not include all the features and functionality of J2EE and .NET, however, the interoperability is constrained to what can be achieved using Web services. In particular, features of J2EE and .NET pertaining to object lifecycle management and persistent sessions aren't supported because Web services standards do not include these features.

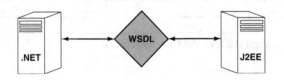

Figure 4-5   The WSDL contract allows disparate systems to interoperate.

Figure 4-6[6] illustrates the fact that when the .NET platform and the J2EE platform share a Web services contract, they communicate using SOAP messages.

---

[6] Note that UDDI is not shown in these illustrations because it represents an optional element of the Web services architecture. Web services descriptions can be shared without using UDDI.

Because SOAP messages are XML documents, each participant needs to be able to understand XML. The WSDL files agreed to by both parties result in the generation of a SOAP message (assuming, of course, that the data type incompatibilities can be resolved) that both sides can understand and exchange to accomplish interoperability. This illustration shows that both ends of the connection need to have access to the same WSDL definitions so that both SOAP nodes can process the messages according to the common WSDL definition and ensure that interoperability via SOAP can be achieved.

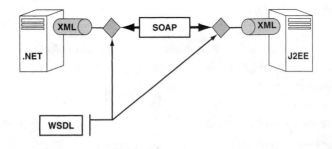

Figure 4-6   The WSDL contract describes how to process the SOAP message.

In some cases, a binary protocol such as .NET Remoting or RMI/IIOP can support additional QoS without relying upon the availability of the full range of WS-* specifications. Binary protocol options are often provided in enterprise service bus (ESB) products. The ESB support of binary protocols relies upon the same WSDL contract as the SOAP over HTTP option, but uses additional transport bindings.

Applying SOA and Web Services for Integration— Service-Enabling Legacy Systems

Web services technologies can be used to create a contract between disparate software systems such as J2EE, CORBA, .NET, WebSphere MQ, and packaged applications. This contract is described using XML and is expressed using a pattern of messages exchanged between the described applications. The contract defines a mutually agreed abstraction of the systems being bridged. Because J2EE, .NET, CORBA, WebSphere MQ, SAP, and virtually any other software system all understand Web services, getting them to interoperate means finding Web services contracts upon which the disparate systems can agree.

One of the advantages of well-defined service contracts is that they can be extended beyond newly developed Web services to also incorporate legacy systems. In particular, legacy systems can be service-enabled by defining WSDL contracts for them and providing SOAP applications that can receive SOAP messages and convert them into message-level or API-level invocations of the legacy systems.

The benefit of this approach is that it allows organizations to cost-effectively reuse valuable legacy assets without adopting expensive and risky "rip-and-replace" strategies.

Almost any legacy system can be service-enabled, including the following:

- Mainframe systems (e.g., CICS and IMS).
- Distributed object applications (e.g., CORBA, DCOM, J2EE).
- Transaction processing systems (e.g., Tuxedo and Encina).
- Packaged applications (e.g., SAP, PeopleSoft, Oracle applications).
- DBMS (e.g., Oracle, Sybase, DB2, SQL Server).
- B2B and messaging systems (e.g., SWIFT, EDIFACT, X12, HL7, WebSphere MQ, JMS, MSMQ).

In the following sections, we give some practical examples of service-enabling legacy systems.

Example #1—CICS and IMS
Mainframe-based legacy applications running on CICS and IMS carry out most of the mission-critical business transactions that are performed each and every day, so it is important to understand how to service-enable these legacy systems. However, unlike CORBA, CICS and IMS do not provide interface

definition languages, nor do they provide reflection capabilities. Instead, things like COBOL Copybooks or 3270 screen buffers usually define the interface to CICS and IMS transactions.[7]

Suppose the interface to a CICS or IMS transaction is defined by a pair of COBOL Copybooks (one defines the input data or request message and the other defines the output data or response message). Because COBOL Copybooks represent COBOL's data model, then the first step in service-enabling the CICS transaction is to map the COBOL Copybooks into XML Schema and then define the service operations using WSDL. Here is a very simple COBOL Copybook:

```
01   REPT.
     02   IMPORT-DATA.
      03   RUSH-IT-ORDER.
          09   MESSAGE-ID                          PIC S9(9).
          09   TIMESTAMP.
             11   FILLER-ZERO-DATE                 PIC 9(8).
             11   FILLER-ZERO-TIME                 PIC 9(12).
          09   PERSON-NUMBER                       PIC X(7).
          09   VALID-FROM-DATE                     PIC S9(8).
          09   SOCIETY-ID                          PIC X(1).
          09   VERTICAL-MARKET                     PIC S9(2).
          09   CALL-NUMBER                         PIC S9(6).
          09   DEAL-CLOSE-PROBABILITY              PIC S9(1)V9(5).
```

And here is a fragment of the corresponding WSDL file where the COBOL naming conventions have been propagated to the XML Schema to make it easier to see the common structure (although this is not necessary and may not be desirable):

```
<types>
    <schema  ...
        <element name="REPTE1" type="xsd1:REPTType"/>
        <complexType name="TIMESTAMPType">
            <sequence>
                <element name="FILLER-ZERO-DATE" type=
                ➡"xsd:unsignedLong"/>
```

---

[7] Note that CICS and IMS are not COBOL-specific transaction-processing monitors. CICS and IMS transactions can be implemented in several different programming languages, including COBOL, PL/I, and C. In this section, we use COBOL and COBOL Copybooks simply as a representative example of how CICS and IMS transactions are implemented.

```
                <element name="FILLER-ZERO-TIME" type=
                ➡"xsd:unsignedLong"/>
            </sequence>
        </complexType>
        <complexType name="RUSH-IT-ORDERType">
            <sequence>
                <element name="MESSAGE-ID" type="xsd:long"/>
                <element name="TIMESTAMP" type=
                ➡"xsd1:TIMESTAMPType"/>
                <element name="PERSON-NUMBER" type=
                ➡"xsd:string"/>
                <element name="VALID-FROM-DATE" type=
                ➡"xsd:long"/>
                <element name="SOCIETY-ID" type="xsd:string"/>
                <element name="VERTICAL-MARKET" type=
                ➡"xsd:byte"/>
                <element name="CALL-NUMBER" type="xsd:int"/>
                <element name="DEAL-CLOSE-PROBABILITY" type=
                ➡"xsd:double"/>
            </sequence>
        </complexType>
        <complexType name="IMPORT-DATAType">
            <sequence>
                <element name="RUSH-IT-ORDER" type="xsd1:
                ➡RUSH-IT-ORDERType"/>
            </sequence>
        </complexType>
        <complexType name="REPTType">
            <sequence>
                <element name="IMPORT-DATA" type="xsd1:
                ➡IMPORT-DATAType"/>
            </sequence>
        </complexType>
    </schema>
</types>

<message name="SendReportRequest">
    <part element="xsd1:REPTE1" name="REPT"/>
</message>

<portType name="ReportPortType">
    <operation name="SendReport">
        <input message="tns:SendReportRequest" name=
        ➡"SendReportRequest"/>
    </operation>
</portType>
```

The complete WSDL definition of the interface to the CICS or IMS transaction
can be given to a developer so that she can import it into her favorite IDE and
build a Web service requester.

At run-time (see Figure 4-7):

1. The Web services requester sends SOAP messages over HTTP to a legacy service gateway.

2. The legacy service gateway converts the SOAP messages into the equivalent COBOL Copybook format (usually a fixed format message) and sends them to the CICS or IMS transaction using whatever access mechanism is in place (e.g., Dynamic Program Link or WebSphere MQ).

3. The legacy service gateway is also responsible for converting any responses from the CICS or IMS transaction into a SOAP message and routing them back to the Web services requester.

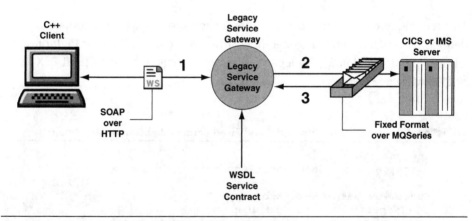

Figure 4-7   Service-enabling CICS and IMS transactions.

Depending on how it is implemented, the legacy service gateway could be a process running on the mainframe host or off-host, or it could be a library that is loaded into the process running the Web services requester.

Ideally, the legacy service gateway should be completely configuration-driven based on information in the WSDL service contract. This can be done if the WSDL service contract contains the logical contract (including the portType) and two bindings—one for SOAP and one for fixed format messages over

WebSphere MQ.[8] For example, see Listing 4-1, which shows a single WSDL file that contains:

1. Report `portType` (lines 4–8).

2. SOAP binding (lines 41–49 and 52–56).

3. Fixed format binding (lines 10–39).[9]

4. WebSphere MQ binding (lines 57–60).

In this way, the existing CICS or IMS transaction is Web services-enabled in a completely configuration-driven manner, and the developer of the Web services requester does not have to write any integration code.

This technique can be extended to other legacy systems whose interface is defined by programming language data structures (e.g., C, C++, or PL/I) or whose interface is defined by legacy message formats (e.g., SWIFT, HL7, X12, or EDIFACT).

Listing 4-1   WSDL File with SOAP and Fixed Format/WebSphere MQ Bindings

```
1. <types>...</types>
2. <message name="SendReportRequest">...</message>
3.
4. <portType name="ReportPortType">
5.     <operation name="SendReport">
6.         <input message="tns:SendReportRequest"
        name="SendReportRequest"/>
7.     </operation>
8. </portType>
9.
10. <binding name="FixedBinding" type="tns:ReportPortType">
```

continues

---

[8] In practice, the WSDL document given to service requesters should not include the fixed format binding because the service requesters don't need to know about the fixed format binding when submitting requests to the legacy service gateway—that is the mechanism by which the legacy service gateway routes requests to the legacy applications, and it should be encapsulated (hidden) from service consumers.

[9] Note that there is not a standard fixed format binding for WSDL.

```
11.    <fixed:binding/>
12.    <operation name="SendReport">
13.     <fixed:operation/>
14.     <input name="SendReportRequest">
15.         <fixed:body>
16.             <fixed:sequence name="REPT">
17.                 <fixed:sequence name="IMPORT-DATA">
18.                     <fixed:sequence name="RUSH-IT-ORDER">
19.                         <fixed:field format="#########-"
                            ➥name="MESSAGE-ID"/>
20.                         <fixed:sequence name="TIMESTAMP">
21.                             <fixed:field format="########"
22.                                 name="FILLER-ZERO-DATE"/>
23.                             <fixed:field format="############"
24.                                 name="FILLER-ZERO-TIME"/>
25.                         </fixed:sequence>
26.                         <fixed:field name="PERSON-NUMBER"
                            ➥size="7"/>
27.                         <fixed:field format="########-"
                            ➥name="VALID-FROM-DATE"/>
28.                         <fixed:field name="SOCIETY-ID"
                            ➥size="1"/>
29.                         <fixed:field format="-##"
                            ➥name="VERTICAL-MARKET"/>
30.                         <fixed:field format="######-"
                            ➥name="CALL-NUMBER"/>
31.                         <fixed:field format="#.#####-"
32.                             ➥name="DEAL-CLOSE-PROBABILITY"/>
33.                     </fixed:sequence>
34.                 </fixed:sequence>
35.             </fixed:sequence>
36.         </fixed:body>
37.     </input>
38.    </operation>
39.   </binding>
40.
41.   <binding name="SOAPBinding" type="tns:ReportPortType">
42.       <soap:binding style="document" transport=
          ➥"http://schemas.xmlsoap.org/soap/http"/>
43.       <operation name="SendReport">
44.           <soap:operation soapAction="" style="document"/>
45.           <input name="SendReportRequest">
46.               <soap:body use="literal"/>
47.           </input>
```

continues

Listing 4-1   WSDL File with SOAP and Fixed Format/WebSphere MQ Bindings (continued)

```
48.        </operation>
49. </binding>
50.
51. <service name="ReportService">
52.        <port binding="tns:SOAPBinding" name="SoapPort">
53.            <soap:address location="http://localhost:9000"/>
54.            <http-conf:client/>
55.            <http-conf:server/>
56.        </port>
57.        <port binding="tns:FixedBinding" name="MQPort">
58.            <mq:client QueueManager="QManager" QueueName=
              ➥"ReportQueue"/>
59.            <mq:server QueueManager="QManager" QueueName=
              ➥"ReportQueue"/>
60.        </port>
61. </service>
```

Example #2—CORBA

CORBA IDL is the OMG-approved interface definition language standard for specifying the interface to CORBA servers. The OMG has defined a specification for IDL-to-WSDL mapping. This IDL-to-WSDL mapping can be used to convert a CORBA IDL into a WSDL service contract including the types, messages, operations, portType, and binding information.

The first step in service-enabling a CORBA server is to convert the CORBA IDL to WSDL. Here is a very simple CORBA IDL with one interface and two methods:

```
interface HelloWorld {
    string sayHi ();
    string greetMe (in string user);
};
```

Here is a fragment of the corresponding WSDL file with one `portType` with two operations:

```
<types>
  <schema
      xmlns="http://www.w3.org/2001/XMLSchema"
      xmlns:wsdl="http://schemas.xmlsoap.org/wsdl/">
      <element name="HW.HelloWorld.sayHi.return"
      ➥type="xsd:string"/>
      <element name="HW.HelloWorld.greetMe.user" type=
      ➥"xsd:string"/>
      <element name="HW.HelloWorld.greetMe.return" type=
      ➥"xsd:string"/>
  </schema>
</types>

<message name="HW.HelloWorld.sayHi"/>
<message name="HW.HelloWorld.sayHiResponse">
    <part element="xsd1:HW.HelloWorld.sayHi.return" name=
    ➥"return"/>
</message>
<message name="HW.HelloWorld.greetMe">
    <part element="xsd1:HW.HelloWorld.greetMe.user" name="user"/>
</message>
<message name="HW.HelloWorld.greetMeResponse">
    <part element="xsd1:HW.HelloWorld.greetMe.return" name=
    ➥"return"/>
</message>

<portType name="HW.HelloWorld">
  <operation name="sayHi">
    <input message="tns:HW.HelloWorld.sayHi" name="sayHi"/>
    <output message="tns:HW.HelloWorld.sayHiResponse" name=
    ➥"sayHiResponse"/>
  </operation>
  <operation name="greetMe">
    <input message="tns:HW.HelloWorld.greetMe" name="greetMe"/>
    <output message="tns:HW.HelloWorld.greetMeResponse" name=
    ➥"greetMeResponse"/>
  </operation>
</portType>
```

The complete WSDL definition of the IDL interface can be given to a developer so that she can import it into her favorite IDE (e.g., Eclipse or Microsoft Visual Studio) and build a Web service requester.

At run-time (see Figure 4-8):

1. The Web services requester sends SOAP messages over HTTP to a legacy service gateway.

2. The legacy service gateway is responsible for converting these SOAP messages into one or more object invocations on the existing CORBA servers.

3. The legacy service gateway is also responsible for converting any responses from the CORBA server into SOAP and routing them back to the Web services requester.

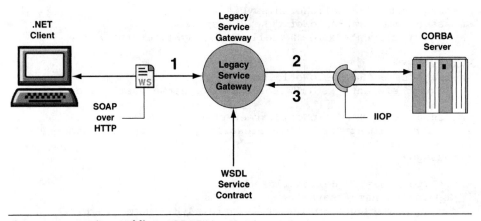

Figure 4-8   Service-enabling a CORBA server.

Depending on how it is implemented, the legacy service gateway could be a library that is loaded in the process running the Web services requester, or it could be a library that is loaded in the process running the CORBA server, or it could be a process running on its own.

Ideally, the legacy service gateway should be completely configuration-driven based on information in the WSDL service contract. This can be done if the WSDL service contract contains the logical contract (including the portType) and two bindings—one for SOAP and one for CORBA/IIOP.[10] For example, see Listing 4-2, which shows a single WSDL file that contains:

1. HelloWorld portType (lines 8–17):

```
8.  <portType name="HW.HelloWorld">
9.      <operation name="sayHi">
10.             <input message="tns:HW.HelloWorld.sayHi"
                ➥name="sayHi"/>
11.             <output message="tns:HW.HelloWorld.
                ➥sayHiResponse" name="sayHiResponse"/>
12.         </operation>
13.     <operation name="greetMe">
14.             <input message="tns:HW.HelloWorld.greetMe"
                ➥name="greetMe"/>
15.             <output message="tns:HW.HelloWorld.
                ➥greetMeResponse" name="greetMeResponse"/>
16.         </operation>
17. </portType>
```

2. SOAP binding (lines 38–50 and 56–58):

```
38. <binding name="HW.HelloWorld_SOAPBinding" type=
    ➥"tns:HW.HelloWorld">
39.     <soap:binding style="document" transport=
        ➥"http://schemas.xmlsoap.org/soap/http"/>
40.     <operation name="sayHi">
41.             <soap:operation soapAction="" style=
                ➥"document"/>
42.             <input name="sayHi"><soap:body use=
                ➥"literal"/></input>
43.             <output name="sayHiResponse"><soap:body
                ➥use="literal"/></output>
44.         </operation>
45.     <operation name="greetMe">
46.             <soap:operation soapAction="" style=
                ➥"document"/>
47.             <input name="greetMe"><soap:body use=
                ➥"literal"/></input>
48.             <output name="greetMeResponse"><soap:body use=
                ➥"literal"/></output>
```

---

[10] Once again, the WSDL document given to service requesters should not include the CORBA binding because the service requesters don't need to know about the CORBA binding when submitting requests to the legacy service gateway—that is the mechanism by which the legacy service gateway routes requests to the legacy applications, and it should be encapsulated (hidden) from service consumers.

```
49.        </operation>
50. </binding>
...
56. <port binding="tns:HW.HelloWorld_SOAPBinding"
    ➥name="SoapPort">
57.        <soap:address location="http://localhost:9000"/>
58. </port>
```

3. CORBA/IIOP binding (lines 19–36 and 53–55):

```
19. <binding name="HW.HelloWorldBinding"
    ➥type="tns:HW.HelloWorld">
20.        <corba:binding repositoryID="IDL:HW/
           ➥HelloWorld:1.0"/>
21.        <operation name="sayHi">
22.            <corba:operation name="sayHi">
23.                <corba:return idltype="corba:string" name=
                   ➥"return"/>
24.            </corba:operation>
25.            <input name="sayHi"/>
26.            <output name="sayHiResponse"/>
27.        </operation>
28.        <operation name="greetMe">
29.            <corba:operation name="greetMe">
30.                <corba:param idltype="corba:string" mode=
                   ➥"in" name="user"/>
31.                <corba:return idltype="corba:string" name=
                   ➥"return"/>
32.            </corba:operation>
33.            <input name="greetMe"/>
34.            <output name="greetMeResponse"/>
35.        </operation>
36.</binding>
...
53. <port binding="tns:HW.HelloWorldBinding" name=
    ➥"HW.HelloWorldPort">
54.        <corba:address location="file:../../HelloWorld.ior"/>
55. </port>
```

In this way, the existing CORBA system is Web services-enabled in a completely configuration-driven manner, and the developer of the Web services requester does not have to write any integration code.

Listing 4-2   WSDL File with SOAP and IIOP Bindings

```
1.  <types>...</types>
2.
3.  <message name="HW.HelloWorld.sayHi"/>
4.  <message name="HW.HelloWorld.sayHiResponse">...</message>
5.  <message name="HW.HelloWorld.greetMe">...</message>
6.  <message name="HW.HelloWorld.greetMeResponse">
    ➡...</message>
7.
8.  <portType name="HW.HelloWorld">
9.      <operation name="sayHi">
10.         <input message="tns:HW.HelloWorld.sayHi" name=
            ➡"sayHi"/>
11.         <output message="tns:HW.HelloWorld.sayHiResponse"
            ➡name="sayHiResponse"/>
12.     </operation>
13.     <operation name="greetMe">
14.         <input message="tns:HW.HelloWorld.greetMe" name=
            ➡"greetMe"/>
15.         <output message="tns:HW.HelloWorld.
            ➡greetMeResponse" name="greetMeResponse"/>
16.     </operation>
17. </portType>
18.
19. <binding name="HW.HelloWorldBinding" type="tns:
    ➡HW.HelloWorld">
20.     <corba:binding repositoryID="IDL:HW/HelloWorld:1.0"/>
21.     <operation name="sayHi">
22.         <corba:operation name="sayHi">
23.             <corba:return idltype="corba:string" name=
                ➡"return"/>
24.         </corba:operation>
25.         <input name="sayHi"/>
26.         <output name="sayHiResponse"/>
27.     </operation>
28.     <operation name="greetMe">
29.         <corba:operation name="greetMe">
30.             <corba:param idltype="corba:string" mode=
                ➡"in" name="user"/>
31.             <corba:return idltype="corba:string" name=
                ➡"return"/>
32.         </corba:operation>
33.         <input name="greetMe"/>
34.         <output name="greetMeResponse"/>
35.     </operation>
36. </binding>
```

continues

Listing 4-2   WSDL File with SOAP and IIOP Bindings (continued)

```
37.
38. <binding name="HW.HelloWorld_SOAPBinding" type="tns:
    ➥HW.HelloWorld">
39.     <soap:binding style="document" transport="http://
        ➥schemas.xmlsoap.org/soap/http"/>
40.     <operation name="sayHi">
41.         <soap:operation soapAction="" style="document"/>
42.         <input name="sayHi"><soap:body use="literal"/
            ➥></input>
43.         <output name="sayHiResponse"><soap:body use=
            ➥"literal"/></output>
44.     </operation>
45.     <operation name="greetMe">
46.         <soap:operation soapAction="" style="document"/>
47.         <input name="greetMe"><soap:body use="literal"/
            ➥></input>
48.         <output name="greetMeResponse"><soap:body use=
            ➥"literal"/></output>
49.     </operation>
50. </binding>
51.
52. <service name="HW.HelloWorldService">
53.     <port binding="tns:HW.HelloWorldBinding" name=
        ➥"HW.HelloWorldPort">
54.         <corba:address location="file:../../
            ➥HelloWorld.ior"/>
55.     </port>
56.     <port binding="tns:HW.HelloWorld_SOAPBinding" name=
        ➥"SoapPort">
57.         <soap:address location="http://localhost:9000"/>
58.     </port>
59. </service>
```

This technique can be extended to any legacy system that provides an interface definition language (e.g., Tuxedo FML) or that provides reflection capabilities (e.g., Java, COM type libraries, RDBMS schema). Of course, this technique is simpler in cases where the mapping to WSDL is already specified in an open standard.

Applying SOA and Web Services for Integration—Enterprise Service Bus Pattern

A common integration challenge involves answering the question "How should the business rules (and technical rules) for satisfying information requests and data transformation be defined and applied while simultaneously reconciling the competing goals of speed, interoperability, portability, and flexibility?"

This challenge surfaces in a number places, including:

- Converting database representations across database systems.

- Converting messages (and files) sent from one system to another.

- Converting data from a public format to an internal format used by a system.

- Converting business documents exchanged between business applications.

- Converting business documents being used for B2B integration.

A common solution to this problem is defining a reusable technical service using the enterprise service bus (ESB) pattern. The ESB (see Figure 4-9) accepts information requests from service requesters (such as "retrieve all information on Fred's Accounts with ABC Bank") and returns the requested information based on metadata describing what information is available from a collection of data services (i.e., services whose primary role is to return data). This example also illustrates how reusable technical services (like an ESB) can be built on top of the Web services platform without being embedded in the Web services platform.

Here are some of the key elements of the ESB pattern:

- **Metadata driven**—The metadata repository contains data access rules about what information is available from the data services (Customer Info "A," Customer Info "B," and Customer Info "C" in Figure 4-9).

- **Transformation rules**—The metadata repository also contains business and technical transformation rules. Business rules for transforming data typically involve semantic conversion of data across systems or applying business operations to the data (extracting line items from a purchase order). Technical rules for transforming data typically involve conversions required for reconciling different programming models (e.g., converting binary Java objects to flat message buffers) and messaging systems (e.g., adding or converting message headers).

- **Declarative versus programmatic**—This allows data lookup rules and transformation rules to be defined in a declarative fashion (e.g., XSLT), but it also allows transformation rules to be defined by writing scripts or code so that complex scenarios can be handled as necessary.

- **Static versus dynamic**—To increase business agility, the ESB supports dynamic updates to the metadata repository so that new information sources can be dynamically added as necessary.

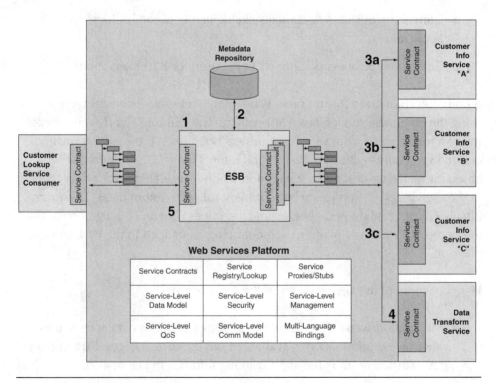

Figure 4-9   ESB pattern example.

The ESB operates as follows (item numbers are keyed to Figure 4-9):

1. Accepts information requests from service requesters.

2. Consults a metadata registry to determine how to assemble the requested information using known data services.

3. Retrieves the data from one or more data service providers (three service providers are shown in Figure 4-9).

4. Applies data transform rules using a data transformation service that removes duplicate data and converts the data that has been collected into the format specified by the service contract.

5. Returns the results to the service requester.

Notice how the ESB is both a service provider and a service requester. Also notice how the ESB differs from a service registry such as UDDI. The ESB accepts requests for information, locates all the data services that are necessary for satisfying that information request (including matching semantic descriptions of information), invokes the appropriate data services, aggregates the results, and returns them to the service requester. A UDDI registry is a service registry that accepts requests for a service and looks them up using a relatively straightforward service classification.

Summary—SOA and Web Services for Integration

Integration is a challenge that has confronted IT departments for decades. Because integration is a multifaceted problem, many different technologies, products, and processes have been used over the years to address it.

XML and Web services provide the technical tools needed for application integration, but they do not provide a structured integration process to guide their use.

WSI and SOI represent two views along a spectrum of integration techniques that use XML and Web services. WSI tends to be more tactical and opportunistic, whereas SOI tends to be more strategic and systematic.

Organizations can choose between WSI and SOI depending on business and technical requirements and goals and the level of formality that they want to incorporate into the integration process. In reality, most organizations will fall somewhere in between these two.

Using Web services for legacy integration and as the basis of an ESB are also important aspects of using SOA and Web services to solve integration problems.

Chapter 5

SOA and Multi-Channel Access

The primary purpose of most organizations (commercial, government, non-profit, and so on) is to deliver services to clients, customers, partners, citizens, and other agencies. Table 5-1 illustrates this for four key industries by listing the services they deliver, the channels they use to deliver these services, and some of the end-user devices and technologies used to deliver these services.

Table 5-1   Some Examples of Service-Oriented Businesses

	Government	Telecom, Communication	Financial Services	Health Care
Service Requesters	citizens and other agencies	customers, business partners	customers, business partners	patients, doctors, insurance carriers, hospitals, government
Services	law enforcement health services disaster management community and social services	local phone service long-distance service mobile/wireless DSL/ADSL/Internet	mortgage/loans credit/debit cards investment management insurance	preventative care emergency care out-patient care nursing care prenatal care

continues

Table 5-1   Some Examples of Service-Oriented Businesses (continued)

	Government	Telecom, Communication	Financial Services	Health Care
Delivery Channels	government office call center mail/fax self-service (eGov) agency to agency	call center self-service (Web, IVR) business-to-business field service technician	retail branch office self-service (Web, IVR) home banking Automated Teller Machine (ATM)	doctor's office emergency ward telephone mail/fax
End-User Devices	office PC home PC telephone web browser mobile/handheld devices	office PC home PC telephone web browser mobile/handheld devices	ATM web browser telephone office PC home PC mobile/handheld devices	office PC home PC telephone medical equipment mobile/handheld devices

In the past, organizations often developed new monolithic applications with a single delivery channel in mind. This can be seen in systems ranging from 3270 applications for money transfer to browser-based applications specifically designed for e-commerce.

The proliferation of delivery channels and end-user devices has given service-oriented businesses the opportunity to better serve their customers anytime and anywhere, but it has also placed an enormous strain on IT departments, as they struggle to convert monolithic applications to make them multi-channel-ready.

It is now necessary for these organizations to deliver these same services and new ones in a consistent manner across all channels. This poses real problems because it is difficult to multi-channel-enable monolithic applications originally built for a single channel. The solution is to use SOA with Web services.

In general, business services change much more slowly than delivery channels (see Figure 5-1). This is because the business services represent long-standing business functions such as account management, order management, and billing, whereas client devices and delivery channels are often based on new devices or new market niches, which tend to change more frequently. In some cases, the rate of change at the presentation layer is 100 times faster than the rate of change at the business services layer.

Therefore, it only makes sense to reuse existing business services when possible. Many of the core business services of large organizations are mission-critical systems running on TP monitors such as CICS, IMS, or Tuxedo. Many core systems also run on SAP, PeopleSoft, Oracle applications, Siebel, CORBA, J2EE, and COM. SOA has proven to provide the right balance between abstraction for dealing with diverse technology and loose coupling necessary for reusing business services for multi-channel applications.

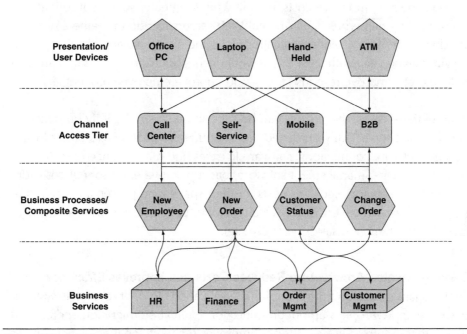

Figure 5-1   **Multi-channel applications call for a service-oriented architecture.**

Business Benefits of SOA and Multi-Channel Access

Multi-Channel Access Reduces Staffing Costs

Evolutionary migration from monolithic applications to multi-channel systems based on an SOA provides the opportunity to reduce staffing costs by moving some service delivery activities from human-intensive processes to less expensive self-service processes.

Multi-Channel Access Eliminates Obsolete and Expensive Infrastructure

Evolutionary migration from monolithic applications to multi-channel systems based on an SOA provides the opportunity to re-engineer existing processes and eliminate obsolete and expensive infrastructure.

For example, eliminating brittle departmental client/server applications and replacing them with more robust, scalable enterprise services can save money by reducing administrative costs and allowing for greater server consolidation. Consolidating numerous departmental Web servers can do the same. In addition, replacing Motif applications (and the expensive and obsolete X/Windows servers) with .NET Framework client applications can simultaneously reduce costs, improve response times, and improve employee productivity.

In all of these cases, the savings can be substantial, given the fully burdened cost for each server (fully burdened costs include amortized costs of hardware, storage, network connections, software licenses and maintenance costs for security software, management software, backup software, personnel costs for system administrators, facilities costs for floor space, and power, air conditioning, and disaster recovery costs, which include replicated hardware/software facilities at a remote disaster recovery site).

Service-Oriented Architecture Reduces Costs and Improves Efficiency

Evolutionary migration from monolithic applications to multi-channels systems based on an SOA opens up opportunities for application migration and consolidation that in turn reduces costs and improves organizational efficiency. This is possible because an SOA defines the business services in a manner that is independent of a particular legacy application or packaged application.

Here is a typical application migration scenario: Consider an existing application that is expensive to maintain and that no longer delivers the functionality needed to meet new business requirements. An SOA infrastructure allows the application to be wrapped as a set of business services and then incrementally replaced with a less expensive, easier-to-maintain application that delivers better overall capabilities.

Here is a typical application consolidation example: Consider an organization that has numerous customer care systems. Each one requires its own separate hardware infrastructure, administrators, user training, and so on. An SOA infrastructure allows all of these customer care systems to be seamlessly consolidated to one or two systems along with the savings in hardware, administrative costs, reduced user-training costs, and reduced software maintenance fees.

A Service-Oriented Architecture for Multi-Channel Access

Organizations need to deliver products and services to customers and partners via multiple channels. A multi-channel access architecture based on service-oriented principles makes the organization more agile by allowing it to deliver all products and services in a consistent manner across all distribution channels.

The multi-channel access pattern is characterized by the need to provide several different types of users with access to a common set of business services where the users employ a diverse set of end-user devices and technologies. Figure 5-2 shows a subset of the delivery channels that might be used in a typical system and some of the related client technology.

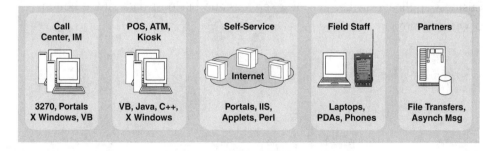

Figure 5-2   Some end-user devices used to access applications.

Architectural Challenges

The main architectural challenge of multi-channel access is mediating between the characteristics of a diverse set of end-user devices and the characteristics of the equally diverse set of internal systems and technologies. Here are some of the characteristics of these systems that need to be considered (more on these later):

- **Connectivity**—For some access channels, we can assume that the user is sitting in front of a PC with a fast and reliable connection, while other access channels are constrained by slow and unreliable connections (dial-up users, mobile users, and field technicians).

- **Security**—For some access channels, we can assume that the user is working inside of a corporate firewall, while other access channels are for requesters that are accessing these services over less secure wireless networks and the Internet.

- **Communication technology**—Different user devices use different communication technology, including standard protocols (e.g., HTTP, Sockets, email, file transfer, Java RMI, CORBA) and proprietary protocols (e.g., MS DCOM, WebSphere MQ, Tibco Rendezvous).

Architecture for Multi-Channel Access

Figure 5-3 shows a layered architecture for providing multi-channel access to business services.

From a business perspective, the architecture is intended to connect client applications at the top of the diagram (i.e., the client/presentation tier) to the business applications (i.e., business services and business data) at the bottom of the diagram.

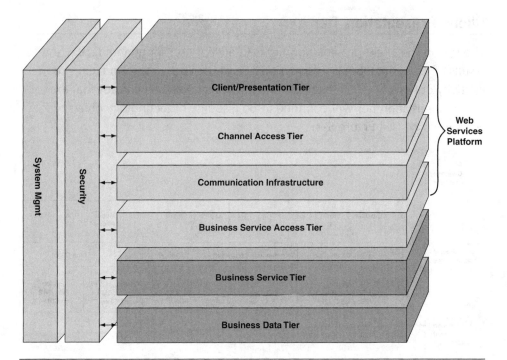

Figure 5-3   Layered architecture for providing multi-channel access.

In between these tiers are the following three layers necessary to support an SOA-based multi-channel access architecture:

1. **Channel access tier**—Mediates between the diverse client applications and user devices and the internal communication infrastructure and business services.

2. **Communication infrastructure**—Provides the enterprise-wide middleware and messaging systems that connect internal systems and provide enterprise qualities of service that these internal systems rely upon.

3. **Business services access tier**—Responsible for providing uniform access to the business services.

Supporting the architecture are security services and system management facilities that span all layers of the architecture.

Client/Presentation Tier

The role of the client/presentation tier is to accept user input and display the results of user interactions. The myriad of end-user devices, form factors, connectivity options, user preferences, and client technologies ensures that the client/presentation tier will continue to be a source of technology diversity for years to come (see Figure 5-4).

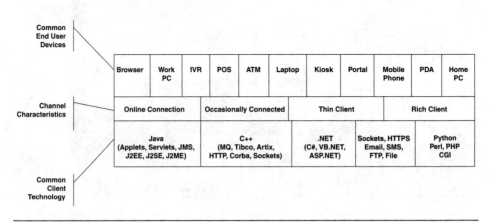

Figure 5-4   Client/presentation tier.

Channel Access Tier

The role of the channel access tier is to mediate between the client applications and the business services (see Figure 5-5). For example:

- **Support all common data formats and protocols**—Including SOAP, XML, name/value pairs, delimited format, fixed width format, Sockets, HTTP, FTP, SMTP, JMS, WebSphere MQ, Tibco Rendezvous, IIOP, and so on, so that a diverse set of clients can be easily supported.

- **Support all common communication interaction patterns**—Including request/response, request/callback, asynchronous messaging, and publish/subscribe so that a diverse set of clients can be easily supported.

- **Payload mapping**—Accept messages from clients in client-specific formats and automatically translate them into the enterprise message standard or the message format defined by the target business service.

- **Protocol bridging**—Receive messages on any transport being used by the client applications and automatically route them to the enterprise's middleware standard including WebSphere MQ, JMS, Tibco Rendezvous, HTTP/S, or CORBA IIOP.

- **Security facilities**—Support all major standards for security including encryption, integrity, authentication (e.g., user name/password, HTTP Basic and Digest Authentication, X.509 certificates, Kerberos security tokens, SAML), authorization (e.g., role-based access control and digital rights management), and single sign-on.

- **Data transformation and validation**—For converting messages received from the client applications into the data formats required by the internal communication infrastructure.

- **Service lookup and service routing**—So that client requests can be routed to the services they require. The service lookup facilities should support load balancing across service instances and service-level failover when a service fails.

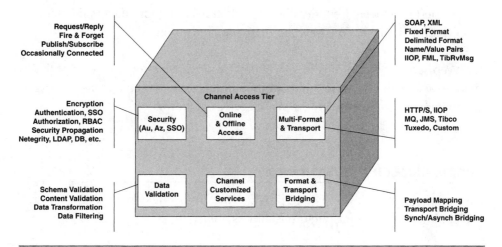

Figure 5-5   Channel access tier.

Typically, the channel access tier is composed of two types of components—service proxies and client gateways:

- **Service proxies**—A service proxy is a programming language object (e.g., Java, C++, or C#) for a service interface that is compiled into the client application. For example, in JAX-RPC, one Java class is created for each WSDL `portType`, which includes one member function for each operation defined in the WSDL `portType`. This simplifies creating client applications because the client program can invoke the service operation without having to create, manage, and manipulate the underlying XML documents. Depending on how it is configured, a service proxy (or associated handlers) can perform some or all of the functions listed previously (security checks, data transformation, data validation, protocol conversion, payload mapping, and so on).

- **Client gateways**—A client gateway is typically a standalone message intermediary, which receives messages from clients on incoming ports and routes them to servers via outgoing ports. Depending on how it is configured, a client gateway will perform some or all of the functions listed previously (security checks, data transformation, data validation, protocol conversion, payload mapping, and so on).

The Web services platform is ideally suited to support the requirements of the channel access tier because the majority of the features of the channel access tier are already included with the Web services platform.

Communication Infrastructure

The communication infrastructure provides the connectivity between systems. The communication infrastructure is a messy place that:

- Needs to support a variety of communication patterns (e.g., request/reply, request/callback, asynchronous messaging, publish/subscribe) and the associated Web services standards (e.g., WS-ReliableMessaging and WS-Eventing).

■ Needs to support message routing.

■ Needs to provide multi-level security (e.g., transport-level security, message-level security, authentication, authorization, role-based access control, or single sign-on).

The best way to do this is using an SOA where there is a clean separation between the logical service contracts and the physical contracts that define the bindings to particular data formats and protocols. Figure 5-6 illustrates this by showing three views of the same system:

■ **Figure 5-6 (a)**—At the highest level of abstraction, the client application (i.e., service requester) uses the business service based on the logical service contract, without any regard for the underlying communication infrastructure.

■ **Figure 5-6 (b)**—At the next lower level of abstraction, we see that the logical connection between the service requester and the business service is realized by the service invocation being routed through the channel access tier and the service access tier. The interfaces between all four tiers (service requester, channel access tier, service access tier, and business service) are defined by service contracts. (However, the service requester only needs to be concerned about the contract it uses because the complexity of the lower levels is hidden from the service requester.)

■ **Figure 5-6 (c)**—At the next lower level of abstraction, we see that the logical connection between the service requester and the business service is realized using several different data formats and transports (again, the complexity of the lower levels is hidden from the service requester). For instance:

■ SOAP over HTTP/S is used between the service requester and the channel access tier.

■ SOAP using WS-ReliableMessaging is used between the channel access tier and the service access tier.

■ COBOL Copybooks over WebSphere MQ is used between the service access tier and the business service.

■ In this case, the channel access tier and the service access tier are responsible for payload mapping, protocol conversion, and routing based
on information in the physical portion of the logical contract and in a
manner that conforms to the higher-level logical contract.

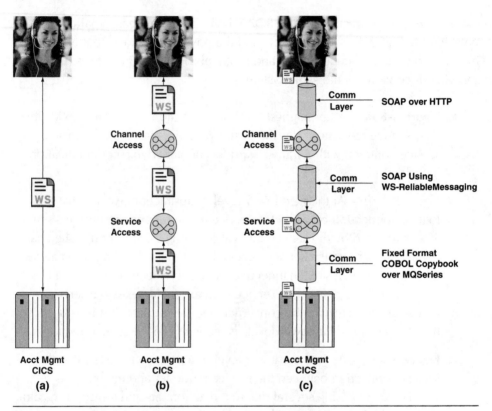

Figure 5-6   Multilayer view of multi-channel communications access.

Business Service Access Tier

The role of the business service access tier is to mediate between the communication infrastructure and the business services (see Figure 5-7).

Several of the key facilities provided by this layer of the architecture are similar to features provided by the channel access tier:

- **Service registration and service lookup**—So that client applications can locate the services they require. The service lookup facilities should support load balancing across service instances and service-level failover when a service fails.

- **Session management**—For handling conversational interactions between client applications and stateful services. (Session management may be also required for stateless interactions—especially when strong authentication is required, such as in WS-SecureConversation.)

- **Data transformation and validation**—For converting messages received from the communication infrastructure into the data formats required by legacy systems.

- **Security services**—Support all major standards for security, including encryption, integrity, authentication (e.g., WS-Security, user name/password, HTTP Basic Authentication, X.509 certificates, Kerberos security tokens), authorization (e.g., role-based access control), and single sign-on.

- **Service enablement**—Facilities for quickly and non-invasively exposing legacy systems as Web services (see the following text for more details).

- **Service orchestration and composition**—Facilities for creating new services by composing existing services using WS-BPEL.

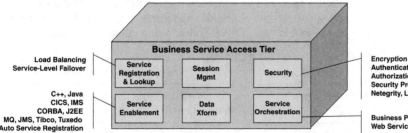

Figure 5-7   Business service access tier.

Many of these services are also included in the channel access tier. The main difference here is that the implementations of these services for the business service access tier must be faster, more scalable, more robust, and more reliable due to the transaction processing load that production-quality business services must handle.

The most important additional service that the business service access tier provides is legacy service gateways for quickly and non-invasively exposing legacy systems as Web services.

Typically, the legacy service gateways provide development-time tools and run-time facilities for turning legacy systems into services that can be invoked using any of the other supported data formats and transports and any of the major communication interaction paradigms. Usually the development tools provide facilities for importing metadata describing the legacy systems and turning them into WSDL service contracts (e.g., WSDL, XML Schema, COBOL Copybooks, CORBA IDL, database schema, and delimited data formats such as comma-separated files). Table 5-2 displays a sampling of legacy systems and possible metadata importers.

Table 5-2   Sampling of Legacy Systems and Possible Metadata Importers

Legacy Service Gateway	Potential Metadata Source	Notes
CICS and IMS	COBOL Copybooks	Routes service invocations to CICS/IMS transactions.
WebSphere MQ	COBOL Copybooks and legacy message formats	Routes service invocations to WebSphere MQ queues and automatically handles correlating WebSphere MQ request/response message pairs.
CORBA	CORBA IDL	Routes service invocations to CORBA objects.
Tuxedo	Tuxedo FML	Routes service invocations to Tuxedo transactions.
TIBCO RV	TibRV message definitions	Routes service invocations to Tibco topics.

Legacy Service Gateway	Potential Metadata Source	Notes
C++	Legacy message formats[1]	Routes service invocations to C++ objects.
Java, EJBs, JMS	Java classes and remote interfaces of stateless session beans	Routes service invocations to JMS topics, Java classes, and stateless session beans.
RDBMS	Database schema	Reads/writes data to/from relational database tables.
Packaged apps	Various	Provides Web services interfaces to package applications such as SAP R/3, PeopleSoft, Siebel, and so on.

Business Service Tier

The role of the business service tier is to implement the business services (i.e., transactions, information updates, information retrievals, and so on) necessary for running the business (see Figure 5-8).

Figure 5-8   Business service tier.

Broadly speaking, these business services can be divided into three categories:

- **Legacy systems**—Existing production systems implemented in C/C++, Java/J2EE, CICS, IMS, CORBA, Tuxedo, SAP R/3, PeopleSoft, Siebel, Tibco Rendezvous, COM/DCOM, and so on. Typically, these systems were not implemented according to an SOA, so they need to be service-enabled using the facilities provided by the business service access tier.

---

[1] Legacy message formats include fixed format messages, name/value pairs, and delimited message formats (e.g., comma-separated messages).

- **Greenfield services**—New services developed to provide new business capabilities or to replace legacy systems that are being phased out. These might be implemented using Java/J2EE, .NET Framework, or C/C++, or by deploying a packaged application. More and more, these tools include capabilities for exposing the new services as Web services.

- **Composite services**—Business services that use one or more other business services. Composite business services should themselves be implemented according to SOA principles so that they can use multiple services implemented using different technologies. Web service orchestration tools based on WS-BPEL should be used to make building composite services easier.

Example—SOA for Developing Composite Applications

A composite application consists of a service requester that uses multiple service providers.

A good business example of this is decoupling mobile telephone product selection and validation from actual provisioning.

Using a service-oriented architecture to perform product and service selection and validation while the customer is on the phone may involve request/response interactions with several backend systems. After the customer has selected the products and services, the customer call can be completed, and the order or orders placed using an asynchronous service request invocation that is moved through a workflow process that performs that actual provisioning.

Figure 5-9 shows a system diagram for this example, and the following list describes the services provided at each layer of the architecture:

- **Client/presentation**—Client application implemented using Web services, the .NET platform, and written in C#, for example.

- **Channel access tier**—Client gateway is a message intermediary that receives messages from clients on incoming ports and routes them to servers via outgoing ports, including performing security checks, data transformation, data validation, protocol conversion, payload mapping, etc.

Security services for role-based access control and single sign-on.

- **Communication infrastructure**—Basic SOAP over HTTP and SOAP using WS-ReliableMessaging.

- **Business access tier**—Service registry (such as UDDI) for service registration, lookup, and load balancing.

Legacy gateways for IMS, CORBA, and WebSphere MQ.

- **Business service tier**—Production servers implemented using IMS, CORBA, J2EE.

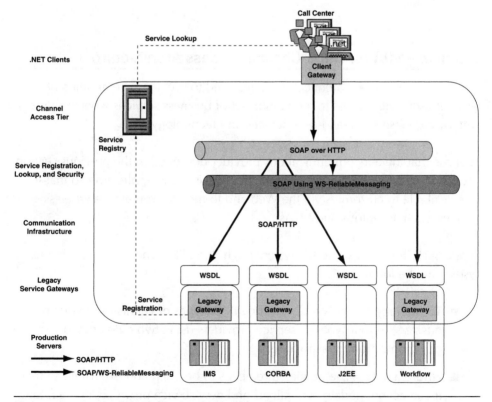

Figure 5-9   Composite application for service selection and provisioning.

By using an SOA, the .NET developers are able to build the composite application knowing only the service contracts for the business services and without knowing anything about the technical details of the service providers, such as the fact that:

■ The business services are implemented using four different technologies.

■ The service selection and validation steps involve accessing IMS, CORBA, and J2EE applications using synchronous, request/response calls.

■ The offline provisioning step involves using SOAP and WS-ReliableMessaging to integrate with a legacy workflow system.

■ Different services are accessed using different communication infrastructure (HTTP and WS-ReliableMessaging).

Example—SOA for Multi-Channel Access Architecture

A multi-channel access architecture is designed to provide several different types of users with access to a common set of business services where the users employ a diverse set of end-user devices and technology.

Suppose that the telecommunications provider described in the previous section needed to extend the service selection and provisioning application so that it was available to customers via the Web and to mobile workers via wireless devices, such as laptops and PDAs.

Figure 5-10 illustrates what this system might look like. The challenges in this system are the following:

■ **Technology diversity**—Connecting three types of clients (or service requesters) to four types of service providers using two different types of communication infrastructure.

■ **Future agility**—The architecture needs to be open and extensible so that it can accommodate new clients and new service providers in the future.

■ **Autonomy**—The architecture should allow individual application teams the greatest amount of autonomy when selecting technologies for developing individual applications while still allowing the independent systems to be quickly combined to deliver new products and services via new channels when necessary.

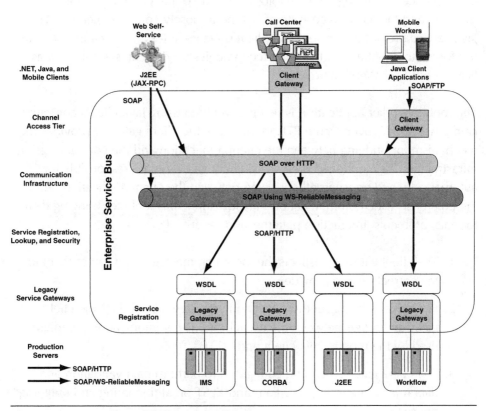

Figure 5-10   SOA for multi-channel application.

With this in mind, let's look at the specifics of this example. Just like the previous example, the back-office applications have been made available as reusable Web services using legacy gateways and are accessible to other applications using SOAP and the internal communication infrastructure, which is based on HTTP and WS-ReliableMessaging.

The customer self-service application was originally developed using J2EE technology. Using a Web services toolkit,[2] the application team can generate JAX-RPC Java service proxies that allow Java service requesters to invoke the back-office services as if they were Java objects. These Java service proxies make it easy to extend the customer self-service application to use the back-office services by hiding the technology diversity of the communication infrastructure and the back-office systems behind a loosely coupled interface. These Java service proxies also give the application team autonomy because they are not forced to adopt any of the other technologies used in the system, such as IMS, CORBA, or WebSphere MQ.

The mobile worker application is being developed using Java clients communicating with SOAP over secure FTP. In this case, the client gateway provides the mechanism for bridging between the client application and the communication infrastructure. As mentioned previously, client gateways are responsible for automatically and transparently bridging between the client applications and the enterprise-wide communication infrastructure—this includes bridging data formats, protocols, interaction patterns, and security. For example:

1. The client gateway inspects the incoming messages and routes them to the correct service provider.

2. For requests being sent to a back-office system over HTTP, the client gateway bridges between the asynchronous communication paradigm used by the mobile Java client and HTTP.

3. The client gateway can be configured to perform data validation and data transformation using XPath and XLST on all incoming and outgoing messages.

4. The client gateway bridges between the mobile security domain managed using Netegrity SiteMinder and the enterprise security domain managed using LDAP.

---

[2] e.g., Artix Encompass, Systinet Developer, or CapeClear Studio.

Much like the Java service proxies, the client gateway makes it easy to extend the mobile worker application to use the back-office services because they also hide the technology diversity of the communication infrastructure and the back-office systems behind a loosely coupled interface. The client gateways also give the application team autonomy because they are not forced to adopt any of the other technologies used in the system such as .NET, HTTP, CORBA, IMS, or WebSphere MQ.

Finally, both the Java service proxies and the client gateways also ensure future agility because they can be easily reconfigured to support additional transports, data formats, security, data validation, and data transformation requirements.

Summary

In this chapter, we discussed applying SOA and Web services to the challenge of providing multi-channel access to business services. Together, SOA and Web services provide an ideal approach to multi-channel access because SOA emphasizes defining loosely coupled business services while Web services provide an open, standards-based approach that enables access to these business services from a wide range of delivery channels and client devices.

We also examined the logical tiers involved in creating multi-channel access for legacy and new services, including the client/presentation tier, the channel access tier, the communication infrastructure, the business service access tier, and the business service tier. When Web services technologies are deployed using such an architecture, they can address the challenges in providing consistent multi-channel access to applications, wherever they are.

Chapter 6

SOA and Business Process Management

Basic Business Process Management Concepts

A business process is a real-world activity consisting of a set of logically related tasks that, when performed in the appropriate sequence, and according to the correct business rules produces a business outcome—"order-to-cash" is an example of a business process. Business processes range from short-lived (taking minutes or hours) to long-lived (taking weeks, months, or even years).

Business process management (BPM) addresses how organizations can identify, model, develop, deploy, and manage their business processes, including processes that involve IT systems and human interaction. BPM has a long tradition, starting with early workflow systems and progressing up to modern Web services orchestration and choreography systems.[1]

---

[1] Note that the terms *orchestration* and *choreography* are sometimes used interchangeably, but you will also see the terms distinguished according to internal and external use (i.e., choreography is sometimes distinguished from orchestration as being more appropriate for extended business-to-business interactions).

The main goals and benefits of BPM include the following:

- Reduce the impedance mismatch between business requirements and IT systems by allowing business users to model business processes and then having the IT department provide the infrastructure to execute and control these business processes.

- Increase employee productivity and reduce operational costs by automating and streamlining business processes.

- Increase corporate agility and flexibility by explicitly separating process logic from other business rules and representing business processes in a form that is easy to change as business requirements change. This allows organizations to be more agile, responding quickly to market changes and quickly seizing competitive advantages.

- Reduce development costs and effort by using a high-level, graphical programming language that allows business analysts and developers to quickly build and update IT systems within a particular problem domain.

Business process automation is the conversion of the activities of an organization from manual or partially computerized systems to enterprise-wide, highly automated systems. Business process automation involves the automation and tracking of business processes, in whole or in part, during which documents, information, and/or tasks are passed from one participant[2] to another for action according to a set of business rules.

Obviously, all IT systems support and implement business processes in one form or another. However, what makes business process management unique is that it explicitly separates business process logic from other business rules (this contrasts with other forms of system development where the process logic is deeply embedded in the application code).

---

[2] Where "participant" means any agent, including humans, organizations, and computer systems.

Business Process Management Systems

Whereas BPM is the discipline associated with defining, managing, and executing business processes as a corporate asset, business process management systems (BPMS) provide the technology that implements one or more of these core BPM functions.

Most business process management systems (whether they are called workflow, process automation, process integration, EAI, B2B, service composition, orchestration, or choreography) provide a process modeling tool, which allows processes to be defined as a graph, where the nodes of the graph represent the tasks to be performed and the arcs of the graph represent control-flow or data-flow dependencies among the tasks. In addition, most process management systems allow the arcs of the graph to be annotated with rules that define, among other things, task pre-conditions, routing logic, escalation rules, time delays, and deadlines.

However, a complete BPMS must do much more than simply execute a process. Figure 6-1 illustrates the basic components of a BPMS.

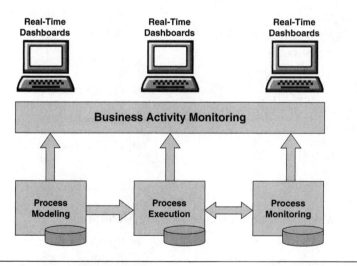

Figure 6-1   Basic components of a BPMS.

The following lists illustrate the wide range of facilities that a complete BPMS system should posses (adapted from Rashid Khan, "Evaluating BPM Software," *Business Integration Journal*, October, 2003).

Process Modeling

- Business process modeler/ graphical designer

- Technical flow modeler

- Business metrics modeling and monitoring

- Collaborative design

- Flexible forms designer and support

- Business process simulation and animation

- Process documentation

- Business analyzer and report generator

- User/role administration

- Security policy administration

Process Execution

- Process engine

- Business rules engine (without requiring scripting or programming)

- Worklist manager

- Escalation and exception handling

- Sub-processes

- Task delegation

- Queues and groups

- Routing—User-based, role-based, rule-based, ad hoc

- Scheduler

- Compensating transactions

- Process recovery

- User-to-user collaboration

Process Monitoring and Business Activity Monitoring

- Business activity monitoring and event management

- Business process monitoring and administration

- Pre-defined dashboards and dashboard designer

- Audit and error logging facility

Infrastructure

- Integration with enterprise management systems

- Web services integration

- Transaction processing

- Web-based architecture

- Failover

- Distributed user administration

- Integration with enterprise security systems

- EAI and third-party application agents

- Database connectivity

- Scalability

- Load balancing

- Org chart and directory integration

Process Modeling

The goal of business process modeling is to capture business requirements at the initial design stage and then make them available to the rest of the development process. Business process modeling begins with business analysts defining their needs using a process-modeling tool. Typically, these tools provide business analysts with a GUI interface (although a spreadsheet-style interface is sometimes provided too) that allows them to drag and drop icons onto a graphical process model of the business process. The process model defines dependencies among tasks, how tasks are sequenced, when and how tasks are enabled, who can perform each task, and other process-related business rules.

Typically, these process models are then given to technical specialists who map the process models to the organization's IT assets, or they are given to software developers who create new software components that fulfill the tasks defined by the business process.

Business analysts and the IT organization may also use the process models to run simulations. Not only are the business processes simulated but also the people and systems related to them are included, too. Business analysts, for example, may use the simulations to look for bottlenecks in the processes, such as how many customer service representatives are required to handle a particular workload. Technical specialists may use the simulations to check performance characteristics, such as how increasing the transaction load will affect server performance.

Process Execution

After the business process has been modeled, simulated, and mapped to new and existing IT assets, it is ready to be deployed. BPM suites include process execution engines that import the process models (typically defined using WS-BPEL) and then execute and manage as many instances of the business process as necessary for supporting the organization's operational requirements.

The process execution engine is responsible for executing the process models and enforcing the business rules associated with the process, such as:

- Invoking tasks or executing tasks in the correct order.

- Assigning and routing tasks to authorized users. In some cases, this also includes allowing the user to manage his or her work queue.

- Tracking the current status of the process, including which tasks have been completed, which tasks are eligible for execution, what deadlines are associated with the process and its tasks, and so on.

- Accessing local and remote IT systems to retrieve information needed by the process, to update information produced by the process, and to execute transactions defined by the process.

- Monitoring process execution, issuing alerts when business rules are violated (e.g., deadlines are missed), and escalating problems to supervisors and managers if they are not corrected on a timely basis.

Because business processes may take weeks or months to complete, it is sometimes necessary for the process engine to simultaneously support multiple versions of the same process.

WS-BPEL is an XML language for defining business process behavior based on Web services. Processes in WS-BPEL consume and provide functionality by using Web service interfaces. WS-BPEL extends the Web services interaction model and enables it to support business transactions. (See the section "Orchestration and Choreography Specifications" for more details of WS-BPEL.)

Process Monitoring

BPM suites include process-monitoring tools that allow business users and IT administrators to monitor and control a business process. This capability includes:

- Seeing a summary of all executing processes.

- Seeing a summary of all completed processes, including historical trends.

- Viewing the status of a process—for example, which tasks have been completed, which tasks are pending execution, which tasks have been assigned to which users, and what deadlines are associated with the process and its tasks.

- Suspending and resuming processes.

- Altering the priority of processes.

- Re-assigning processes.

Process monitoring tools typically include multiple interfaces, such as graphical views, tabular views, and forms-based views.

Business Activity Monitoring

Business activity monitoring (BAM) analyzes events generated by business processes and information collected about business processes to provide real-time feedback on higher-level business functions and business performance metrics. BAM is becoming a standard component of business process management suites.

BAM is aware of the context of the executing business processes because it can correlate the information and events it collects with the associated process models. Therefore, BAM has immediate knowledge of process deviations and can send alerts to interested parties.

As part of a BPM suite, BAM has access to multiple systems involved in a given business process and can combine this information to create real-time digital dashboards that provide real-time feedback for the enterprise.

A BAM dashboard gives stakeholders in an organization access to information that helps them track and manage key performance indicators (KPI). Organizations can provide different company stakeholders with BAM dashboards (sometimes called enterprise performance management dashboards) customized to their needs. A sales view, for example, could enable salespeople to see orders and related details. An operations view would show shipments and picking errors. The CEO could see daily and monthly totals, actual versus planned results, year-over-year comparisons of KPIs, and more in real time.

What's Missing from WS-BPEL?

There is an important difference between BPM and WS-BPEL; specifically, something's missing from WS-BPEL and the associated BPMS tools. Although WS-BPEL is vital to the Web services stack, it should not be viewed as a complete BPM solution for Web services. We have reviewed the key elements of a BPM solution, including process modeling, process simulation, process documentation, process execution, process monitoring and control, and business activity monitoring. WS-BPEL is a language for representing a process flow in a form suitable for a WS-BPEL engine to read and interpret. WS-BPEL does not pretend to address or standardize any other aspects of a BPM solution, such as process modeling or process monitoring, although we are sure that over time, it will influence process modeling tools, process monitoring tools, and so on. In some of these areas, other standards have been proposed, such as BPMN and BPML for process modeling, but their adoption is not yet widespread.

Example Business Process

Figure 6-2 shows an example business process for opening a customer account. In general, a business process includes activities to be performed, links between the activities that determine the order in which activities can be performed and the data that is passed between activities, and business rules for enabling transitions between activities.

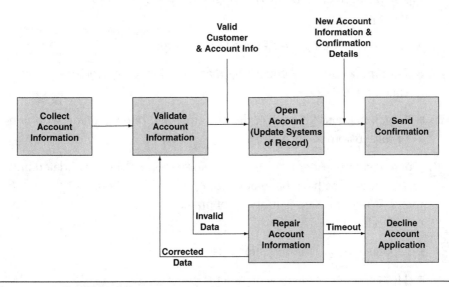

Figure 6-2   Simple business process.

The steps in the business process are:

1. **Collect account information**—Gather all necessary customer and account information to open the account. When this step is further elaborated, it might involve one or more of the following:

   ■ Customer enters data via Web site.

   ■ Customer provides data to a customer service representative over the phone.

- Customer provides data on a written form, and a data entry clerk enters it into a computer system.

- Customer already has an account, so the customer information is extracted from a database.

2. **Validate account information**—After the information has been collected, it needs to be validated, and business rules need to be checked. When this step is further elaborated, it might involve one or more of the following:

- Ensure all required fields have been entered.

- Perform consistency checks such as verifying the customer's home state and ZIP Code.

- Check the credit history of the customer and rate the credit worthiness of this customer.

3. **Open account**—After the customer information has been validated and all business rules have been applied, open a new account for the customer. When this step is further elaborated, it might involve one or more of the following:

- Update customer information system.

- Update order management system.

- Update billing system.

- Update sales force automation system and inform sales representative of new account.

- Inform business partners of new customer and the customer's credentials, such as credit limit.

4. **Send confirmation**—After the customer account has been successfully opened, send a confirmation to the customer along with details of his or her new account. When this step in the process is further elaborated, it might involve one or more of the following:

- Send a letter to the customer thanking him or her for opening this new account.

- Send an email to the customer thanking him or her for opening this new account.

- If the customer is a Gold customer, then have a customer service representative call the customer and thank him or her for opening this new account.

5. **Repair account information**—If the customer and account information cannot be validated or doesn't satisfy all the business rules, then try to correct the information or obtain more information that satisfies the business rules. When this step in the process is further elaborated, it might involve one or more of the following:

   - Send an email to the customer asking for information that was omitted from the account registration form or asking for more information on the customer's credit history.

   - Have a customer service representative call the customer and ask for the missing information or ask for more information on the customer's credit history.

6. **Decline account application**—If the customer and account information cannot be repaired so that it satisfies all business rules for opening a new account, then decline the customer's request to open a new account.

It is almost always the case that what one person views as a process, someone else views as a single task. For example, take the "Open Account" business process defined previously:

- Opening an account would be a single activity to a business analyst whose job is defining a relationship banking system.

- However, the "Collect Account Information" activity is a complex process to a business analyst who is responsible for managing all the customer access channels including bank branches, Web site, call center, and interactive voice response systems.

Luckily, most business process management systems and Web services composition languages allow one process to invoke other processes so that processes can be composed in a hierarchical manner. Composite applications can be used to meet a wide range of business requirements. See the section "Defining Atomic and Composite Services" for further information on composite applications.

Combining BPM, SOA, and Web Services

This section discusses the benefits of using BPM, SOA, and Web services in combination. The benefits include a more flexible and agile implementation of a BPM system and the ability to more easily create, manage, and maintain composite applications.

Benefits of BPM, SOA, and Web Services

Most organizations have a diverse application and technology landscape (see Figure 6-3). Typically there are numerous application silos (so named due to their stand-alone nature, which includes everything from application GUIs to application-specific business logic to application databases), and sharing information among applications is difficult due to differences in technology platforms and data models.

Moving to an SOA and Web services introduces a services layer (see Figure 6-4). The services layer consists of line of business services that are aligned to a particular business domain (including data models suitable for each business domain), reusable technical services that can be shared across multiple business domains, and the Web services platform, which allows services to be defined and utilized in a manner that is independent of the underlying application and technology platforms.

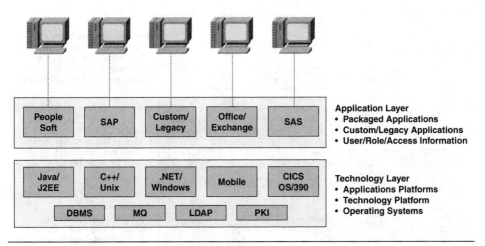

Figure 6-3   Typical application and technology landscape.

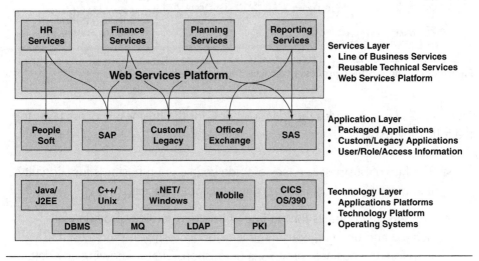

Figure 6-4   Services layer based on SOA and Web services.

The next layer is the business process layer (see Figure 6-5).

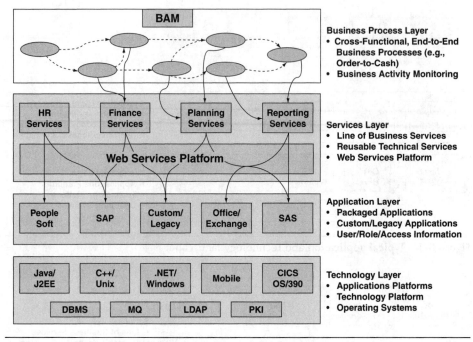

Figure 6-5   The business process layer uses the services layer.

The services layer provides the ideal platform for the business process layer for the following reasons:

- The line of business services provide coarse-grain business functionality that maps to the business tasks in a business process.

- The service contracts for the line of business services provide well-defined and unambiguous interfaces for accessing the services, and therefore the business process is not responsible for knowing any details of the underlying application and technology platforms.

- The service registry and service discovery facilities provided by the service layer ensure that the business process layer can dynamically locate and access services as necessary.

- The service-level data model is defined based on the business domain and is independent of the data model used by any particular application.

Furthermore, XML is used as the canonical format for exchanging data between tasks in the business process and when a business task invokes a service because XML is independent of the internal data formats used by the underlying applications.

- The service-level security model provides single sign-on and role-based access control to ensure that process tasks are authorized to use services, and it protects the business process layer from having to deal with the various security interfaces provided by the underlying application and technology platforms.

- The service-level management model generates run-time statistics regarding service usage, which can be used by BAM tools that are part of the business process layer.

In the past, most systems did not provide a services layer based on an SOA and Web services. BPM without a services layer is complex and brittle because the process layer is required to access the underlying business applications directly (see Figure 6-6).

This approach is more complex because the process layer must directly access existing applications using one or more interfaces defined by the application (e.g., APIs, messages, or database tables). This requires the process implementer to learn about these application interfaces and requires steps to be added to the business process to compensate for poorly defined application interfaces or for transforming application specific data into a canonical format that the business process can use.

This approach is more brittle (i.e., more likely to break) because the process is tightly coupled to specific applications and specific application interfaces. This means that something as simple as installing a newer version of an application (with revised APIs, messages, or database tables) could break all the processes that access it. This tight coupling also makes this approach harder to change. For instance, replacing an existing application with a new application from another vendor impact requires modifying all processes that access the old application.

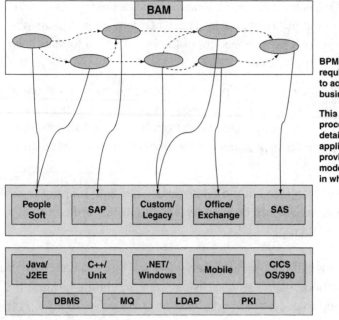

Figure 6-6   BPM without services is brittle.

Implementing a process layer without a services layer has inhibited the widespread adoption of BPM.

Defining Atomic and Composite Services

This section takes a closer look at the design and implementation of solutions based on BPM, SOA, and Web services using an example that involves making business services available to internal and external users based on existing legacy systems and newly developed line of business services.

Figure 6-7 illustrates the initial system consisting of a legacy HR system, a legacy finance system, an existing enterprise security system for managing user/role/entitlement information (e.g., LDAP), and an existing enterprise system management system.

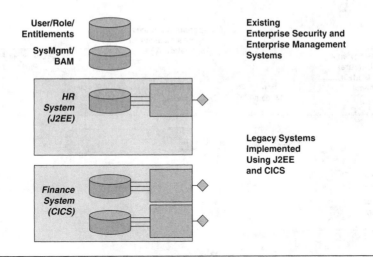

User/Role/
Entitlements

SysMgmt/
BAM

HR
System
(J2EE)

Finance
System
(CICS)

Existing
Enterprise Security and
Enterprise Management
Systems

Legacy Systems
Implemented
Using J2EE
and CICS

Figure 6-7   Example of legacy systems to be process- and service-enabled.

The HR system is implemented using J2EE technology and consists of an application database and an application object model, and it provides an EJB-based interface. The finance system runs on the mainframe; it is implemented using CICS transactions against mainframe databases and is accessed by off-host client applications via WebSphere MQ.

The first step in delivering reusable services using an SOA is defining business domain data, service, and process models, as shown in Figure 6-8.

The service-level data model defines the business-level data that will be exchanged among services and made available to service requesters. The service-level data model includes data definitions (XML Schema), data validation rules (XML Schema constraints and XPath), and data transformation rules (XLST). Ideally, the service-level data model is created based on an existing industry schemas, although in practice, it may have to be derived from existing data structures, object models, and database schemas, in which case, the data modeler must carefully abstract these low-level data definitions to create a service-level data model that is truly application- and technology-independent.

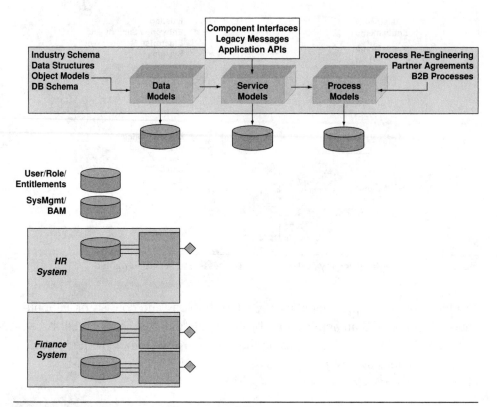

Figure 6-8   Data, service, and process modeling.

The service model defines the service contracts (WSDL plus optionally WS-Policy) for the line of business services. The service contracts define the following:

■ The input and output parameters for the services (based on the document types defined by the service-level data model).

■ The security profile for the services (e.g., entitlements, access control lists, privacy, and non-repudiation).

■ The qualities of service for the services (priority, guaranteed delivery, transactional characteristics, and recovery semantics).

■ The service-level agreements (e.g., response time and availability).

Typically, there are two broad categories of services: *atomic* services (services that cannot be decomposed into finer-grain services) and *composite* services (services created by composing two or more other services). Like the service-level data model, ideally the service model is created based on existing industry service definitions, although in practice, it may have to be derived from existing component interfaces (e.g., COM/DCOM type libraries, CORBA IDL, Java objects), legacy message formats, or existing application APIs.

The process model defines the business processes implemented by the solution using WS-BPEL (see the section "WS-BPEL" later in this chapter). Each process definition includes the process tasks, the control flow between tasks, the data flow between tasks, and other business rules associated with the process (e.g., process- and task-level pre-conditions, process- and task-level deadlines, rules for assigning tasks to users, rules for assigning tasks to services, and rules for routing alerts and escalating issues). The process model is typically created based on existing process definitions, re-engineered process definitions, partner agreements that define interactions around a process, or industry process definitions.

Ideally, the service-level data model is created first and is used as the basis for defining the service model, which in turn is used as the basis for defining the process models. However, the models can be defined in any order, and typically, the models are defined in an iterative manner.

Figure 6-9 illustrates defining atomic services based on the data and service models. In this example, three of the services are defined by creating legacy service wrappers for the legacy systems. The legacy services wrappers provide a Web services interface (SOAP and WSDL) to a legacy system, and they are responsible for receiving incoming SOAP messages, translating them into a format that the legacy system can understand, and then routing the request to the appropriate legacy system (e.g., invoking the appropriate EJB or placing a message on the appropriate WebSphere MQ queue). In this example, one of the services is defined by implementing a new J2EE component and exposing it as a Web service.

Figure 6-9 also shows the Web services platform providing core facilities for defining, registering, securing, and managing the atomic services. The Web services platform takes advantage of existing enterprise security systems that support SAML, XKMS, XACML, WS-Security, as well as a directory service (such as LDAP or ADS) that contains user/roles/entitlement information. Similarly, the Web services platform takes advantage of existing enterprise management systems that support WSDM (such as CA Unicenter, HP Openview, or IBM Tivoli) for monitoring and managing the services.

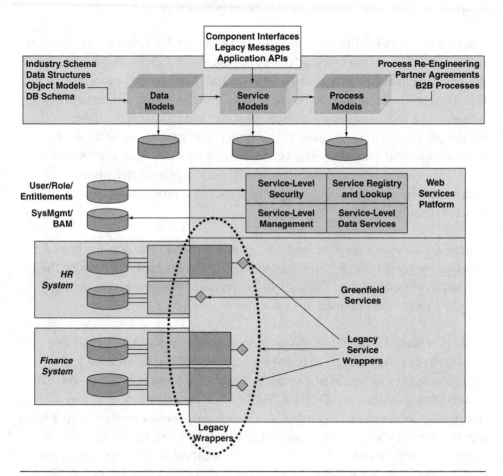

Figure 6-9   Creating atomic Web services based on data and service models.

Figure 6-10 shows the next layer in the SOA for defining composite services.

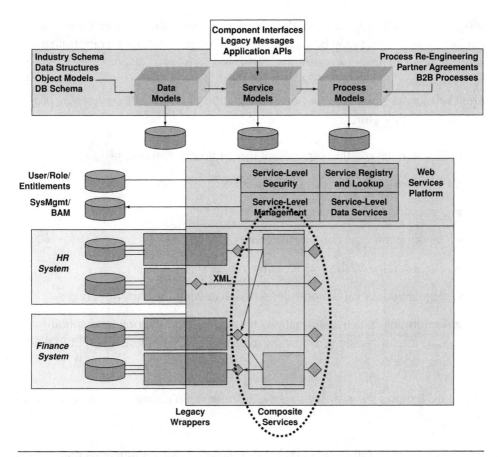

Figure 6-10   Creating composite Web services.

Composite services are Web services that use (or are composed of) other services. Composite services are like any other Web service in that they have a WSDL service contract and are invoked using SOAP messages. Composite services can be created by explicit programming, such as an EJB exposed as a Web service that consumes other Web services. Composite services can also be created using Web services orchestration and WS-BPEL. In this case, the developer typically defines the composite service using a Web services orchestration product that provides a graphical user interface for composing Web services (which also generates a WS-BPEL process definition) and a run-time engine that executes the WS-BPEL process definition. The advantages of composing Web services using WS-BPEL are simplicity and flexibility because the composite service can be changed without deploying any new code. In some cases, explicit programming may be better—especially for very simple composite services or for performance-sensitive composite services.

The Web services platform supports the creation of composite services by providing the facilities for:

- Discovering existing services (at design time and run-time).
- Registering the new composite service.
- Accessing the existing services securely.
- Securing the new composite service.
- Orchestrating Web services using WS-BPEL.
- Applying data validation rules when accessing the existing services.
- Performing data transformations for aggregating, filtering, and splitting data after it is received from existing services but before it is sent to existing services.

Figure 6-11 shows the next layer in the SOA for defining and executing business processes.

Business processes implement complex, multistep business functions that typically involve multiple participants, including internal users, external customers, and partners. The run-time semantics of the business process are defined using WS-BPEL, and the process engine is responsible for executing the process tasks and enforcing the associated business rules according to the WS-BPEL script.

Each task in the business process is either performed by a Web service or by a user. When a task is implemented by a Web service, the process engine is responsible for locating and invoking the Web service. When a task is implemented by a user, the process engine is responsible for routing the task to an authorized user. The business process may also define how transactions should be handled and the recovery semantics when failures occur (e.g., whether ACID transactions or compensating transactions are required). The business process itself is also a Web service so that any service requester, including another business process, can initiate it.

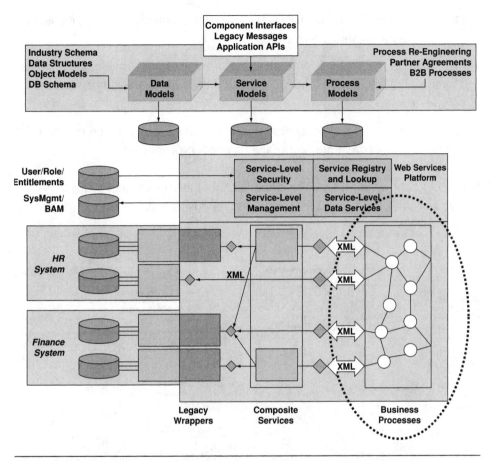

Figure 6-11   Creating business processes that use composite and atomic services.

Once again, the Web services platform supports the creation and execution of business processes by providing the facilities for:

- Discovering existing services (at design time and run-time).

- Registering the new business process as a Web service.

- Accessing existing services securely.

- Securing the new business process.

- Orchestrating and choreographing Web services using WS-BPEL.

- Allowing the business process to apply data validation rules when accessing the existing services.

- Allowing the business process to perform data transformations (e.g., data aggregation, filtering, and splitting) as data is being passed between process tasks.

- Generating run-time statistics regarding service usage, which can be used by BAM tools that are part of the business process layer.

Figure 6-12 shows the next layer in the SOA that allows services requesters to access and utilize the Web services (including business processes exposed as Web services).

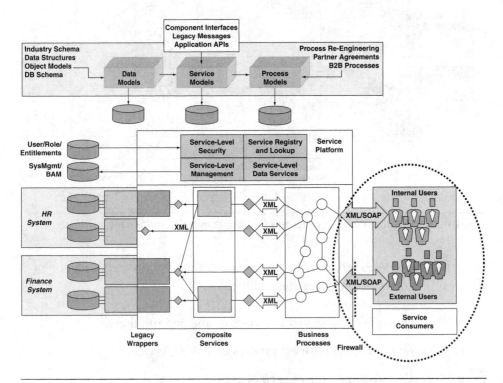

Figure 6-12   Making business services available to internal and external users.

Any authorized service requester (including IT systems, end-user applications, and other Web services) can access any service at any time and from anywhere, including atomic services, composite services, and business processes exposed as Web services. Sometimes only a fraction of the services are made available to service requesters outside of an organization (e.g., customers and partners), and typically these service requesters must comply with more stringent security requirements than internal service requesters.

Orchestration and Choreography Specifications

Web services are emerging as the cornerstone for architecting and implementing business processes and collaborations within and across organizational boundaries. Two languages for Web service composition have emerged:

- **Business Process Execution Language (WS-BPEL)**—Developed by BEA, IBM, Microsoft, and Siebel and subsequently submitted to the WS-BPEL Technical Committee at OASIS.

- **Choreography Description Language (WS-CDL)**—Developed by the Web Services Choreography Working Group at W3C, based on an input specification written by Intalio, Sun, BEA, and SAP.

The goal of these languages is to glue Web services together in a process-oriented way.

Comparing Web Services Orchestration and Choreography

The terms *orchestration* and *choreography* are frequently used to describe two approaches to composing Web services. Although the two terms overlap somewhat, Web services orchestration (WSO) refers to composing web services for business processes, whereas Web services choreography (WSC) refers to composing Web services for business collaborations (see Figure 6-13).

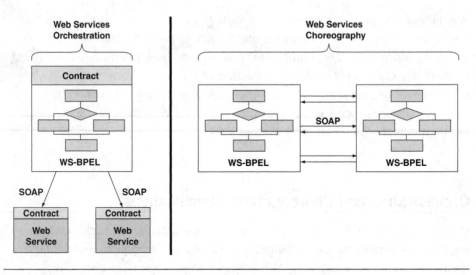

Figure 6-13   Comparing orchestration and choreography.

More specifically:

- Web services orchestration is used for defining composite services and internal processes that reuse existing Web services. WSOs can be used to support the preparation of information to exchange externally in WSCs.

- Web services choreography is used for defining how multiple parties collaborate in a peer-to-peer manner as part of some larger business transaction by exchanging messages with trading partners and external organizations, such as suppliers and customers.

In the case of WSO, the focus is on creating a composite service in a declarative (non-programmatic) manner. A WSO defines the services that compose the orchestration and the order in which the services should be executed, including parallel activities and conditional branching logic. In this way, the orchestration can be viewed as a simple process that is itself a Web service. WSO flows typically include control points for branching, parallel processing options, human response steps, and predefined steps of various types such as transformation, adapters, email, and Web services.

In the case of WSC, the focus is on defining how multiple parties collaborate as part of some larger business transaction. WSC allows each party to describe its part in the interaction in terms of the public message exchanges that occur between the multiple parties as Web services, rather than a specific business process that a single party executes, as is the case with WSO.

When defining business interactions using WSC, a formal description of the message exchange protocols used by business processes during their interactions is needed that models peer-to-peer message exchanges, both synchronous and asynchronous, within stateful, long-running processes involving two or more parties.

The definition of such business protocols involves precisely specifying the visible message exchange behavior of each of the parties involved in the protocol, without revealing internal implementation details. There are two reasons for separating the public aspects of business process behavior from internal or private aspects:

- One is that organizations do not want to reveal their internal business processes and data management to their business partners.

- The other is that separating public processes from private processes provides the freedom to change private details of the internal process implementation without affecting the public business protocol.

The key difference between WSO and WSC is that WSC is a peer-to-peer model, where there may be many parties collaborating in a business process, whereas a WSO is a hierarchical requester/provider model, where the WSO alone defines what services should be called and when they should be called, and the WSO does not define a collaboration among multiple parties.

Whereas WS-BPEL is focused on WSO and the composition of individual Web services and can be used to drive WSC-style interactions across enterprise boundaries, CDL is focused on WSC and the definition of cross-enterprise relationships, regardless of the underlying technology used to implement the organizational behavior. CDL, on the other hand, is not well suited for WSO and for assembling specific Web services into composites. CDL can certainly reference

Web services endpoints as the entry points of collaboration across enterprises, but its focus is definitely more on defining the relationship between companies. CDL defines its relationship to WS-BPEL, however, while the reverse isn't true (at least not at the time of this writing).

Can Both WSO and WSC Be Specified Using a Common Language?

There's no doubt about the different characteristics of these interactions (those necessary to submit and acknowledge the request of a purchase order and those necessary to process the purchase order itself). However, disagreement remains over whether both types of interactions can be specified using a single language. Many WS-BPEL advocates would say that WS-BPEL is the only language required for the spectrum of interactions and executions, while others take the position that a complementary language is required and that a single language cannot handle everything, especially details related to the definition of the parties involved in the collaboration. Industry adoption and real-world use will tell the tale. We expect some combination of the two to prevail because we do not expect WS-BPEL or any single language to be universally used.

WS-BPEL

Web Services Business Process Execution Language (WS-BPEL) is a process-oriented composition language for Web services.

WS-BPEL is service-oriented and relies on WSDL. A WS-BPEL process can be exposed as a WSDL-defined service and can be invoked like any other Web service. Furthermore, WS-BPEL expects that all external Web services included in a web services composition be defined using a WSDL service contract. This approach allows a WS-BPEL process to invoke other WS-BPEL processes and also allows a WS-BPEL process to call itself recursively.

Is WS-BPEL the Best or Worst of the Combination?

WS-BPEL is said to combine the best of WSFL and XLANG because it allows for a mixture of block-structured and graph-structured process models. However, the fact that WS-BPEL is based on WSFL and XLANG, which themselves are based on different paradigms, leads to a situation where WS-BPEL has overlapping constructs. Therefore, developers using WS-BPEL are faced with multiple ways of accomplishing the same task (i.e., when to use XLANG-style or WSFL-style), which introduces an additional and unnecessary level of complexity to process design. The developers of WS-BPEL at OASIS will have to work hard to avoid producing the worst of both worlds instead of the best.

The WS-BPEL specification replaces IBM's WSFL (Web Services Flow Language) and Microsoft's XLANG (Web Services for Business Process Design). XLANG was a block-structured language with basic control flow structures such as sequences, switches (for conditional routing), whiles (for looping), and alls (for parallel routing). In contrast, WSFL was graph-oriented and relied mainly on the concept of control links.

WS-BPEL defines a set of basic tasks for creating Web service compositions:

- **Invoke task**—Allows the business process to invoke a one-way or request-response operation on a `portType` offered by a Web service.

- **Receive task**—Allows the business process to do a blocking wait for a message to arrive.

- **Reply task**—Allows the business process to send a message in reply to a received message.

- **Wait task**—Tells the process to wait for some time.

- **Assign task**—Copies data from one place to another.

- **Throw task**—Indicates that an error condition has occurred.

- **Terminate task**—Terminates the entire orchestration instance.

Structured tasks are used to combine the primitive tasks into more complex processes:

- **Sequence task**—Define an ordered sequence of tasks.

- **Switch task**—Ability to select a particular branch based on conditional logic.

- **Pick task**—Block and wait for a suitable message to arrive or for a time-out alarm to go off. When one of these triggers occurs, the associated activity is executed, and the pick completes.

- **While task**—Define a group of tasks that should be repeated while a condition is satisfied.

- **Flow task**—Indicate that a collection of steps should be executed in parallel (links can be used to define execution order within a particular flow).

WS-BPEL treats all state uniformly as a collection of WSDL message types. A collection of messages that constitute the state of a business process is called a *container.* The messages held in a container are often those that have been received from Web services partners or that are to be sent to Web services, but WS-BPEL does not require this. Containers can hold messages that act as temporary variables for computation and that are never exchanged with partners.

WS-BPEL includes the idea of a container for each task in the flow, each of which has a schema definition. A message is given correspondence to a container, which is basically a Web service with additional information about how to process it, how to prepare it for processing (any pre-conditions), and what to do after processing it (any post-conditions); this container then determines the next task or step in the activity to be executed (which could be the result of a conditional expression).

All data access and data handling in WS-BPEL is defined using standards such as XPath and XSLT and is based on the WSDL service contracts (and the underlying WSDL message definitions, WSDL part definitions, and XML Schema definitions) of the services being composed as part of the process.

Licenses for WS-BPEL

Something interesting about WS-BPEL is that both Microsoft and IBM have disclosed on the OASIS Web site that they might have patents upon which anyone implementing WS-BPEL would infringe. This obviously raises the question about intellectual property (IP) on specifications such as WS-BPEL. If open specifications are to promote competition, IP rights have to be assigned to standards bodies, not kept within the private companies competing with each other. If a vendor must license patent rights in order to implement a specification, that's an inhibitor to widespread adoption and a permanent encumbrance to competition. Some industries have managed to foster and adopt licensing models around intellectual property that have benefited everyone, such as the electronics industry's endorsement of the compact cassette, VHS video format, compact disc, and digital video disc. But in the software industry, patents and what they mean, or what's acceptable as a patent, is the source of perennial dissatisfaction because it seems that anything can be patented. For the market to succeed, it is important to create a situation in which Web services standards are freely implementable and have the same status as Web standards such as HTML and HTTP.

A WS-BPEL variable identifies the specific data exchanged in a process. When a WS-BPEL process receives a message, it populates the appropriate variable so that subsequent requests can access the data. The assignment task is used to create new messages or to modify existing ones, using parts of other messages, XPath expressions, XSLT expressions, or literal values. Therefore, the assignment task allows messages received from one service to be transformed and used as input to operations of another.

WS-BPEL provides the ability for activities to be scoped and for fault handlers and compensation handlers to be defined for these scopes. Fault handlers and compensation handlers are like catch clauses in object-oriented programming languages such as Java and C++ and can be triggered when a throw task is executed.

During its lifetime, a business process instance typically holds one or more conversations with partners involved in its work. In such cases, it is often necessary to provide application-level mechanisms to match messages and conversations with the business process instances for which they are intended. WS-BPEL addresses correlation scenarios by providing a declarative mechanism to specify *correlation sets*. Each correlation set in WS-BPEL is a named group of properties that, taken together, serve to define an application-level conversation within a business protocol instance.

Consider the usual supply-chain situation where a buyer sends a purchase order to a seller. The seller needs to asynchronously return an acknowledgment for the order, and the acknowledgment must be routed to the correct business process instance at the buyer. The obvious and standard mechanism to do this is to carry a business token in the order message (such as a purchase order number) that is copied into the acknowledgment for correlation. The token can be in the message envelope in a header or in the business document (purchase order) itself. In either case, the exact location and type of the token in the relevant messages is fixed and instance-independent. Only the value of the token is instance-dependent. Therefore, the structure and position of the correlation tokens in each message can be expressed declaratively in the business process description. The WS-BPEL notion of a correlation set allows a WS-BPEL-compliant infrastructure to use correlation tokens to provide instance routing automatically.

Is WS-BPEL an Executable Language?

Some people view WS-BPEL as the XML script that a business process engine executes, while others view it more as an interchange language. That is, if one business process engine wants to execute a proprietary language but export a process flow for use by another process engine, the engine can convert the proprietary script into WS-BPEL. Similarly, if the target engine wants to convert the WS-BPEL to a proprietary format for execution, it can. Other implementers take the view that the language is fine to execute the way it is. The question is whether or not the different approaches will impact portability and interoperability.

In this example, WS-BPEL defines the process flow. WSDL describes the Web service endpoint to which the customer can submit the PO document. WS-Policy defines the security, reliability, and transactional requirements the service requester must use in communicating with the provider. The document is sent using SOAP and formatted using XML according to a predefined XML Schema shared between the customer and the supplier so that the supplier can determine whether the order is valid. WS-Security can be used to check the authorization of the customer to submit purchase orders and decrypt the document so that it can be processed. WS-Addressing provides the callback address for the customer so that the order can be reconfirmed once the supplier knows it can be filled and shipped by a certain date. The WS-Composite Application Framework drives the compensating transactions to undo the work of specific tasks or to cancel the entire process. WS-ReliableMessaging guarantees that the PO document is received by the supplier and that the invoice or cancellation message is received by the customer. (Details on all of these specifications are provided in Part II of this book.)

WS-BPEL can be used to define both orchestrations (called executable processes) and choreographies (called abstract processes). In an executable process, the orchestration defines the specific activities to be carried out and the specific services to be invoked to complete the business process. In an abstract process, the choreography specifies the public message exchanges between two or more parties—the choreography is not executable and does not define the process flow's internal details. The interface of the choreography is defined by the set of all receive and reply activities present in the process.

WS-BPEL Implementations Vary

It is often said that "WS-BPEL is the kind of language that you implement the way you want to." This in part means that the specification is so large and comprehensive that many implementers may choose just to implement a part of it. Another possible interpretation is that the specification is very loose, and implementers will naturally interpret it differently.

Although a WS-BPEL process is defined based on the `portTypes` defined in one or more WSDL documents, a WS-BPEL process is defined in the abstract by referencing only the `portTypes` of the services involved in the process, not their possible deployments. Defining business processes in this way allows the reuse of business process definitions over multiple deployments of compatible services.

WSDL 1.1 or WSDL 2.0?

Although it's true enough that WSDL 1.1 and WSDL 2.0 are very similar, the use of either with WS-BPEL may be very different. The way the working group schedules seem to go, WS-BPEL and WSDL 2.0 may be ready at the same time. This is a common problem in standards, in which you (as a specification author) would like to refer to the newest version of a standard, even before it's completed, but you can't. You just don't know how it might change. In this case, it's very possible that when WS-BPEL is done, it may have to be immediately revised to include mappings to WSDL 2.0.

WS-BPEL is currently defined to work with WSDL 1.1, and the examples in this section are based on WSDL 1.1. WS-BPEL should also be compatible with WSDL 2.0, however, because the basic constructs are the same. WSDL 2.0 offers several extensions to WSDL 1.1 that might be beneficial to WS-BPEL, such as the definition of several new message exchange patterns and a features and properties extension for messages, interfaces, and operations that allows assertions such as security and transaction requirements to be included directly into the WSDL file instead of in associated policy schemas. But because this is all XML, the real consequence of where things are defined has more to do with how the various pieces of XML are assembled together and processed rather than in which file they are defined.

What follows is a set of examples using pseudo-code generic enough to illustrate the way in which WSDL and WS-BPEL are related and work together to achieve the goals and objectives of business process automation using Web services. The examples below follow the process flow illustrated in Figure 6-2.

First, the messages are defined:

```
<xs:element name="opanA:CustomerInfo" type="openA:tCustomerInfo"/>
    <xs:complexType name="openA:tCustomerInfo">
        <xs:sequence>
            <xs:element   name="AccountNumber" type="xs:double"/>
            <xs:element   name="CustomerName" type="xs:string"/>
            <xs:element   name="CustomerAddress" type=
            ➡"xs:string"/>
            <xs:element   name="CustomerType" type="xs:string"/>
        </xs:sequence>
    </xs:complexType>
```

This example illustrates a very simple definition of a customer information record that might be used in the initial step of the process flow. The record structure can be defined in the WSDL file itself or in an associated file that's included by reference or actually imported into the file. (WSDL 2.0 supports Document Type Definitions (DTDs) and RelaxNG schemas in addition to XML Schemas for message type definitions.)

Definitions such as these are typically assigned to messages. Namespaces are used to qualify the element and attribute names of imported data types and structures.

The association of application data to messages in WSDL V2 is accomplished within the `<types>` section. In WSDL 1.1, there's an explicit mapping of message names to schema data. For example:

```
<message name="CustomerMessage">
        <part name="CustomerInfo" type="openA:tCustomerInfo"/>
</message>
```

This associates the `CustomerInfo` schema data type with the `CustomerMessage` WSDL message type.

A namespace definition is also required for using the `CustomerInfo` data type. For example:

```
xmlns:openA="http://www.bank.com/xsd/AccountManagement"
```

Then the `portTypes` (called `Interfaces` in WSDL 2.0) are defined for the messages, including the names of the operations and their input and output messages. For example:

```
<portType name="CollectAccountInfo">
    <operation name="CheckInfo">
        <input message="openA:CustomerInfo"/>
        <output message="openA:ValidInfo"/>
        <fault name="InvalidData"
            message="openA:CustomerDataError"/>
    </operation>
</portType>
```

The bindings are in the physical part of WSDL, and they are omitted here because they use SOAP, SMTP, HTTP, or other communications transport without affecting the logical part of WSDL or WS-BPEL definitions.

Structures called partner links are added below the WSDL port types to link the WS-BPEL process definitions to the port types. For example:

```
<plnk:partnerLinkType name="CheckCustomer">
    <plnk:role name="AccountManagement">
            <plnk:portType name="openA:CollectAccountInfo"/>
    </plnk:role>
</plnk:partnerLinkType>

<plnk:partnerLinkType name="ValidateAccount">
    <plnk:role name="ValidRequest">
    <plnk:portType name="openA:ApproveApplication"/>
    </plnk:role>
    <plnk:role name="InvalidRequest">
    <plnk:portType name="openA:RejectApplication"/>
    </plnk:role>
</plnk:partnerLinkType>
```

These partner links relate WSDL operations to steps within a WS-BPEL process and serve to bridge the description of the service and its interfaces to the description of the process flow defined to consume those services.

The WS-BPEL portion of the extended WSDL is identified using a process name.
For example:

```
<process name =  "OpenAccount"
      targetNamespace="http://www.bank.com/wsdl/accountManagement
      xmlns=http://www.bank.com/2005/05/schemas/AccountService.xsd
      xmlns:openA=http://www.bank.com/wsdl/OpenAccount
      abstractProcess="no"
```

An abstract process is not directly executable, and the abstractProcess field is
set to yes when WS-BPEL is used to define choreography rather than orchestration. Any additional namespaces required for the definitions in this section are
typically included here. Following the process name, the partner links for this
particular flow are referenced to point back to the particular part of the link to
the WSDL that this specific flow needs to use. For example:

```
<partnerLinks>
      <partnerLink name="CollectAccountInformation"
      ➥partnerLinkType="openA:GetAccountInfo"
      <partnerLink name="ValidateAccountInformation"
      ➥partnerLinkType="openA:CheckAccountInfo"
      <partnerLink name="OpenAccount" partnerLinkType=
      ➥"openA:OpenAccountOk"
      <partnerLink name="SendConfirmation" partnerLinkType=
      ➥"openA:ConfirmOpen"
      <partnerLink name="RepairAccountInformation"
      ➥partnerLinkType="openA:RepairInformation"
      <partnerLink name="DeclineAccountApplication"
      ➥partnerLinkType="openA:DeclineApplication"
</partnerLinks>
```

This example illustrates that six partner links are needed for the six steps in the
flow, including CollectAccountInformation, ValidateAccountInformation,
OpenAccount, SendConfirmation, RepairAccountInformation, and
DeclineAccountApplication.

Following the list of partner links is the declaration of variable names—that is,
XML Schema, XML Simple Type, and/or WSDL message definitions that are
needed for this process. For example:

```
<variables>
  <variable name="customerData"
  ➥messageType="openA:CustomerRecord"/>
```

```
    <variable name="validData" messageType="openA:CustomerRecord"/>
    <variable name="accountData" messageType="openA:AccountRecord"/>
    <variable name="confirmationData"
➥messageType="openA:ConfirmationRecord/>
    <variable name="faultData" messageType="openA:FaultRecord"/>
</variables>
```

If any fault handlers are required for the process, those are defined next. For example:

```
<faultHandlers>
    <catch faultName="openA:InvalidCustomer" faultVariable=
    ➥"BadData">
      <reply partnerLink="ValidateAccountInformation"
       portType="openA:RejectApplication"
       operation="sendRejectionMessage"
       variable="CustomerData"
       faultName="cannotOpenAccount"/>
    </catch>
</faultHandlers>
```

This fault handler is set up to catch any problem with validating customer data when trying to open an account, such as bad credit data or past problems with the bank.

Finally, the process flow sequence is defined to put the operations into the execution relationship. For example:

```
<sequence>
  <receive partnerLink="CollectAccountInformation" interface=
  ➥"openA:AccountManagement" operation="InputData"
  ➥variable="customerData"/>
  <assign>
    <copy>
      <from variable="customerData"/>
      <to variable="accountData"/>
    </copy>
  </assign>

  <invoke partnerLink="ValidateAccountInformation" interface=
  ➥"openA:AccountManagement" operation="ValidateData" variable=
  ➥"accountData"/>
  <assign>
    <copy>
      <from variable="accountData"/>
      <to variable="validData"/>
```

```
    </copy>
  </assign>

  <receive partnerLink="openAccount" interface="openA:
  ➥AccountManagement" operation="openAccount" variable=
  ➥"validData"/>
<sequence>
```

This example illustrates how the process flow would first receive the customer data input from the collect customer information function and next invoke the validate account information function to check the data. Depending on the results of the validation, the flow would continue toward approval or toward trying to clean up the bad data, if possible. WS-BPEL offers several conditional verbs for this kind of branching, including switch, pick, and while commands.

WS-BPEL correlation sets identify data shared by the execution of multiple Web services in the process flow and a compensation handler within the fault handler executes any compensation logic that might be able to undo the results of a previous step, such as closing an account that was improperly opened.

Aside from the complexities of incorporating WS-BPEL syntax into WSDL files, the relationship to the process flow construct of other technologies such as reliability, security, and transactions may have to be separately understood and individually defined to get an overall flow design to work correctly.

Choreography Description Language
The Web Services Choreography Working Group at W3C is developing the Web Services Choreography Description Language (WS-CDL). WS-CDL is designed to complement WS-BPEL and other extended Web services technologies by defining the executable processes needed to implement a piece of a business choreography or business-to-business (B2B) scenario.

A typical B2B scenario such as that defined within RosettaNet's Partner Information Process (PIP) and ebXML's Business Process Specification Schema (BPSS) involves the submission of an XML document such as a purchase order from one trading partner to one or more other trading partners for execution. WS-BPEL could define the flow of execution, messages in the flow, and other actions such as fault handlers and compensations. While WS-BPEL's abstract processes are intended for B2B interactions, WS-CDL provides additional capabilities beyond WS-BPEL, including how different business process engines might talk to each other, such as a trading partner scenario involving a WS-BPEL engine on one side and a RosettaNet engine on another, or a RosettaNet engine on one side and a plain application server on the other (i.e., without a business process management engine).

Metadata such as trading partner name, security information to be shared, policy information on non-repudiation, acknowledgment policy, human approval policies, and so on cannot be defined with WS-BPEL alone when WS-BPEL is used in conjunction with other technologies in a wide-business process collaboration across multiple companies, such as in an extended supply-chain scenario.

WS-CDL is intended for use in B2B scenarios in which it isn't possible to define a single controlling entity for the entire interaction, and it may be necessary to define the rule for sharing control of the overall flow. WS-CDL defines how and when to pass control from one trading partner to another.

WS-CDL provides a "global" definition of the common ordering conditions and constraints under which messages are exchanged that can be agreed upon by all the Web services participants involved in the interaction. Each participant can then use the global definition to build and test solutions that conform to it. Business and government agencies may not want to cede control to an external business process engine and may want to use WS-CDL for negotiating a smooth handoff of control. WS-CDL is not an executable language but rather a declarative language for defining interaction patterns to which multiple parties can agree.

A WS-CDL document is a named set of definitions that can be referenced parties, using a *package* element as a root that contains one or more collaboration type definitions.

The syntax of the package construct is as follows:

```
<package
    name="SupplyChain"
    author="Ericn"
    version="1.1"
```

```
      targetNamespace=www.iona.com/artix/examples
      xmlns="http://www.w3.org/2004/04/ws-chor/cdl">
      importDefinitions*
      informationType*
      token*
      tokenLocator*
      role*
      relationship*
      participant*
      channelType*
      Choreography-Notation*
</package>
```

The package model defines the participants in collaboration and their respective roles and relationships. Once agreed upon, packages are exchanged a cross trust boundaries among the collaborating companies to share explicit definitions.

The package construct allows aggregating a set of choreography definitions, where the elements `informationType`, `token`, `tokenLocator`, `role`, `relationship`, `participant`, and `channelType` are shared by all the choreographies defined within this package.

Example of Web Services Composition

In this section, we'll compare and contrast the different approaches to using WS-BPEL to define the flow illustrated in Figure 6-2. In general, there are two approaches to implementing the same business process:

- Orchestration-centric.

- Choreography-centric.

These approaches are described in further detail in the following subsections.

Orchestration-Centric Approach

This approach is called orchestration-centric because it defines the entire process in a top-down manner, with the top-level flow being an orchestration, each task in the orchestration being either a Web service or a sub-orchestration that is called by the top-level orchestration, and each task in the sub-orchestrations being either a Web service or an orchestration that is called by the sub-orchestrations, and so on.

The following example shows the WS-BPEL pseudo-code for the `OpenAccount` process (this pseudo-code shows the essential logic of the Web services orchestration using WS-BPEL keywords but without the XML syntax):

```
receive 'OpenAccountRequest'

invoke CollectAccountInfo
invoke ValidateAccountInfo
assign AccountInfoInvalid = ValidateAccountInfoResponse
while AccountInfoInvalid = true
          invoke RepairAccountInfo
          pick onRepairAccountInfoCB
              invoke ValidateAccountInfo
              assign AccountInfoInvalid =
              ➥ValidateAccountInfoResponse
          otherwise // timeout - assume AccountInfo can't be
          ➥repaired
              invoke DeclineAccountApplication
              terminate
          end pick
end while
invoke OpenAccount
invoke SendConfirmation
```

Figure 6-14 shows a drawing of the `OpenAccount` process in terms of how it orchestrates the execution of a series of Web service requests.

In this approach, the `OpenAccount` process is implemented as a WS-BPEL orchestration that has the following characteristics:

- The orchestration is initiated when an `OpenAccountRequest` is received.

- The orchestration invokes Web services (such as `OpenAccount` and `CollectAccountInformation`) to fulfill the steps in the orchestration.

- The orchestration defines the business logic for the `OpenAccount` process, including control logic (e.g., control of the while loop that handles invalid account information) and data flow.

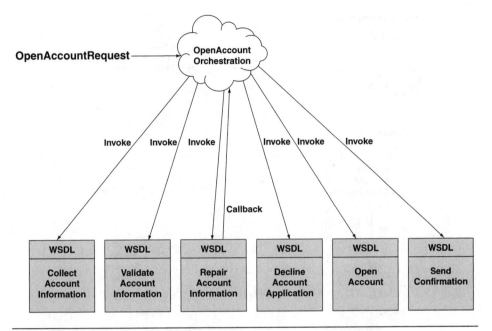

Figure 6-14   OpenAccount **process using Web services orchestration.**

Loops and conditional processing constructs are not shown but are assumed to exist and to be handled by the orchestration control point rather than within any of the individual services.

Choreography-Centric Approach

This approach is called the choreography-centric approach because it links together all the business tasks in the top-level business process using a series of choreographies, with no single engine being in control. In this approach, the interactions are peer-to-peer (each choreography operates as a peer to the other choreographies), instead of the more command-and-control style of approach typified by the orchestration-centric approach.

Figure 6-15 shows a drawing of the OpenAccount process using the choreography-centric approach.

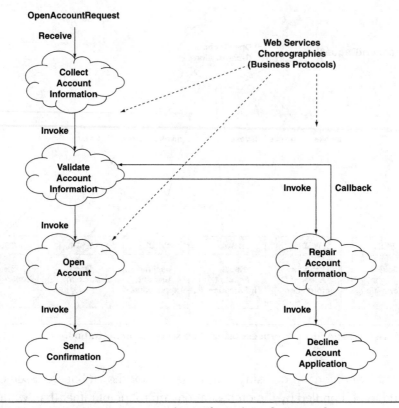

Figure 6-15   OpenAccount **process using Web services choreography.**

For instance, the interaction between each pair of tasks is defined as a choreography:

- CollectAccountInformation and ValidateAccountInformation.

- ValidateAccountInformation and RepairAccountInformation.

- ValidateAccountInformation and OpenAccount.

- OpenAccount and SendConfirmation.

- RepairAccountInformation and DeclineAccountApplication.

Comparing Orchestration-Centric and Choreography-Centric Approaches

In general, the choreography-centric approach is more loosely coupled. It is particularly well suited when portions of the process span administrative and organizational boundaries, which makes it difficult (if not impossible) to synchronize internal processes; however, it is much more important to define and specify the business protocol linking the partners (even if the "partners" are simply departments in the same company).

One key difference is that the orchestration approach assumes a single, central point of control over the entire scope of the process execution, while the choreography approach assumes that execution control is shared, potentially across multiple business process engines or various other technologies.

Part I Summary: Benefits of Combining BPM, SOA, and Web Services

The following section discusses the individual strengths provided by BPM, SOA, and Web services, and the section, "Complementary Features and Benefits of BPM, SOA, and Web Services," discusses how these approaches and technologies complement each other and how combining them overcomes limitations that they face when used by themselves.

Individual Features and Benefits of BPM, SOA, Web Services, and XML

Table 6-1 discusses the unique strengths provided by BPM, SOA, and Web services.

Table 6-1   Individual Features and Benefits of BPM, SOA, Web Services, and XML

	Unique Features and Benefits
BPM	Strong focus on process modeling makes business processes explicit so that they are easier to understand, refine, and optimize.
	Modeling tools allow business analysts to communicate business needs and requirements.

continues

Table 6-1   **Individual Features and Benefits of BPM, SOA, Web Services, and XML (continued)**

Unique Features and Benefits

BPM	Process logic is maintained separately from the underlying applications and is not hard-coded into these applications, thus making it easier to quickly modify business processes as business needs and requirements change.
	Process automation streamlines business processes and reduces process cycle times.
	Process automation ensures that processes are executed in a consistent fashion—for example, ensuring that all necessary steps are completed, that tasks are only routed to authorized users, and that government regulations are enforced.
	BAM tools provide real-time information on business processes for decision makers and relate that information to key business performance metrics.
SOA	Strong architectural focus (e.g., SOA governance, development processes, service and data modeling, and tool support) is ideal for creating long-term strategic value.
	Services provide an ideal level of abstraction for aligning business needs and technical capabilities (compared to procedures, objects, or components).
	Services provide an ideal level of abstraction for creating reusable, coarse-grained business functionality (compared to procedures, objects, or components).
	Loosely coupled services reduce vendor lock-in and simplify application migration and application consolidation.
	Well-defined service contracts clearly separate the service interface from the underlying details of the service implementation.
	Service-level data model defines documents to be exchanged among service requesters and service providers in a manner that is aligned with a particular business domain and that is independent of a specific application or technology platform.
Web services	Pervasive, open standards for distributed computing and document exchange.
	Web services are more pervasive and extensible than earlier distributed computing technologies such as COM/DCOM, CORBA, Java RMI, DCE/RPC, WebSphere MQ, and Tibco.

Unique Features and Benefits	
Web services	Web services are supported by all major ISVs, including platform vendors (e.g., IBM, Microsoft, SAP, PeopleSoft, Oracle, Sun, and BEA).
	Tool support for Web services and related technologies is thriving and growing.
	Extended Web services standards hold the promise of providing most of the elements of a Web services platform.
	EAI products relied on proprietary data formats and message buses, which hampered interoperability with other products and created vendor lock-in. XML and Web services allow the same open, standards-based technologies to be applied across all business domains, thus simplifying future interoperability.
XML	Widely accepted standard for defining business documents and exchanging information.
	Extensible so that business domain-specific schemas can be defined, but they are still based on the same core technologies.
	XML is supported by all major ISVs, including platform vendors (e.g., IBM, Microsoft, SAP, PeopleSoft, Oracle, Sun, and BEA).
	Tool support for XML and related technologies is thriving and growing.
	EAI products defined proprietary data formats and provided proprietary tools for data transformation. XML is supported by open, standards-based technologies such as XML Schema, validating parsers, XPath, XSLT, XQuery, and XHTML that support data validation, data transformation, and displaying XML data.
	Earlier standards for data exchange (e.g., EDI, HL7, SWIFT, and FIX) tended to be focused on a particular problem domain or business domain and were only supported by ISVs focused on that domain. XML is extensible so that business domain-specific schemas can be defined, but they are still based on the same core technologies.

Complementary Features and Benefits of BPM, SOA, and Web Services

Table 6-2 presents ways in which BPM, SOA, and Web services complement one another and how they improve on earlier technology.

Table 6-2   **Ways in Which BPM, SOA, and Web Services Complement One Another**

	Inhibitor or Limitation	Enabler or Compensating Feature
BPM	Earlier BPM systems tended to focus on one area (modeling, workflow, EAI, B2B, document management, and so on) to the detriment of broader functionality.	BPM systems have matured, and many products provide broader functionality that can be applied across a range of application types.
BPM	Earlier BPM systems needed to provide proprietary integration technology (including adapters for databases, legacy systems, packaged applications, and so on), which tended to be brittle and incomplete. Furthermore, these adapters often required custom coding to make them work.	SOA and SOI provide the ideal level of abstraction for defining reusable business functionality that completely encapsulates underlying applications and technology platforms from the BPM system.
BPM	Earlier BPM systems defined proprietary formats and techniques for representing a business process.	WS-BPEL provides a standard for service composition, service orchestration, and service choreography.
BPM	Earlier BPM systems defined proprietary formats for representing process-level data and custom techniques for manipulating it (e.g., validation rules and transformation).	XML is a widely accepted standard for defining business documents and exchanging information. XML is supported by related technologies such as XPath, XSLT, XQuery, and XHTML.
SOA	Earlier technologies used for SOA (e.g., CORBA, J2EE, WebSphere MQ) were tied to a specific technology platform, and it was difficult to the SOA beyond that expand technology platform.	Services implemented using Web services are platform-independent, including independent of OS platforms, application platforms, and middleware technologies.
SOA	Earlier technologies used for SOA (e.g., CORBA, J2EE, WebSphere MQ) did not provide strong support for modeling service-level data or for data manipulation (e.g., validation rules and transformation).	XML for service-level data model— XML is richer and more pervasive than earlier approaches to service-level data modeling.

	Inhibitor or Limitation	Enabler or Compensating Feature
SOA		XML is supported by related technologies such as XPath, XSLT, XQuery, and XHTML.
SOA	Earlier technologies used for SOA (e.g., CORBA, J2EE, WebSphere MQ) did not provide support for service composition, service orchestration, and service choreography.	WS-BPEL provides comprehensive, standards-based facilities for service composition, service orchestration, and service choreography. At a technology level, there is a strong and clear alignment between WS-BPEL, WSDL, and SOAP—in the past, the process execution engine could not rely on pervasive standards such as WSDL for defining interfaces to legacy systems and SOAP for providing message-level interoperability.
SOA	Earlier technologies used for defining service contracts (e.g., CORBA IDL) were not extensible to support alternative transports and alternative data encoding systems.	WSDL and SOAP are easily extended to support alternative transports. WS-BPEL extends WSDL and SOAP for process modeling and service composition, service orchestration, and service choreography.
Web services	A strong architectural foundation has not yet been established for Web services.	Users of Web services benefit from the strong architectural focus of SOA.
Web services	Inconsistency across specifications led to interoperability problems.	WS-I continues to profile Web services specifications to improve interoperability and reduce inconsistenciesand ambiguities.
Web services	Core Web services standards (SOAP, WSDL, UDDI) are inadequate for providing a complete Web services platform.	Extended Web services standards provide all the key facilities of a Web services platform.

The convergence of BPM, SOA, Web services, and XML promises to significantly improve corporate agility, reduce time-to-market for new products and services, reduce costs, and improve operational efficiency of IT systems.

Part II

Extended Web Services Specifications

This part of the book discusses the major extended Web services specifications, focusing on those most significant for SOA-enabled applications. The book does not describe every proposed Web services specification. Instead, we have picked the most important specifications for SOA-enabled applications.

What Are Extended Specifications?

An additional level of Web services technology is evolving that includes security, transactions, reliability, orchestration, and metadata management for extended SOA-based applications that involve integration and business process management. As Web services products include more and more of these features, an SOA based on Web services can be used for more and more kinds of applications.

The widespread adoption of extended technologies is a prerequisite for success in large-scale Web services projects, and understanding the extent to which the various specifications are supported is important when using products from multiple vendors. Care should be taken to minimize dependency on vendor-specific features or to isolate them for easy replacement when standards are completed and available.

Extended specifications are proposed primarily in the following areas:

- **Metadata management**—WS-Addressing, WS-MessageDelivery, WS-Policy, Web Services Policy Language, and WS-MetadataExchange for defining ways in which cooperating Web services can discover the features each other supports and interoperate.

- **Security**—WS-Security, XML Signature, XML Encryption, and other specifications for ensuring privacy, message integrity, authentication, and authorized access.

- **Reliability**—WS-Reliability and WS-ReliableMessaging for ensuring that messages are delivered and processed.

- **Notification**—WS-Eventing and WS-Notification for defining additional message exchange patterns such as publish/subscribe.

- **Transactions**—WS-Transactions family and WS-Composite Application Framework for coordinating the work of multiple independent Web services into a larger unit.

- **Orchestration**—WS-BPEL and WS-CDL for combining multiple Web services to perform a larger unit of work.

The degree to which extended functionality is required varies significantly from application to application; care is needed when assessing what's required from each of these areas for any particular project, particularly when more than one is used in combination.

The extended features provided by these specifications are intended to be composable, meaning that it should be possible to combine them as necessary to meet specific requirements. By using a combination of WSDL and policy assertions, it should be possible for a requester to determine which extended features a provider supports and which options within each provider it might require. One of the primary mechanisms for composing these extended features is incrementally adding new headers to existing SOAP messages or inserting them in new SOAP messages. The specifications do not define any order in which these features must be included or processed. We've listed them in the order in which we believe it's important to consider them in a project.

Chapter 7

Metadata Management

Metadata is data about data, or more precisely, data about a software entity associated with it in some way. For example, a file is an entity, and a file record layout is metadata associated with the file that tells you how to interpret the contents of the file. A Web service may have a variety of metadata associated with it, including data types and structures for messages, message exchange patterns for exchanging messages, the network addresses of the endpoints that exchange the messages, and any requirements for extended features such as security, reliability, or transactions.

Web services metadata is an important part of basic and SOA-based Web services solutions. In general, the more complex the application of Web services, the greater the need for metadata and comprehensive metadata management solutions.

Web services metadata and metadata management technologies include the following:

- **UDDI**—A registry and repository for storing and retrieving Web services metadata.

- **XML Schema**—For defining data types and structures.

- **WSDL**—For defining messages, message exchange patterns, interfaces, and endpoints.

- **WS-Policy**—For declaring assertions for various qualities of service requirements, such as reliability, security, and transactions.

- **WS-Addressing**—For defining Web service endpoint references and associated message properties.

- **WS-MetadataExchange**—For dynamically accessing XML, WSDL, and WS-Policy metadata when required.

These different kinds of metadata work together to define the characteristics of any Web service, from simple to complex. The metadata items are contained in XML files of varying definition and are typically stored in a directory, such as UDDI or LDAP, or in plain files for easy retrieval. All of the metadata items benefit from the use of consistent design and naming conventions, especially for enterprise solutions.

Naming Conventions and Easy Retrieval

When thinking about metadata and its management, it's at least as important to develop a consistent means of storing and retrieving the metadata as it is to define it in the first place. One of the reasons UDDI failed to gain broad adoption is that it doesn't provide sufficient methods for effectively categorizing and identifying metadata for easy search and retrieval. It's an old saying in the database world that you have to know how you're going to retrieve something before you figure out how you're going to store it, and this definitely holds true for metadata. How you name your service is important, for example. You don't want to call the "customer lookup" service the "customer lookup service" because that's redundant, but you might want to call it the "customer ID lookup" if it uses the customer ID as the search field. Another service might be the "customer name lookup." Similarly, it's important to use good names for data items so that whoever ends up requesting the service can easily understand the data that the service provides. These conventions are a part of any large project, of

continues

course, but they are especially important for services designed for reuse and interoperability. The consumers of services will find it especially important to clearly understand and recognize such metadata items as the service description name, XML Schema name, service operations names, and security policy name.

To organize Web services metadata, you generally start with the WSDL file and add information to or extend it. The WSDL defines the characteristics of the interaction between the service requester and provider. The description may include only information pertinent to the core Web services specifications or it may also include extended feature requirements. The requirement for extended features is typically defined using policy information referenced as a set of declarations asserting the requirements of the service provider that the requester must match in order to achieve full interoperability. (Some headers may be defined as optional, allowing interoperability to continue without the extended features.)

Before a Web service is invoked, the requester needs access to sufficient metadata to generate a SOAP message, including optional and required headers, to meet the description of the service that the provider publishes. If the provider's service is a basic Web service, sufficient metadata simply includes the message data format, message exchange pattern, and provider's network address. If the provider's service uses extended features, the requester may need to locate and obtain additional metadata, such as policy schemas for security, reliability, or transactions, and endpoint references with their optional associated properties. For example, the requester may need to register with a transaction coordinator and obtain a transaction context before invoking the provider's service if it requires a transaction. In short, a requester may need access to any or all of the various pieces of metadata associated with the provider's service in order to successfully and completely use it.

This information can be made available to the requester in a variety of ways, including a URL for download, UDDI directory reference, or email delivery. The way it typically works today (that is, without a widely adopted registry standard) is that the WSDL is posted at an accessible URL, and the URL is made available to the requester by some out-of-band means, such as a listing on a Web site, an email attachment, or a printed address on paper. The requester might also be given a general address at which multiple WSDL files and associated policy and message schemas are stored. In this case, the protocol described in WS-MetadataExchange can be used to query the node for available information, such as the WSDL and policy information. Action URIs can also be used to help obtain metadata if the requester has the WS-Addressing information for the location of the WSDL and policy schema information.

Often, the relationship of metadata that is available for a service depends on the definition of a specific Web service. In practice, many of the significant Web service providers on the Web with publicly available services such as Amazon.com, Google.com, and others provide both a SOAP/WSDL implementation and a "plain" HTTP-based implementation. In other words, some Web services metadata includes the definition of how to exchange the XML data either way, using SOAP messages or plain HTTP GETs and POSTs.

The Simple Approach to Metadata Management

The fundamental metadata required to execute a Web service typically includes the WSDL file and the endpoint address at which the SOAP listener is available to receive (and optionally return) messages. The question typically arises as to how this information is discovered and managed.

The basic requirement is to publish the metadata for a Web service so that the service requester can find and use it. Initially, UDDI was proposed to meet this requirement, but as we have mentioned, UDDI did not succeed in realizing its original vision. UDDI was designed to support dynamic discovery, in which the lookup of Web services metadata was a seamless part of a Web service execution. The original vision of UDDI was that a Web service requester could supply some general information, such as a business name, business classification, or business location, and receive a valid Web service description with which to execute the request.

However, for various reasons including the difficulty of creating meaningful categorization information for the Web, UDDI did not achieve its goal of becoming the registry for all Web services metadata and did not become useful in a majority of Web services interactions over the Web.

Many other proposals were presented for Web services metadata management, including DISCO, Microsoft's original discovery specification, and WS-Inspection, a later effort by IBM. More recently, Microsoft and IBM have published WS-MetadataExchange as an alternative mechanism for Web services metadata discovery.

Even though UDDI did not manage to establish itself as the central registry for Web services metadata, it did manage to establish itself at the center of the debate over the ultimate solution—if it's not UDDI, then what is it? In general, it seems that some companies are using UDDI, but others are extending registry solutions already in place such as LDAP, Java Naming and Directory Interface (JNDI), relational databases, or the CORBA Trader. Still another alternative in some limited use is the ebXML Registry.

Any registry used for Web services metadata needs to support the general feature list of UDDI—that is, storage and retrieval of descriptions (or pointers to them) and associated metadata such as policies. UDDI is also encumbered by the failure of its original vision because upward compatibility has to be preserved (a questionable assumption, however, given UDDI's disappointing adoption rates).

Although the idea of dynamic discovery using UDDI did not really work out, most Web services toolkits (and there were 82 registered on Xmethods.net at the time of writing) can accept a WSDL file imported from a location on the Internet and generate a compatible SOAP message from it to successfully interact with the published service. There are some restrictions and incompatibilities across Web service implementations, which SOAPBuilders and WS-I have attempted to address. The compatibility of metadata and the interpretation of the various specifications determine the extent of possible interoperability. In general, compatibility of metadata tends to be higher for simpler services. For example, widespread interoperability and the ability to automatically generate a SOAP message and access a service tends to be higher when the service and its data types and structures are simple. In general, simple types are widely inter-operable, whereas complex types such as arrays and structures are not as widely interoperable.

Using Plain SOAP and WSDL

The original specifications—SOAP and WSDL—support a very simple metadata management system for basic operations. The endpoint at which a Web service listener is positioned is also typically the endpoint at which the metadata is published. A Web services toolkit can perform an HTTP GET to download the WSDL file and issue an HTTP POST to execute the service.

Many Web sites are dedicated to providing a list of available Web services, including:

- **Xmethods.net**—A sponsored site on which anyone can publish his or her Web service, including a "try it" service and a link to Mindreef's SOAP Scope for analyzing messages and WSDL files.

- **Bindingpoint.com**—A Web site operated by Acclaim IT in the UK, listing basic Web services that presumably can be aggregated into solutions with the help of Acclaim's integration services.

- **GrandCentral.com**—A Web site with a combination of hosted and sponsored Web services supporting synchronous and asynchronous invocation patterns for the same services.

- **Strikeiron.com**—A Web site featuring a collection of Web services for rent and other services associated with developing, deploying, and hosting services.

- **Remotemethods.com**—Another sponsored site listing many of the same Web services that you can find from the other sites.

Most of the Web services on these various Web site directories are simple Web services for calculating interest rates, foreign currency conversion, weather reports, stock quotes, sending SMS messages to phones, validation of bank information, TV station listings, and so on. But a growing number of the services are commercial in nature—that is, the sites offering them require a fee for their use. For example:

- An EDI conversion service to transform Electronic Data Interchange (EDI) files into flat files, for $70 month from Free EDI Online.

- XwebServices.com—a variety of Web services for use in Web site hosting, including shopping cart services for $20 a month for up to ten thousand hits per month and $.025 per hit thereafter.

- Credit-card processing services from Payment Resources International, Infodial, and others that require an account with the processing firm and a per-transaction fee.

Other Web services programs are sponsored by well-known Web sites, including:

- **Amazon.com**—The kit is freely downloadable, although a fee is required to use it for purchases. More than 50,000 users had registered and paid the fee at the time of writing, creating hundreds of virtual storefronts for Amazon.com and other merchandise.

- **Google.com**—The kit is also freely downloadable and free for certain services, in beta at the time of writing.

- **eBay.com**—A program fee is required to obtain and use the kit, and a per-transaction fee is required to use it. At the time of writing, eBay claimed that their top 50 affiliates (that is, users of the Web services APIs) were earning $1 million a year in commissions.

Most of these programs support both Java and .NET programming environments for access to the APIs, and Amazon.com makes a point of providing what they call "REST"-oriented Web services (that is, plain HTTP and XML without the SOAP and WSDL formatting). Amazon.com says that the HTTP/XML flavor of their Web services is popular among Web site designers and developers familiar with markup languages displayed in browsers. The SOAP/WSDL versions of the services are popular among more traditional enterprise users such as Java and

Visual Basic developers, who like the structure and appreciate the processing hints provided in SOAP and WSDL that can make it easier to map the XML messages into and out of the programs they write.

For these types of Web services, the simplest metadata is sufficient: a Uniform Resource Locator (URL). For example:

```
http://webservices.primerchants.com/creditcard.asmx
```

This is the URL for the credit-card processing service provided by Payment Resources International. It is free for trial, and two of its operations are available for testing purposes. If you really want to use the service, however, you have to open an account with Payment Resources, which results in a per-transaction fee for every credit card purchase they process.

By convention, the WSDL file is available at the same location using a ?WSDL parameter at the end of the URL. For example:

```
http://webservices.primerchants.com/creditcard.asmx?WSDL
```

Dereferencing (that is, clicking on) the URL results in downloading the WSDL file for the service. One of the great things about Web services in general is that the WSDL is readable in a browser, and you can easily download and check out the WSDL files for Web services published on the Web before you use them.

Like Amazon.com, Payment Resources provides basic HTTP support in addition to the SOAP/WSDL option.

In summary, the most popular options for metadata management and discovery are Web page directories with various listings. It is also very common for two enterprises to privately exchange metadata when making a Web service available for business-to-business communication, the way you might directly give your fax number to a business partner.

This level of metadata management is sufficient for the basic Web services operations that can be supported by a single endpoint, including one-way and request/response messages formatted either according to RPC conventions (that is, procedure/argument notation) or as complete XML documents (typically with associated DTD or schema for validation and parsing).

However, there are some built-in restrictions and limitations to what can be accomplished using the basic SOAP and WSDL (and even plain HTTP) specifications. For example, here is the port element portion of the Payment International credit card service:

```
<port name="CreditCardSoap" binding="s0:CreditCardSoap">
  <soap:address location="http://webservices.primerchants.
  ➥com/creditcard.asmx" />
</port>
<port name="CreditCardHttpGet" binding="s0:
➥CreditCardHttpGet">
  <http:address location="http://webservices.primerchants.
  ➥com/creditcard.asmx" />
</port>
<port name="CreditCardHttpPost" binding="s0:
➥CreditCardHttpPost">
  <http:address location="http://webservices.primerchants.
  ➥com/creditcard.asmx" />
</port>
```

As you can see, all of the services in this example are provided at the same location:

```
http://webservices.primerchants.com/creditcard.asmx
```

The .asmx indicates this is a .NET implementation, which requires the services to be dispatched through IIS in order to find them.

Figure 7-1 illustrates the basic metadata management mechanism for Web services. The provider shares the description file with the requester so that the requester can generate the SOAP message or messages that the provider expects to receive. The requester also has to be ready to receive any messages that might be returned from the provider, depending on the specified message exchange pattern(s).

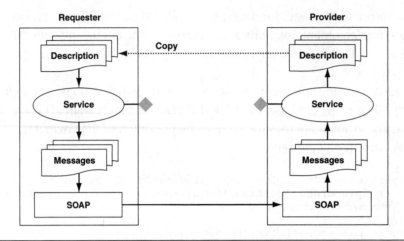

Figure 7-1   Web service description files are copied from provider to requester.

Simple MEPs such as one-way and request/response can easily be accomplished using the same URI. For example, once the requester receives a URI for
the provider's service, it can obtain a copy of the WSDL file by issuing an HTTP
GET, and when the WSDL file is downloaded, the requester can send the SOAP
message to the provider using an HTTP POST and receive any reply message on
the HTTP response.

However, the creators of the Web services specifications envisage additional,
more complex usage patterns for Web services, including message exchange
patterns such as publish/subscribe and broadcast, using multiple endpoints
within a composite application to handle complex interactions and flows, and
more easily mapping services to multiple transports, and thus need additional
metadata management solutions.

Metadata Specifications

This section describes the various metadata and metadata management technologies and how they fit together to describe a Web service.

XML

The main use of XML in Web services metadata is for defining data types and structures for SOAP messages (although of course, all Web services specifications also have associated XML Schemas to validate them).

For example:

```
<xs:schema targetNamespace="http://www.mybank.com/2005/05/schemas/
➥AccountService.xsd"
xmlns:xs=http://www.w3.org/2001/XMLSchema


<xs:element name="CustomerInfo" type="tCustomerInfo"/>
    <xs:complexType name="tCustomerInfo">
        <xs:sequence>
            <xs:element   name="AccountNumber" type="xs:double"/>
            <xs:element   name="CustomerName" type="xs:string"/>
            <xs:element   name="CustomerAddress" type=
            ➥"xs:string"/>
            <xs:element   name="CustomerType" type="xs:string"/>
        </xs:sequence>
    </xs:complexType>

<xs:element name="ConfirmationInfo" type="tConfirmationInfo"/>
    <xs:complexType name="tConfirmationInfo">
        <xs:sequence>
            <xs:element   name="AccountNumber" type="xs:double"/>
            <xs:element   name="ConfirmationCode" type=
            ➥"xs:string"/>
            <xs:element   name="ConfirmationType" type=
            ➥"xs:string"/>
        </xs:sequence>
    </xs:complexType>

<xs:element name="DataError" type="tDataError"/>
    <xs:complexType name="tDataError">
        <xs:sequence>
            <xs:element   name="Field" type="xs:string"/>
            <xs:element   name="ErrorDescription" type=
            ➥"xs:string"/>
        </xs:sequence>
    </xs:complexType>
```

This example illustrates data types and structures for a customer information message, a confirmation message, and an error message that can be used in conjunction with a composite Web service application to open a bank account.

The first message captures the customer information to be validated. The second message represents a response indicating succesful validation, and the third message represents a response indicating an error in the customer data. These basic types of information can be included in WSDL in various ways:

- In WSDL 1.1, the information can be added directly into the file or imported (although the import mechanism is not well-defined and docs not appear to be used very often).

- In WSDL 2.0, the information can be added directly in the file or by a well-specified import mechanism.

The basic building blocks of a Web service interaction are the XML messages exchanged between services in a pattern or sequence (with branches, exceptions, and fault processing).

WSDL 2.0

The Web Services Description Language (WSDL) was originally published in March 2001 and submitted to the W3C, where the WSDL working group developed WSDL V2.[1]

This section focuses on the changes in WSDL 2.0 because WSDL 1.1 is well documented.

For example, WSDL 2.0 supports Document Type Definitions and RelaxNG schemas in addition to XML Schema for defining data types and messages.

In WSDL 2.0, there's a better way to handle importing and including schema information, and some of the terms have changed:

- Interfaces replace portTypes.

- Endpoints replace ports.

---

[1] WSDL 2.0 is scheduled to become a W3C recommendation in late 2004.

A features and properties section has been added to most syntax structures for the declaration of policy information, such as security and transactional requirements, essentially creating attributes for messages, operations, interfaces, and endpoints. They've also defined some MEPs formally for combining in and out messages into patterns. In addition, faults were added in case messages can't be returned.

The major WSDL 2.0 syntax elements are as follows:

```
<types>
    (include schemas)
<interfaces>
   <operations>
        input=
        output=
<binding>
<service>
   <endpoint name
```

Features and properties can be added into any of the major syntax elements. WSDL files can be created by combining files containing any of the major elements for reusability of the definitions.

WSDL 2.0 includes the following message exchange patterns:

- **In-only**—Exactly one message received and no faults out.

- **Robust in-only**—Exactly one message received and a fault if not.

- **In-out**—Exactly two messages: a message received and a response sent.

- **In-optional-out**—One or possibly two messages, depending on whether or not a response is generated.

- **Out-only**—Exactly one message sent, no fault.

- **Robust-out-only**—Exactly one message sent, and a fault if not.

- **Out-in**—Exactly two messages: a message sent and a response received.

- **Out-optional-in**—One or two messages, depending on whether a response is generated.

The MEPs are essentially two sets of four patterns depending on whether the intial message direction is inbound (i.e., the service receives the initial message) or outbound (i.e., the service sends the initial message). In today's world, the outbound message pattern would be very hard to achieve because there is no good way for the provider to obtain the requester's address. However, WS-Addressing provides the ability to define additional endpoint information that can be passed or discovered by the provider to accomplish the pattern.

After the schemas are defined, the type definitions are available for use in WSDL 2.0 messages as a direct child of `definitions`—that is, using the `types` element to enclose message definitions. There are two ways to enclose mes-sages defintions within `types`—use the `xs:import` mechanism provided by XML Schema, or embed the schemas within `xs:schema` elements. Both can be combined in the same WSDL file.

Faults can now be defined for interfaces:

```
< interface   name = "reservation" >
    <fault name = "inValidCreditCardFault"
            element = "ghns:invalidCreditCardError">
        <documentation>
            fault declaration for invalid credit card
            ➡information.
        </documentation>
    </fault>
    <fault name = "inValidDataFault"
            element = "ghns:invalidDataError">
        <documentation>
            fault declaration for invalid data.
        </documentation>
    </fault>
  </interface>
```

Faults are new in WSDL 2.0. A good question is how you know whether to use SOAP faults of WSDL faults or another fault mechanism altogether, but at least several options are supported.

UDDI

Universal Description, Discovery, and Integration (UDDI) was ratified as an OASIS standard in May of 2003. The UDDI program at OASIS is standardizing

V3. This section focuses on the differences in V3 compared to V2 since V2 is well documented.

As illustrated in Figure 7-2, a registry can be used as an intermediate storage mechanism between the requester and the provider. The provider can publish the description (and associated policy and data schemas) to the registry, and the requester can search the registry for the metadata it requires. Web services specifications support both a registry model (based on UDDI) and an ad-hoc model (based on out-of-band exchange of URLs and the use of WS-MetadataExchange to query Web based addresses and retrieve their metadata).

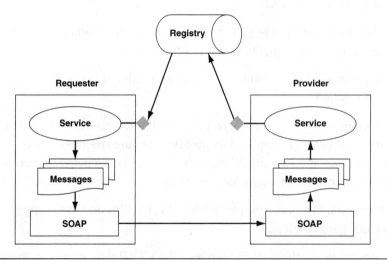

Figure 7-2   Registries are used for storing and retrieving service metadata.

Many other registries are used for storing and retrieving Web service metadata, including LDAP directory services, the CORBA naming service, and other homegrown repositories for Web services metadata. This is a classic piece of distributed computing architecture, and Web services provide several alternatives, including UDDI V3.

Implementations of UDDI have tended to settle on UDDI V2, which is referenced by the WS-I basic profile. However, implementations of V3 are starting to appear on the market.

Compared to V2, UDDI V3 adds significant features, including:

- The ability to support registry federation and transfer of entries from one registry to another—Includes the ability to generate IDs and allow them to be shared across registry implementations, and to move registry entries from one host system to another.

- New IDs based on URIs—Instead of relying solely on generated UUIDs, UDDI V3 allows the use of URIs similarly to the way XML namespaces use them, as unique prefixes to registry keys. Using those keys in the public UDDI requires a registration and approval process so that the URIs are not spoofed.

- Digital signatures to ensure the authenticity and validity of entries and to help improve the quality of data in the registry.

- Better support for combining private and public UDDIs in a comprehensive solution.

- Definition of policy for asserting the conformance of a particular UDDI implementation to some of the optional features defined in the V3 specification, such as a publish/subscribe feature for notifying related registries of the impact of changes for a given entry.

- Additional categorization for finding WSDL files and for locating businesses geographically.

- Constraints on the XML Schemas in the UDDI data model so that it is easier to compare one to another.

Private implementations of UDDI are more widely used than public implementations. UDDI V3 is an effort to address some of the issues preventing adoption of the public version and also to provide better support for private implementations.

The public UDDI registry continues to be operated by Microsoft, IBM, and SAP. Bindingpoint.com still uses it, for example, whereas Xmethods.net uses its own private implementation of UDDI V2 adapted from WebMethods' implementation.

The subscription feature is designed to support a multi-registry configuration (that is, a system of federated registries) in which the same entry might be present in more than one physical registry. When an entry is changed in one registry, the subscription feature allows an event to be published to the other registry. Notifications can be sent via email or SOAP. When SOAP is used, the endpoint has to be able to understand the UDDI format of the subscription message.

The security implementation requires the ability to support canonicalization and normalization. In addition, enhancements to the inquiry APIs allow better searching and provide the ability to return large record sets.

UDDI May Overlap Other Specifications

UDDI V3's new subscription mechanism seems to overlap WS-Notification and WS-Eventing and perhaps an update to the UDDI standard will be necessary when one of these specifications (or both) is widely adopted. UDDI V3 also includes an <accessPoint> definition mechanism in the subscription feature that seems to overlap with WS-Addressing. These overlaps between specifications highlight yet another reason Web services standardization needs leadership and architecture.

Addressing

Two specifications define additional information for Web services references: WS-Addressing and WS-MessageDelivery.

As shown in Figure 7-3, when a Web service interaction spans more than a single requester and provider (i.e., involving multiple providers), an addressing mechanism is required so that the initial provider can forward the request to the next provider, and so on. When the final provider (sometimes called the ultimate receiver) is reached, addressing information in the SOAP headers is used to return the reply to the initial requester.

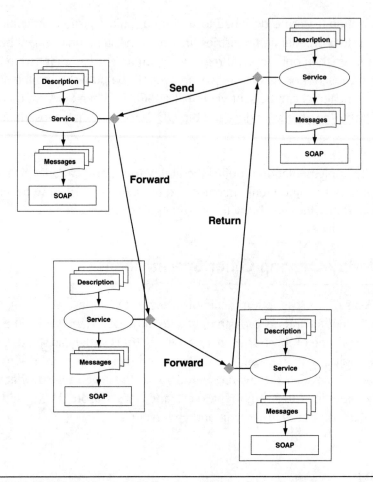

Figure 7-3   Addressing information allows complex exchange patterns.

A formal address also helps a message get back to the requester if there's a network failure and the response is lost. Addressing is also a requirement for many other specifications, including WS-BPEL, WS-AtomicTransactions, WS-Notification, WS-Eventing, WS-CAF, and WS-MetadataExchange.

This model works for intermediary processing as well, although intermediary processing is defined as transparent to the message content and is allowed to operate on the content of SOAP headers only.

WS-Addressing

WS-Addressing defines two mechanisms for SOAP headers that are typically provided by transport protocols and messaging systems:

- **Endpoint references**—Where to find a service on the network and any associated properties that may be necessary to interact successfully with that endpoint.

- **Message information headers**—Identifies the sender and optional reply address (when different).

Defining these mechanisms at the SOAP header level provides a better abstraction of the SOAP message from the underlying transport and makes multi-transport implementations of Web services easier. For example:

```
<wsa:ReplyTo>
  <wsa:Address>
   http://www.iona.com/Artix/BankExample
  </wsa:Address>
</wsa:ReplyTo>
  <wsa:To>
    http://www.iona.com/Artix/TransferFunds
  </wsa:To>
<wsa:Action>
  http://www.iona.com/Artix/Samples/Transfer
</wsa:Action>
```

This example illustrates the WS-Addressing namespace `wsa` and shows the address from which the message is being sent (`http://www.iona.com/Artix/BankExample`), along with the address to which the reply is to be sent (`http://www.iona.com/Artix/TransferFunds`) and the action to be taken (`Transfer`). The body of the message would include the amount to transfer. Additional addresses could be included to route the message reply anywhere on the network.

WS-Addressing headers define an address for a Web service endpoint and also for an individual message destination. The message information headers carry information about where the message is from, where it's going, and where the reply (if any) should be sent.

For example:

```
<Header>

  <wsa:ReplyTo>
     <wsa:Address>
         http://www.iona.com/artix/examples/BankTransfer
     </wsa:Address>
  </wsa:ReplyTo>

  <wsa:To>
       http://www.NattyBank.com/accounts/Inbound
  </wsa:To>

  <wsa:Action>
        http://www.iona.com/newcomer/transferMillions
  </wsa:Action>

</Header>
```

This example illustrates a message sent from www.iona.com's bank transfer application to the Natty Bank's accounts department. The requested action is to transfer millions of dollars into Newcomer's bank account. The Action URI provides a way to express a semantic operation to be performed upon the message. This is optional, but many extended specifications are starting to use it as a way to send a message to a generic service and supply an option for how to use the generic service for one of the specific operations it supports, such as retrieving policy information.

The WS-Addressing action feature is important as Web services progress because the HTTP binding SOAP action is removed as of SOAP 1.2 and deprecated in the WS-I basic profile. The SOAP action had been used to carry the operation or queue name associated with the target service. Similarly, reference properties can be used to carry additional information about a queue, such as priority, ordering, or error queue name.

If SOAP is to be truly transport-independent, it needs a transport-independent way of defining the exact address of the executable entity to which a message is being sent and to which a message is returned. It's also important to define a mechanism to support advanced message exchange patterns, which are becoming important for the new class of applications growing up around the concepts of SOA and BPM.

Addressing metadata is used to identify the target of a SOAP message, in particular, the:

- TCP address of the computer hosting the service (derived from the domain portion of the URL, which is what the domain part of iona.com or other Internet address translates to).[2]

- Location on the computer of the service to be executed (often found by registering a Web service with a Web server, for example).

- Specific operation within the service to handle the message—receiving the message, processing the input data—and optionally returning a reply.

The addressing information ensures that a SOAP message is routed to the right program, object, or queue. The more information available in the address, the better control a requester has over specifying the exact location of the service provider, and the better an SOA or BPM solution can support complex interactions.

In addition, several other extended specifications rely upon a granularity of addressing typically available only within the transport layer. If Web services are to be truly transport-independent, addressing information needs to be included within the messages themselves. Earlier attempts at providing this information include WS-Referral and WS-Routing, which focused more on point-to-point interactions than on categorizing addressing information according to its purpose.

For the newer versions of Web services specifications, it's necessary to replace the SOAP action header with addressing information in the header of the SOAP message. Instead of relying on transport level information such as this to obtain the information necessary to dispatch the message to the right service, addressing information is used to include the dispatching information in the message header.

---

[2] See www.DNSstuff.com for translating domain names to IP addresses and vice versa.

Examine the Message to Route It?

A big question in messaging is whether or not you have to examine the message in order to find out where to route it. Either the addressing information has to be included within the message (as it is in the SOAP headers with WS-Addressing), or it has to be contained within some information associated with the message. Addressing information can also be provided as a configuration or management property associated with a message. A configuration or management property associated with the message typically results in some transport-specific information being passed along with the message, such as the SOAP action field in HTTP. If the information is contained in the transport, the message could be passed transparently, and the SOAP envelope would not have to be opened until it reached its destination. Of course, SOAP 1.2 headers can also instruct intermediaries to open the message to inspect, act upon, and/or replace headers. This is an age-old dilemma in messaging systems: whether to associate the metadata with the message somewhere outside the message (such as in a transport-specific mechanism) or to open the message to perform security checks, routing, load balancing, and other operations not directly related to processing the payload. Like many of these classic trade-offs, there's no single correct answer. Of course, all this would be moot if everyone would just use HTTP for everything—and though it sounds unlikely, it could happen one day.

One way to implement message dispatching to the correct execution environment is to inspect the SOAP message headers containing addressing information and use the addressing information to route the message internally to the correct program or queue. This allows the development of transport-independent dispatch mechanisms, or multi-transport mechanisms.

Multi-Transport Addressing

Although WS-Addressing and WS-MessageDelivery are supposed to contain sufficient information for multi-transport operation, in practice, you often

continues

need to use the extensibility points within the mechanisms in order to really include all the information necessary to use a specific transport. For example, WebSphere MQ uses many properties and configuration settings associated with its queues to enable them to perform operations such as priority checking and transaction control. In message queuing systems, the queue is the destination of the message, and you may need to place some of these properties and configuration settings in the extensibility areas of WS Addressing and WS-MessageDelivery in order to propagate them correctly. It's just not possible for a simple addressing reference to contain all the features of all the possible transports that someone might want to use for Web services.

WS-MessageDelivery

WS-MessageDelivery defines delivery properties, message identification, and message referencing for Web services message exchange patterns such as callback and broadcast. The message delivery properties are designed to work with WSDL-defined and other message exchange patterns. The WS-MessageDelivery specification defines a Web service reference, abstract message delivery properties, a SOAP binding, and its relationship to WSDL.

For example:

```
<wsmd:MessageOriginator>
    <wsmd:uri>http://www.iona.com/Artix/BankExample </wsmd:uri>
</wsmd:MessageOriginator>

<wsmd:MessageDestination
    wsmd:wsdlLocation="http://www.NattyBank.com/wsdl

    <wsdl11:service name="myservice" wsmd:portType=
➥"myns:myPortType">
        <wsdl11:port name="myport" binding="myns:myBinding">
            <soapbind:address location="http://example.com/wsdl/
            ➥impl"/>
        </wsdl11:port>
    </wsdl11:service>

</wsmd:MessageDestination>

<wsmd:ReplyDestination>
```

```
    <wsmd:uri>http://www.iona.com/Artix/BankExample/reply
    ➡</wsmd:uri>
</wsmd:ReplyDestination>

<wsmd:FaultDestination>
    <wsmd:uri>http://www.iona.com/Artix/BankExample/fault
    ➡</wsmd:uri>
</wsmd:FaultDestination>

<wsmd:MessageID>
    uuid:58f202ac-22cf-11d1-b12d-002035b29092
</wsmd:MessageID>

<wsmd:OperationName>TransferMillions</wsmd:OperationName>
```

This example illustrates the major parts of WS-MessageDelivery—the message originator and destination, the reply destination, a fault destination, and an operation name. These are all comparable to the major parts of WS-Addressing. However, WS-MessageDelivery adds a message ID in the form of a UUID.

How Do MEPs Get Defined?

Message exchange patterns are a core feature of Web services, yet it isn't at all clear how and where they get defined. The original SOAP and WSDL specifications defined only two MEPs—one-way and request/response—but they contained placeholders for additional, more complex MEPs such as publish/subscribe and broadcast. The SOAP 1.2 and WSDL 2.0 specifications define eight MEPs, but they are all variations of one-way and request/response. Some of the more complex MEPs are defined in WS-Eventing and WS-Notification and these specifications illustrate how to use WS-Addressing features for those MEPs. WS-MessageDelivery defines a callback MEP, and other specifications such as WS-CAF and WS-C use callbacks. Whether such an MEP has to be formally defined or can be left up to the imagination of the user remains an open question. Certainly with WS-Addressing extensibility, it's possible to create any MEP that you want to. At least in the case where another specification defines its own MEP using the addressing specification, interoperability will be ensured.

As Web services are increasingly used for composite applications, SOA implementations, and BPM flows, they also increase their requirement for the ability to deliver a message to an address participating in one or more of the various MEPs. These requirements include asynchronous responses and message correlations to validate MEPs, guarantee their execution when specified, and span transport protocols in a multi-transport environment. Different messages in an MEP may be sent over different transports, and therefore, a common referencing mechanism is required. In addition, communication with mobile devices may involve specific addressing requirements when a complete transport stack is unavailable. It's also possible to imagine applications built using composite MEPs that need addressing and referencing support.

Policy

A policy is an assertion about a service that describes one or more characteristics that a provider instructs a requester to follow. Policies can be expressed in a variety of ways, from simple statements of fact such as "strong authentication is required using Kerberos" to a set of rules evaluated in priority order that determine whether or not a requester can interact with a provider.

Metadata about services is also often called properties—for example, in the .NET Framework or J2EE, a transactional property can be set that defines whether or not a transaction is required in order to invoke an object successfully. Objects might also have properties that require some kind of security information, such as an authentication token, to be checked for authorization to access the object. Policies are the way in which Web services accomplish similar functionality.

Policies are also intended as a vehicle to express service level agreements (SLAs), which are important in an SOA because they describe requirements for load balancing, availability, service delivery guarantees, and response time.

Policy Technology Is Immature

One of the most important aspects of SOA involves the metadata available for a service so that a variety of clients can interact with it. In object technology, it was easier to resolve the problem because the same object model was used for both the provider and requester. It's important in a reusable world that any given service supports the highest possible levels of reuse to the widest possible variety of other services, without compromising the integrity of the service. Policy expressions are considered the way to accomplish this, but the initial specifications are very rough, and at least three distinct approaches have emerged. The W3C has initiated a program to resolve the differences in approach to policy and to produce a standard that can be widely adopted and used. One big question is whether policies belong in WSDL or not (likely not because it seems like an advantage to be able to change them independently of the service description and potentially associate multiple different policies with the same service depending on when and where it's deployed). Another big question is whether policies are expressed in the form of rules that a requester has to evaluate before sending a message to a provider, or whether the policies are expressed in the form of checklist items to be matched up between requester and provider. WSPL takes the former approach, while WS-Policy takes the latter. One thing is clear as of this writing—a lot of work remains before the goal can be realized of configuring and accessing services using metadata associated with them rather than proprietary tools and products.

Policy assertions inform the requester about any additional information beyond "plain" WSDL (such as requirements for extended features) that may be needed to successfully invoke the provider's service. Additional information can include alternate transports, security requirements, whether or not a transaction is needed or accepted, and whether reliable messaging is required. The provider's service must publish the policy assertion information so that the requester can access it. A policy assertion provides the metadata in a way the service requester can understand and consume, similarly to the way in which the requester understands and consumes a provider's WSDL. A policy assertion groups policies in a recognizable XML grammar and qualifies policies using priorities and equation tests.

When a requester obtains the set of policy assertions from the provider (or from a policy repository), the effective policy (i.e., the one the requester will actually use) is calculated using the assertion information and a set of rules defining how the assertions are to be evaluated. Some policies might have higher priority than others, some are in effect only when others are in effect, and some might not be necessary at all under certain conditions.

In a policy-enabled world, the first message to a provider may request a copy of the provider's policy information so that the request to actually execute the service can be formatted correctly. Of course, if the requester cannot understand the policy information it retrieves, then it probably will not be able to successfully invoke the service. WS-MetadataExchange provides a protocol for inquiring about a service's policy information.

Three mechanisms for expressing policy exist in various Web services specifications:

- **WS-Policy Framework**—Developed by BEA, IBM, Microsoft, and SAP.

- **Web Services Policy Language**—Created as a subgroup within the XACML Technical Committee at OASIS.

- **WSDL 2.0 features and properties**—Created by the WSDL Working Group at W3C.

These specifications are described in the following subsections.

WS-Policy

WS-Policy refers to a set of three specifications:

- **WS-PolicyFramework** (often called WS-Policy for short because it's the "enclosing" specification for the other two)—Defines the overall model and syntax that can be extended by other specifications (such as WS-SecurityPolicy).

- **WS-PolicyAssertions**—Defines a basic set of assertions for policies, including whether an assertion is required or not.

- **WS-PolicyAttachment**—Defines how to attach policy assertions to WSDL files.

WS-PolicyFramework

The WS-PolicyFramework specification defines a policy expression as an XML serialization consisting of three components:

- A top-level container element.

- Policy operators that group assertions.

- Attributes that determine policy usage.

The top-level container element is:

```
<wsp:Policy xmlns:wsp="..." xmlns:wsse="...">
 . . .
</wsp:Policy>
```

The top-level element encloses the policy assertions and identifies the namespaces being used. In this example, there are two namespaces: one for WS-Policy and the other for WS-Security.

The following is an example of policy operators:

```
  <wsp:ExactlyOne>

    <wsp:All wsp:Preference="100">
    . . .
    </wsp:All>

    <wsp:All wsp:Preference="1">
    . . .
    </wsp:All>

  </wsp:ExactlyOne>
```

Policy operators enclose assertions, defining priority using the preference attribute and how many assertions from the list are to be enforced. Options include exactly one, all, or one or more.

Determining Effective Policy

The combination of a preference number and the option for how many assertions to choose are supposed to allow the requester to figure out which policies the provider really requires, which are optional, and which are just recommended. The looseness of the definitions may make it very difficult for a given requester to arrive at a precise definition of what the provider expects to receive. The world of distributed computing is full of these kinds of ambivalences, such as the "transaction maybe" property on EJBs and .NET objects. In other words, if you are calling me in a transaction, I'll join in, but if not, then that's OK, too. The flexibility is intended to allow the broadest range of requesters to invoke a provider's service, ruling requesters in rather than out. A policy that's too restrictive is obviously not helpful to the principles of broad reusability and multi-channel access considerations. On the other hand, a service may have a definite requirement for security or reliability that needs to be expressed in a way that's meaningful to a requester. It's finding the middle ground between the advanced features that are really required by a provider and the ones that are just "nice-to-have" that causes the difficulty. Behind all of the ambivalence is the fact that policy is a way to describe rules and requirements for the usage of advanced features, and it's being defined (as it must be to complete the metadata picture) before the advanced features are widely adopted and used. After the advanced features shake out a bit, the policy picture will become a whole lot clearer. Which security format will everyone really adopt? Which transaction model will really turn out to be the most useful for service orientation? These fundamental questions of adoption, which are only settled by real world usage, are crucial to settling the policy discussion.

The following is an example of attributes that determine policy usage for WS-Security:

```
<wsse:SecurityToken>
  <wsse:TokenType>wsse:Kerberosv5TGT</wsse:TokenType>
</wsse:SecurityToken>
<wsse:Integrity>
  <wsse:Algorithm Type="wsse:AlgSignature"
```

```
        URI=http://www.w3.org/2000/09/xmlenc#aes />
</wsse:Integrity>

<wsse:SecurityToken>
  <wsse:TokenType>wsse:x509v3</wsse:TokenType>
</wsse:SecurityToken>
<wsse:Integrity>
  <wsse:Algorithm Type="wsse:AlgEncryption"
        URI="http://www.w3.org/2001/04/xmlenc#3des-cbc" />
</wsse:Integrity>
```

By enclosing these assertions within the ExactlyOne operator (as previously illustrated), the requester knows to pick one of these encryption algorithms for ensuring message integrity because by defining these assertions, the provider is saying that it can accept encrypted messages in either the AES or 3DES format. The preferences of "100" and "1," respectively, indicate the provider's preference, with "100" indicating a higher preference for AES-based encryption.

An assumption of the policy model is that every Web service can (and probably should) have an associated policy, consisting of one or more assertions. In that case, policies can be compared across services to determine compatible subsets. In other words, a policy comparison can determine whether or not two services can interoperate.

Simple assertions are comparisons of the same type in which it can be determined if the two (or more) assertions have equal values. For example, two integrity assertions can be compared to see whether or not they specify the same encryption algorithm. When policy assertion types aren't as easily matched, complex comparisons may be possible. Policies can be shared using the PolicyReference element.

WS-PolicyAssertions
To really make a system of policy assertions and comparisons work, a standard set of assertions is needed. The WS-PolicyAssertion specification defines an initial set of assertions for simple policies, including the following:

- TextEncoding—Defines supported character set encodings such as ASCII or UTF-8.

- **Language**—Defines the supported and preferred natural languages for internationalization (may be dependent upon or related to supported character sets).

- **SpecVersion**—Defines the supported specifications and their versions.

- **MessagePredicate**—Defines a predicate expression that must evaluate to true as a way to flag acceptable messages.

These assertions can be used to identify the character sets, languages, and specification versions (that is, SOAP 1.1 or SOAP 1.2) that the service supports. The `MessagePredicate` is intended (but not required) to identify an XPath expression requiring certain specified message parts to be present in order to have the service accept and process the message.

WS-PolicyAttachment
The purpose of the WS-PolicyAttachment specification is to define how a policy is associated with an endpoint reference, Web service description, or UDDI entry.

WS-Addressing can be used to specify an endpoint reference with which to associate a policy assertion. WSDL extensibility points are used to associate WS-Policy assertions with a WSDL file.

WS-PolicyAttachment defines a generic mechanism for associating policy assertions with XML elements, but it also specifically defines the association with WSDL 1.1 using extensibility points on the following syntax items:

- The five elements that are used to define a `portType`:

    - `portType`.

    - `portType/wsdl:operation`.

    - `portType/wsdl:operation/wsdl:input`.

    - `portType/wsdl:operation/wsdl:output`.

    - `portType/wsdl:operation/wsdl:fault`.

- ■ The five elements that are used to define a `binding`:

  - ■ `binding`.

  - ■ `binding/wsdl:operation`.

  - ■ `binding/wsdl:operation/wsdl:input`.

  - ■ `binding/wsdl:operation/wsdl:output`.

  - ■ `binding/wsdl:operation/wsdl:fault`.

These options are presented in order of granularity, as association with an enclosing element such as `portType` is inherited by the enclosed elements.

The WS-Policy specifications include a general recommendation that any policies be signed to prevent tampering and that they include a security token to allow an authorization check.

Figure 7-4 illustrates the association of policy information with the WSDL file. The shaded area represents the policy information. The policy information has to be available to the requester, just like the basic information about the Web service. The WS-PolicyAttachments specification defines how the assertions are associated with the WSDL file, and the WS-MetadataExchange can be used for discovering such referred policy schemas for a given WSDL file.

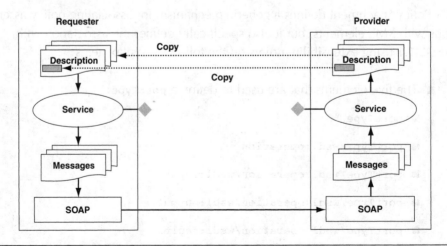

Figure 7-4   Policy information associated with WSDL is copied.

Because Web services include the ability to generate a conformant message when given a description, the policy information is made available in a compatible XML format. The requester can use WS-MetadataExchange or possibly UDDI to discover what additional policy metadata might be associated with the provider's service, or the provider can find a way to inform the requester using an out-of-band technology such as email or fax.

Do Properties Belong in WSDL?

Given the mechanism in WS-PolicyAttachments for extending WSDL syntax elements with policies by reference, the question naturally arises as to whether or not it make sense to simply extend WSDL 2.0 to handle policy information and thereby obviate the need for yet another WS-* specification. The answer is that the features and properties part of WSDL 2.0 provides a specific extensibility point for policy information. However, the authors of the WS-PolicyFramework object to the inclusion of features and properties in WSDL since the WS-PolicyFramework already provides a solution. Of course, there's a difference between defining a formal extensibility point for policy within WSDL and defining the policies themselves. With all the discussion about the right way to model and process policy information, the way to attach policies seems like the least of anyone's worries.

Web Services Policy Language (WSPL)

The Web Services Policy Language (WSPL) is a policy profile for the OASIS Extensible Access Control Markup Language (XACML), but it has general applicability. WSPL can associate generic policy information with any Web services endpoint.

WSPL works by defining a sequence of rules that the requester processes to determine which extended features need to be included in the request message, or which service-level agreements the provider asserts. WSPL is modeled as a tree structure with an enclosing `PolicySet` element. Policies within the set are intended to represent a single aspect of the service and may contain a sequence of one or more rules, which represent the attributes of the policy. The WSPL model assumes that conflicts among rules and attributes are resolved using a mechanism such as a rules conflict resolution engine.

As shown in Figure 7-5, the WSPL model involves a tree of XML elements that enclose rules to be applied.

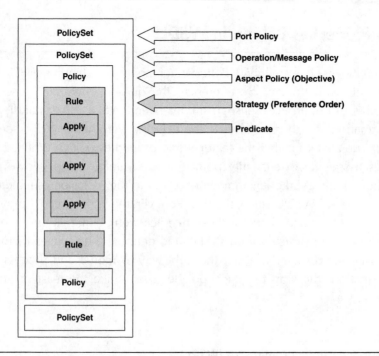

Figure 7-5   WSPL model encloses rules within policies.

The `PolicySet` element is associated with a WSDL 1.1 `portType`. `PolicySets` can be nested to define policy targets at a lower level of granularity.

Comparing WS-PolicyFramework and WSPL

Basically in WS-PolicyFramework, the same syntax can be applied to different items in a WSDL file, whereas in WSPL different syntax is defined for the different parts of the WSDL file. Also in WSPL, the priority of rules is assigned by the order in which they're specified, whereas WS-PolicyFramework attempts to create a generic mechanism for weighting policies with numeric values (even though there's no reference scale or guidance on what any numbers might mean; this is entirely up to the user) and assertions about picking from the list. WSPL is also modeled more like rules processing than WS-PolicyFramework, which defines a system of searching for matches between requester and provider capabilities.

WSDL 2.0 Features and Properties

The features and properties syntax in WSDL 2.0 associates policy information with various WSDL element levels, according to the desired granularity. The presence of a feature indicates that a service supports it, while a property is used to specify whether the feature is required or optional. Features can include reliability, security, transactions, correlation, and routing. Each feature is identified using a name in the form of a URI.

The set of available features is determined by combining all features and properties element on the following components:

- Interface.

- Interface operation.

- Message reference.

- Binding.

- Binding operation.

- Binding message or fault reference. The elements of the Property component include:

  - `<name>`—An absolute URI format.

  - `<required>`—A Boolean that, if true, means that the provider requires the feature.

  - `<value>`—The property's value (i.e., its content).

  - `<value constraint>`—A type definition that can be used to constrain the value of property, such as to within a certain range (i.e., between 1 and 100).

The features and properties mechanism in WSDL 2.0 can be used for a variety of purposes, including the expression of policies. However, it does not include many of the characteristics of either WS-Policy or WSPL for defining precedence, nesting rules, or selecting among various assertions.

Comparing the Policy Specifications

All three approaches to defining policy have their merits, and expectations are that they will be combined into a common approach over time.

As illustrated in Figure 7-6, the policy approaches vary in their use of addressing, support for UDDI, extensibility, resolution, operators, and weighting mechanism. The only point of commonality is on the attachment, excepting WSPL, which doesn't include a binding attachment.

The W3C has initiated a program to investigate and hopefully converge these and other policy proposals.

	WS-Policy	WSPL	WSDL
Operators	All, ExactlyOne, OneOrMore	Equal, greaterThan, set-equals, etc.	None
Usage	Required, rejected, observed, +++	Required, may	Required, may
Weighting	Numeric	Preference Order	None
Addressing	Inline, URI, UDDI, WS-Addressing	Inline	Inline
Predicate	Optional	Rule required	Optional
Attachment	Port, op, msg, binding	Port, op, msg	Port, op, msg, binding
Resolution	None—flattens to choice	Disjunctive Normal form	None
Extensibility	Yes	No	Yes

Figure 7-6   Comparing policy approaches.

WS-MetadataExchange

The WS-MetadataExchange specification creates an interaction protocol for discovering and retrieving Web services metadata from a specific Internet address. For a given URI, WS-MetadataExchange defines how to query the network endpoint for WSDL and associated policy information. WS-MetadataExchange is not simply a system of additional SOAP headers—it's a definition of a complete messaging protocol to be carried out independently of and (like discovery) prior to any requester-provider interaction pattern.

WS-MetadataExchange works by sending a SOAP message request to a Web services provider that has published its metadata in a network-accessible location, defined using WS-Addressing. The WS-MetadataExchange implementation at the provider node is responsible for accepting the WS-MetadataExchange

message, parsing it to discover what metadata is being asked for, and providing
the requested metadata in a reply message.

For example:

```
<s12:Envelope
   xmlns:s12='http://www.w3.org/2003/05/soap-envelope'
   xmlns:wsa='http://schemas.xmlsoap.org/ws/2003/03/addressing'
   xmlns:wsx='http://schemas.xmlsoap.org/ws/2004/02/mex' >
   <s12:Header>
     <wsa:Action>
      http://schemas.xmlsoap.org/ws/2004/02/mex/GetPolicy/Request
     </wsa:Action>
     <wsa:MessageID>
      uuid:73d7edfc-5c3c-49b9-ba46-2480caee43e9
     </wsa:MessageID>
     <wsa:ReplyTo>
      <wsa:Address>
             http://www.iona.com/Artix/Examples/Bank
      </wsa:Address>
     </wsa:ReplyTo>
     <wsa:To>http://www.NattyBank.com/Transfer</wsa:To>
     <ex:MyRefProp xmlns:ex='http://www.iona.com/refs' >
      78f2dc229597b529b81c4bef76453c96
     </ex:MyRefProp>
   </s12:Header>
   <s12:Body>
    <wsx:GetPolicy />
   </s12:Body>
</s12:Envelope>
```

This example illustrates the use of a SOAP 1.2 message together with WS-
Addressing that specifies the endpoint location for the message and also specifies the action URI to be executed at the remote node. The action is a "get
policy request." The additional information in the request message includes
the message ID, the address of the requester, the address of the provider, and
the location in which the provider has placed the metadata, called refs in the
example.

The response is returned to carry the requested data back to the originator of the message exchange. For example:

```
<s12:Envelope
  xmlns:s12='http://www.w3.org/2003/05/soap-envelope'
  xmlns:wsa='http://schemas.xmlsoap.org/ws/2003/03/addressing'
  xmlns:wsp='http://schemas.xmlsoap.org/ws/2002/12/policy'
  xmlns:wsx='http://schemas.xmlsoap.org/ws/2004/02/mex' >

<s12:Header>
  <wsa:Action>
   http://schemas.xmlsoap.org/ws/2004/02/mex/GetPolicy/Response
  </wsa:Action>
  <wsa:RelatesTo>
   uuid:73d7edfc-5c3c-49b9-ba46-2480caee43e9
  </wsa:RelatesTo>
  <wsa:To>http://www.example.com/MyEndpoint</wsa:To>
</s12:Header>

<s12:Body>
 <wsx:GetPolicyResponse>
  <wsp:Policy
   xmlns:wsse='http://schemas.xmlsoap.org/ws/2002/12/secext' >
   <wsp:ExactlyOne>
    <wsse:SecurityToken wsp:Usage="wsp:Required">
    <wsse:TokenType>
      wsse:Kerberosv5TGT
    </wsse:TokenType>
    </wsse:SecurityToken>
    <wsse:SecurityToken wsp:Usage="wsp:Required">
    <wsse:TokenType>
      wsse:X509v3
    </wsse:TokenType>
    </wsse:SecurityToken>
   </wsp:ExactlyOne>
  </wsp:Policy>
 </wsx:GetPolicyResponse>
</s12:Body>
</s12:Envelope>
```

The example includes the action URI indicating that the message is a "get policy response." The response includes sufficient information to correlate the response with the original request. In the body of the message, the provider's policy information is returned. This example illustrates that the security policy stating that either a Kerberos or X.509 security token is required to invoke the provider's service.

Summary

Metadata is data that describes data and other software artifacts such as service descriptions, network addresses, and policy assertions. Managing, obtaining, and using metadata effectively is critical to successful SOA-based applications, including automated business process management, allowing service requesters to discover sufficient information about service providers to generate conformant messages.

Important aspects of metadata management include identifying and using a registry and/or repository accessible to everyone who needs it, whether they are inside the company or an external trading partner.

Commercial Web sites listing Web services for sale or rent have become popular ways of listing and discovering services available over the Internet. Companies can construct applications using a combination of these publicly available services and privately developed services to complement them. When using a combination of publicly available and privately developed Web services, it's important to define and use consistent metadata, including addressing, policy, and descriptions of data and service characteristics.

An important relationship exists between the metadata about a service and the operation of an SOA. A common definition of data to be shared among services, using XML Schema, is essential. Beyond that, it's necessary to create a well-defined service description, including at least WSDL and possibly additional information associated with the WSDL. And finally, after policies are in place for security, transaction, and reliability requirements, it's important to clearly publish these so that service requesters can obtain them and generate conformant, interoperable messages using the right patterns.

Chapter 8

Web Services Security

Web services provide significant new benefits for SOA-based applications, but they also expose significant new security risks. Creating and managing a secure Web services environment involves dealing with various Internet, XML, and Web services security mechanisms. Other security mechanisms may be already in place within the execution environment, especially when existing systems become service-enabled to join the SOA.

The general approach is relatively straightforward, taking into account:

- Transport-level security such as firewalls, virtual private networks, basic authentication, non-repudiation, and encryption.

- Message-level security such as using authentication tokens to validate requester identity and authorization assertions to control access to provider services.

- Data-level security such as encryption and digital signature to protect against altering stored and/or transmitted data.

- Environment-level security such as management, logging, and auditing to identify problems that need to be fixed and establishing trusted relationships and communication patterns.

Achieving the right mixture of the various technologies and levels of protection, and figuring out what threats to protect against and how, typically takes some time and effort. A good solution protects programs and data against unauthorized access, guards against the possible consequences of in-flight message interception, and prevents a variety of malicious attacks that have become all too familiar in the Internet world.

This chapter:

- Describes the various threats and challenges that need to be guarded against.
- Summarizes the basic Web services security technologies.
- Provides detail on some of the more important technologies and standards.

Most of the technologies described in this chapter were designed and developed specifically for use with Web services. However, several of them are generic security mechanisms that can be applied to Web services. As a rule, the WS-Security framework describes how to incorporate these other security technologies into Web services by defining a place for them within SOAP headers.

Figure 8-1 illustrates the fact that WS-Security provides a framework into which other security technologies are plugged. For example, WS-Security does not define any authentication ticket mechanism; instead, it defines how to use plain user name/password, Kerberos, and X.509 tickets within the context of a SOAP header. WS-Security also defines how to use XML Signature, XML Encryption, and SAML within SOAP headers.

Other Web services security specifications, such as WS-Trust, WS-Secure-Conversation, and WS-Federation, define protocols that help establish agreements between requesters and providers about the kinds of security they will use. Finally, WS-SecurityPolicy is used to declare a provider's requirements for security support, such as strong authentication.

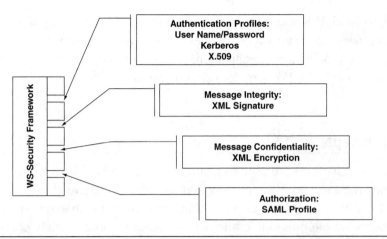

Figure 8-1   Relationship of WS-Security framework to other specifications.

Overarching Concern

Security is sometimes called an "overarching concern" because everything involved in the Web services environment needs some level of protection against the many threats and challenges that IT departments must deal with on a regular basis.

For example, SOAP messages need to be secure, WSDL files may need to be secured against unauthorized access, firewall ports may need additional mechanisms to guard against heavy loads and to inspect Web services messages, and so on. Because Web services are designed for interoperability, an important goal of the security technologies is to enable execution environment technologies to continue to work while adding security mechanisms to the Web services layers above them.

An XML appliance may also be deployed to inspect messages arriving at the edge of the network (that is, where it meets the Internet); if so, this device must be deployed with an understanding or assessment of its relationship to other security mechanisms.

The starting point is ensuring network layer protection using IP Security (IPsec), Secure Sockets Layer (SSL), and basic authentication services, which provide a basic level of protection.

At the next level, WS-Security provides the framework for protecting the message using multiple security technologies. Most of the technologies are defined outside of the WS-Security specification; in that case, WS-Security tells you how to use them within the Web services environment.

Core Concepts

Two basic mechanisms are used to guard against security risks: signing and encrypting messages for data integrity and confidentiality, and checking associated ticket and token information for authentication and authorization. These mechanisms are often used in combination because a broad variety of risks must be taken into account.

As illustrated in Figure 8-2, WS-Security headers can be added to SOAP messages before they are sent to the service provider. The headers can include authentication, authorization,[1] encryption, and signature so that the provider can validate the credentials of the requester before executing the service. Invalid credentials typically result in the return of an error message to the requester. The requester typically adds the authentication and authorization information in the form of tokens. Thus, there's a need to share and coordinate security information, such as tokens, between requester and provider or across a chain of requesters, providers, and possibly SOAP intermediaries.

To successfully manage encryption and authentication for end-to-end message exchange patterns, the WS-Security specification defines several SOAP header extensions. For example:

```
<wsse:Security
  xmlns:wsse="http://schemas.xmlsoap.org/ws/2002/12/secext">
  <wsse:UsernameToken>
   <wsse:Username>Ericn</wsse:Username>
   <wsse:Password>8Bcnu6</wsse:Password>
  </wsse:UsernameToken>
</wsse:Security>
```

---

[1] Note that as of the time of writing, WS-Authorization was not yet completed.

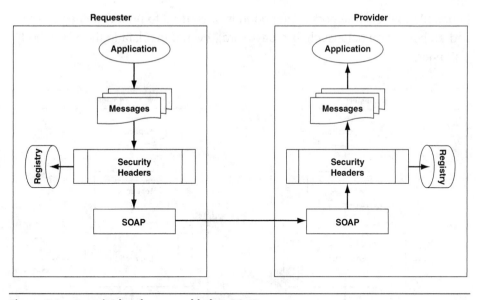

Figure 8-2   Security headers are added to SOAP messages.

The example shows the WS-Security namespace `wsse` and the use of the clear text user name/password authentication feature. The inclusion of WS-Security headers in a SOAP message ensures that the user name/password shown in this example is available for processing by intermediaries as well as at the ultimate destination of the message. Further information on these topics is provided later in this chapter.

If the service provider requires a Kerberos token, the WS-SecurityPolicy declaration associated with the provider's WSDL might look like this:

```
<SecurityToken wsp:Requirement=Kerberos
   <TokenType>... </TokenType>
   <TokenIssuer> ... </TokenIssuer>
</SecurityToken>
```

As shown in Figure 8-3, a key pair (or other encryption mechanism) can be used to encrypt a message before transmission and decrypt it after it's received but before it's processed by the application. Encryption means sending information in code, much like the military does to protect confidential information during wartime. To snoop on an encrypted transmission, someone would have to be able to break the code. Encryption is often used to protect authentication and authorization data (such as a password), even if the data in the SOAP body isn't encrypted.

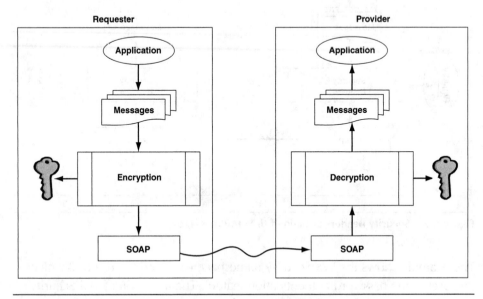

Figure 8-3   Encryption protects messages from snooping.

The encryption information can be sent in a WS-Security header so that a provider knows what encryption algorithm was used to encrypt the message. As with authentication, several standards exist for encryption. Some of the common ones include Secure Shell (SSH) and RSA, named for its inventors, Ron Rivest, Adi Shamir, and Leonard Adelman. RSA developed and first implemented the concepts behind public key cryptography (also called PCKS), which allows services to communicate securely by using a private key and by the exchange of a public key. The private key, which isn't shared, is used in the encryption algorithm, while the public key, which can be shared, is used to decrypt the message. In Web services specifications, the XML Key Management Specification (XKMS) can be used to manage the distribution of public and private keys to enable this style of secure communication.

These basic types of security technologies are also often used in combination with other extended technologies, such as reliable messaging and transactions, to improve the security of an overall system. Transaction processing technologies require additional messages for coordinating transaction protocols, and these often require security to prevent their disruption.

Web services management is often very concerned with security. In addition to securing the management infrastructure itself from unauthorized use (i.e., to prevent anyone from gaining administrative control over the Web services deployment), it's important to be able to monitor and manage the security infrastructure. Web services management tools typically implement some level of security functionality using SOAP intermediaries or SOAP interceptors.

Identity

Identity management for Web services is similar to identity management for any IT system in that the subject (whether a person, machine, program, or abstraction such as a process flow) is given a unique or unambiguous name within the security domain whose validity can be checked. The identity of a Web service requester is sometimes critical for a provider to establish trust because whether or not the requester is allowed to access the provider's service (or any other service, data resource, or device managed by the provider's service) depends upon the identity of the requester.

Identity management is complex for Web services, just like it is for the Web, because Web services can span departments and enterprises. Typically, identity management is performed locally, departmentally, or within an enterprise by ensuring that each employee's user name is unique on the network. Employees are responsible for keeping their passwords private because passwords are used to authenticate the user's identity and to determine the applications, directories, and data the user is allowed to access.

Identity management may need to be performed within a broader scope, such as the Microsoft Active Directory or a corporate-wide LDAP solution. When an identity has to be uniquely managed across the Internet and across enterprises, the level of administration difficulty increases, as does the need for trust. Various initiatives, such as those sponsored by the Liberty Alliance, are focused on establishing mechanisms for identity management for the Internet.

Authentication

Authentication is the process through which an authority verifies a subject's identity, based on some set of proof such as a password or personal identification number (PIN). The authentication process creates a *principal*, which is an object that represents the authenticated subject, such as a credential or token that the subject can use later. On the Web, the subject is typically a user, but for Web services, it can be a machine, program, or other abstract entity represented by the Web service requester. Web services typically use some form of the user name/password mechanism for basic authentication, but stronger forms such as signatures also may be used.

Authentication can be described as the process of confirming that you (or your proxy service requester) are who you say you are. On the Web, this is most often seen as a popup user name/password box, which is called forms-based authentication, which uses a cookie returned on subsequent invocations.[2] Only you know the correct user name and password, so you are authenticating yourself as someone who is allowed to access the Web site. The Web site will have to set up and manage a directory of authorized user name/password combinations so that it can verify the information you submit.

Web services requesters can include authentication information using user name/password information in SOAP headers that the service provider can check against its directory of authorized user name/password combinations. The user ID and password can also be sent via HTTP (no SOAP header required). The provider typically carries out a further refinement of this model to support specific checks for authorization to access specific services or specific data resources. Sometimes requesters are assigned certain roles that can be used as indexes into authorization information—meaning authorization is sometimes carried out according to specific roles such as administrator, clerk, or manager, but again, this is typically managed by the provider and may not appear in the SOAP header (and certainly not in the WS-Security header if it appears at all).

---

[2] Cookies are not supported in Web services because they are not in XML format and cannot be used across multiple service executions.

Authentication is needed in Web services to verify the identities of the service provider and service requestor. In some cases, mutual authentication may be needed (that is, the provider must authenticate the requester and vice versa).

Digital Signature

A digital signature signs a message digest using a public/private key pair. A hash algorithm creates the message digest, and the encryption algorithm signs the digest (with the private key). The receiver decrypts the signature using the public key, recomputes the message digest, and compares the two. If the message has been altered, the results won't match, and the provider knows the message has been tampered with. As in other encryptions, symmetric or asymmetric key algorithms can be used to compute the signature, although for signing the user of asymmetric keys is more typical.

Summary of Challenges, Threats, and Remedies

This section summarizes the major challenges and threats that need to be addressed using Web services and other security mechanisms and identifies (where possible) the technologies necessary to guard against each challenge or threat.

Web services, because they represent an abstract interfacing and messaging layer, cannot and should not include some of the security mechanisms available within the underlying platforms on which Web services execute. It would be a mistake to try to replicate into the Web services environment such operating system-level protections as memory protection, file or device protection, or even network-level protection.

In general, to guard against the broad variety of threats and challenges, security solutions must be implemented through the transport layer, the Web services layer, and the data layer, and also must be mapped into and out of the underlying execution environment to ensure either that the defined security policy is enforced or that when it is not, there is an audit log entry of the failure or policy breach.

Understanding the Security Architecture

It's important to view the Web services security challenges and threats within their overall architectural context and determine solutions based not simply on a given technology but rather on looking at the overall solution context. That is, you can't just say "use SSL" without understanding the threat you're trying to defend against and without understanding the overall security context into which you'd like to deploy SSL. SSL may be sufficient, but it may not. Multiple security technologies often must be used in conjunction to provide a comprehensive solution to the big security concerns, and it is therefore important to understand how the technologies work together.

The following sections detail some of the specific challenges and threats that the overall Web services security environment must address.

Message Interception

The potential for SOAP message interception and decoding gives rise to a category of security threats that must be guarded against when deploying Web services, including message replay, alternation, and spoofing.

Unless specifically encrypted, Web services messages are transmitted in plain text, which can easily be intercepted and read. An intercepted message can be modified, potentially affecting all or part of the message body or headers. Additional bogus information could be inserted into a message header or body parts. Any message attachment could also be modified or replaced. Altering the message or the attachment could cause bogus information to be sent to and received from a Web service, possibly including a virus. Reading an intercepted message can also give anyone access to confidential information within a message or message attachment, such credit card information, social security numbers, bank account numbers, and so on.

Protecting against message interception includes the use of encryption and digital signatures to preserve confidentiality and integrity.

Person in the Middle Attacks

Because SOAP messages can be routed through intermediaries, and because intermediaries are able to inspect the messages to add or process headers, it's possible for a SOAP intermediary to be compromised. Messages between the requestor and the ultimate receiver could therefore be intercepted while the original parties still believe they are communicating with each other.

Mutual authentication techniques can protect against this type of threat, but signed keys or derived keys provide even better protection.

Spoofing

Spoofing is a complex challenge in which an attacker assumes the identity of one or more trusted (i.e., authenticated) parties in a communication in order to bypass the security system. The target of the attack believes it is carrying on a conversation with a trusted entity. Usually, spoofing is a technique to launch other forms of attack such as forged messages that request confidential information or place fraudulent orders.

It's possible for spoofed Web service messages to include SQL or script tampering to attack through JSP or ASP script execution.

Mutual authentication techniques can protect against this type of threat.

Replay Attacks

A replay attack is one in which someone intercepts a message and then replays it back to the receiver. Replays could also be used to gather confidential information or to invoke fraudulent transactions.

Strong authentication techniques together with message time stamp and sequence numbering can protect against this type of threat.

Denial-of-Service Attacks

When an unauthorized intermediary or other attacker intercepts a SOAP message, the attacker can resend it repeatedly in order to overload the Web services execution environment and effectively deny service to legitimate services that are trying to get through. An attacker can also blast a ton of messages to a Web service after the attacker gets its address. Even if the messages are rejected, the site can get overloaded with error processing.

In general, if someone wants to launch this type of attack, there's no real defense. However, firewall appliances are growing in popularity because they can help mitigate denial-of-service attacks.

Finding the Right Balance

For Web services, as with any application, it's necessary to establish the proper balance between business requirements, protection, performance, and ease of administration. Security mechanisms each carry a performance price not only in terms additional processing overhead when executing a service but also to the IT staff who must design, develop, and administer them. Encryption includes an obvious overhead because it takes time to encrypt and decrypt messages. Sending a user name/password on each message also adds to the overhead of processing a message. It's for these reasons that many of the various technologies have been developed, but this also means that the user needs to understand not only what each technology provides, but also what it costs, and whether or not there are other security mechanisms that can be used and that will satisfy the business requirements while imposing less of a burden.

Securing the Communications Layer

The first level that needs to be secured is the communications transport. In the case of Web services, this is almost always TCP/IP, and this is certainly the case when using HTTP.

Firewalls map a publicly known IP address to another IP address on the internal network, thereby establishing a managed tunnel and preventing access by programs at unauthorized addresses. Web services can work through existing firewall configurations, but this often means increased protection has to be added to firewalls to monitor incoming SOAP traffic and log any problems. Another popular solution involves the use of XML firewalls and gateways that are capable of recognizing Web services formats and performing initial security checks, possibly deployed as intermediaries or within a "demilitarized zone" (i.e., between firewalls).

IP Layer Security

Security mechanisms for the Internet include the IP layer with IP security (IPsec). IPsec provides packet-level authentication and encryption and is typically implemented at the operating system level. IPsec is a facility available to all applications using the Internet, including Web services. However, in practice this means that the IPsec connection is typically part of a separate security setup between the communicating parties. In other words, for Web services to use IPsec, the IPsec communication session has to be established in advance of invoking a Web service, typically by the transport or the user, because nothing in the Web services layer is used to establish an IPsec session.

IPsec is most often used in virtual private network (VPN) applications and between firewalls, which many companies use to secure the communications between remote users and corporate systems. Other VPN technologies are also widely used as a security foundation for Web services invocations, just as they can be used for any other Internet-based application.

Transport-Level Security

At the next level is transport layer security. Typically, this is provided by Secure Sockets Layer/Transport Layer Security (SSL/TLS, usually referred to simply as SSL), which is often seen on the Web as HTTPS. This security level can be implemented in the network application, rather than in the operating system, and Web services can easily and directly use it by requiring HTTPS as a transport. Implementations of SSL for other transports, such as IIOP and RMI/IIOP, also provide the capability for Web services to take advantage of this important privacy mechanism when used over other transports.

SSL provides encryption and strong authentication and may be sufficient for many applications. SSL authentication can be used to provide strong, mutual authentication—much stronger than HTTP Basic, HTTP Digest, or WS-Security user name token authentication. However, SSL is transport-based rather than application-based, so it secures the network nodes rather than the service requester or provider. SSL provides authentication, message confidentiality, and message integrity, but these capabilities are limited to the transport level and cannot be applied to the application level. SSL also does not offer any protection for XML data in storage. It also does not directly support any of the advanced authorization checking such as role-based authorization that many applications may require, although it is possible to map the SSL strong authentication information to a local principal and use that in an application-defined role-based authorization scheme to determine access privileges. But these are application-specific scenarios, not general solutions.

The simplest starting point for Web services security typically is the user name/password checking associated with HTTP that is common to many Web sites. However, basic authentication may not be sufficient for Web services. A password can be encoded using Base64 or another simple obfuscation algorithm even without SSL, but obfuscation does not provide true encryption and therefore is not very secure. When a potential attacker figures out the encoding mechanism or algorithm used for the obfuscation, the message can be intercepted and tampered with. Additional, stronger authentication mechanisms include:

- At the transport level: HTTP Basic, HTTP Digest, and SSL.

- At the application level: User name/password, X.509, Kerberos, SPKM, SAML, and XrML.

What makes an authentication mechanism stronger is mainly its resistance to interception. An authentication token is harder to intercept when it's encrypted or encoded, or when (as with Kerberos and X.509) it's issued by a third party, such as an authentication authority, with whom the application can check to be sure the token is correct.

SSL cannot handle composite applications, however, or complex MEPs. Furthermore, SSL encryption is all or nothing, unlike XML Encryption, which can be applied to any part of an XML document.

Message-Level Security

The next level of security above the transport level is message-level security, where the security protections are provided by the WS-Security framework and associated specifications. The WS-Security framework defines SOAP headers that include the necessary information to protect messages. The WS-Security specification defines the security header for SOAP messages and what can be included within the header. Associated specifications define the contents of the SOAP security header and the processing rules associated with those contents.

Because Web services expose access to programs and data stores, their use creates additional requirements for security protection. Furthermore, complex Web services may span multiple network locations discovered dynamically or composed into a larger interaction such as a process flow. Web services need an end-to-end security model for the entire conversation because sensitive information could be passed from service to service. A Web service interaction also may potentially involve multiple parties using different security-related technologies.

The WS-Security Framework

WS-Security (Web Services Security) is the name of a set of specifications[3] that augment SOAP message headers to incorporate solutions to many common security threats, in particular those related to the requirements of Web services messaging.

Because SOAP is a particular form of an XML document designed for messaging and interoperability, WS-Security needs to define how XML Encryption and XML Signature should be used with SOAP—this is one of the major motivations for WS-Security.

---

[3] See http://www.oasis-open.org/committees/tc_home.php?wg_abbrev=wss.

The WS-Security specifications protect against:

- **Message alteration**—By including digital signatures for all or parts of the SOAP body and the SOAP header.

- **Message disclosure**—By supporting message encryption.

The WS-Security framework can also be used to:

- Preserve message integrity through the use of strong key algorithms.

- Authenticate messages through the use of various token mechanisms such as Kerberos and X.509.

The specifications are divided between the core framework and profiles of other technologies that are defined to fit within the framework. Much of the work of the WS-Security Technical Committee at OASIS is involved in adding profiles to the WS-Security suite of specifications.

At the time of writing, the WS-Security framework consists of the following specifications:

- Web Services Security: SOAP Message Security.

- Web Services Security: User name Token Profile.

- Web Services Security: X.509 Token Profile.

- Profiles for the use of other technologies with the framework are under development, including SAML, Kerberos, and XrML (Extensible Rights Markup Language for role-based authorization and control of access to digital media and services content).

The WS-Security set of specifications defines the overall framework for including these various types of security information into SOAP headers and then defines (or profiles) other technologies so that both requesters and providers can share a common understanding of their use.

The WS-Security framework is designed to work with SOAP 1.1 and SOAP 1.2[4] by defining the security tokens and encryption mechanisms that go in the SOAP headers.

WS-Security provides a general-purpose mechanism for associating security tokens with messages. No specific type of security token is required by WS-Security. It is designed to be extensible (e.g., to support multiple security token formats).

For example:

```
<?xml version="1.0" encoding="utf-8"?>
<s11:Envelope
  xmlns:s11="http://schemas.xmlsoap.org/soap/envelope/"
  xmlns:wsse="http://www.docs.oasis-open.org/wss/2004/01/
              oasis-200401-wss-wssecurity-secext-1.0.xsd">
  <s11:Header>
   <wsse:Security>
     ...
   </wsse:Security>
  </s11:Header>
  <s11:Body>
   ...
  </s11:Body>
</s11:Envelope>
```

This example illustrates a SOAP 1.1 message (indicated by the s11: namespace prefix) and shows the OASIS standard namespace for the WS-Security security header (indicated by the wsse: namespace prefix). The namespace for SOAP 1.2 is as follows:

```
xmlns:S12="http://www.w3.org/2003/05/soap-envelope"
```

WS-Security describes a mechanism for encoding binary security tokens within the header. The specification describes how to encode X.509 certificates and Kerberos tickets as well as how to include opaque encrypted keys. It also

---

[4] Note that SOAP with Attachments is supported for SOAP 1.1 only because SOAP 1.2 includes its own binary message attachment format (MTOM—message transmission optimization mechanism).

includes extensibility mechanisms that can be used to further describe the characteristics of the security tokens that are included with a message.

A security token is a credential that proves identity. When using Kerberos, X.509, SAML, or XrML, you've already proven your identity at least once. The question is whether the service will accept this credential (typically based on the trust relationship that exists between the issuing authority and the service and on the freshness of the credential). Sometimes the service requires additional proof (such as a signature) or multiple forms of proof. WS-Trust provides a protocol for the service to request additional proof. Assuming that the service accepts the credentials, it then determines whether the subject has permission to access the requested resource.

There are many different ways of managing these tokens on a network, and there are also different ways of proving an identity. With a user name, for example, an accompanying password proves that this is really your identity. A Kerberos ticket, however, is encrypted by its issuer using a key that the service provider can verify. Additionally, a digital signature might be sent along with a certificate to authenticate an identity.

WS-Security therefore needs to support multiple approaches for conveying and authenticating identity. WS-Security doesn't define how to perform authentication but rather defines how to transmit a variety of different security tokens within the security header. The service provider typically uses the information in the header to authenticate the identity of the requester, but authentication tokens can also be used in other ways.

Although it allows any type of security token, the WS-Security specification explicitly defines four options (user name, binary, XML, and token reference). The simplest (although not always the most secure) option is to send a security token containing a user name and password. To allow this, WS-Security defines a `<UsernameToken>` element that can contain a user name and password.

Because sending unencrypted passwords across a network isn't a very effective authentication mechanism, the `UsernameToken` element is most likely to be used to authenticate SOAP messages sent across an encrypted connection, such as one that uses SSL.

A second option is to send a binary security token, such as the one containing a Kerberos ticket. For example:

```
<wsse:Security
  xmlns:wsse="http://www.docs.oasis-open.org/wss/2004/01/
                oasis-200401-wss-wssecurity-secext-1.0.xsd">
  <wsse:BinarySecurityToken
        ValueType="http://www.docs.oasis-open.org/wss/2004/07/
        ➥oasis-
          000000-wss-kerberos-token-profile-
          1.0#Kerberosv5_AP_REQ"
    EncodingType="http://www.docs.oasis-open.org/wss/2004/01/
      ➥oasis-200401-wss-wssecurity-secext-1.0.xsd#Base64Binary">
      QMwcAG ...
  </wsse:BinarySecurityToken>
</wsse:Security>
```

As this example shows, a Kerberos ticket is sent using the `<BinarySecurity-Token>` element. This element's `ValueType` attribute indicates that this is a Kerberos Version 5 service ticket, which is used to authenticate a client to a particular service. The ticket is encoded using `base64`. Other encoding options have been proposed but not yet defined.

The fourth option is to send a reference to a security token rather than the token itself. WS-Security defines the `<SecurityTokenReference>` element that contains a URI for a security token. The service provider can dereference the URI to obtain the token from its location on the Internet.

Message integrity is provided by leveraging XML Signature in conjunction with security tokens (which may contain or imply key data) to ensure that messages are transmitted without modification. The integrity mechanisms support multiple signatures, including any that might be added by SOAP intermediaries, and are extensible to support additional signature formats.

A signature provides additional proof that the token is valid. The signature verifies the claim that a particular security token represents the producer of the message by using the token to sign a message (demonstrating knowledge of the key). The `<ds:KeyInfo>` element in the signature provides information to the provider as to which key was used to create a signature. The following example illustrates that the sender created the signature using the referenced token (usually a binary token):

```
<ds:KeyInfo>
        <wsse:SecurityTokenReference>
                <wsse:Reference URI="#MyID"/>
        </wsse:SecurityTokenReference>
</ds:KeyInfo>
```

XML Encryption provides message confidentiality in conjunction with security tokens to keep portions of SOAP messages confidential. The encryption mechanisms support additional encryption technologies, processes, and operations by multiple actors. The encryption information references a security token when that token is used to encrypt the data.

WS-Security can handle multiple options for carrying authentication information and ensuring message integrity and confidentiality, but the requester and provider still need a way to agree on which option or options are being used. That's where WS-SecurityPolicy comes in.

WS-SecurityPolicy

Like the WS-Security framework, WS-SecurityPolicy is intended to work with both SOAP 1.1 and 1.2. WS-SecurityPolicy is a policy assertion language that can be used within the WS-PolicyFramework (see Chapter 7, "Metadata Management"). WS-SecurityPolicy can be used to develop an XML-based assertion associated with a Web service endpoint or WSDL file using WS-Policy-Attachment (again, see Chapter 7). A service requester can discover the WS-SecurityPolicy association using the WS-MetadataExchange protocol or can otherwise dereference a URL pointing to the XML file in which the WS-SecurityPolicy assertion is stored.

Decoding the WS-SecurityPolicy assertion tells the service requester what security features are required by the service provider, such as the authentication token format and whether or not the message has to be signed using an XML signature. For example:

```
<wsp:Policy
    xmlns:wsp="http://schemas.xmlsoap.org/ws/2002/12/policy"
    xmlns:wssp="http://schemas.xmlsoap.org/ws/2002/12/secext">
```

```
      <wsp:All>
         <wssp:Integrity wsp:Usage="wsp:Required">
         <wssp:Algorithm Type="wssp:AlgSignature"
             URI="http://www.w3.org/2000/09/xmldsig#rsa-sha1"/>
      </wssp:Integrity>
    <wssp:SecurityToken>
        <wssp:TokenType>wsse:X509v3</wssp:TokenType>
    </wssp:SecurityToken>
  </wsp:All>
 </wsp:Policy>
```

This example shows that the provider requires message integrity using the referenced XML Signature algorithm and requires authentication using X.509 tokens.

By specifying the token type within the `Integrity` element, you are saying that the signature must be created using this type of token. Although not included in this example, the SOAP body contains the Request Security Token (RST) and the Request Security Token Response messages.

WS-Trust

Sometimes it's necessary for a service provider and service requester to communicate out of band (that is, outside of the normal Web service invocation message exchange) to exchange security credentials. For example, a requester may need to obtain a provider's public key for encryption before sending the message. The WS-Trust specification defines the protocol for assessing and brokering a trusted relationship such as this.

WS-Trust establishes a protocol for:

- Issuing, renewing, and validating security tokens.

- Assessing or brokering trust relationships.

WS-Trust defines the process of exchanging and brokering security tokens so that the requester can obtain the necessary security information to construct trusted messages.

As illustrated in Figure 8-4, WS-Trust defines a SOAP message exchange proto-col according to which a service requester and provider can communicate with each other to exchange authentication and authorization credentials.

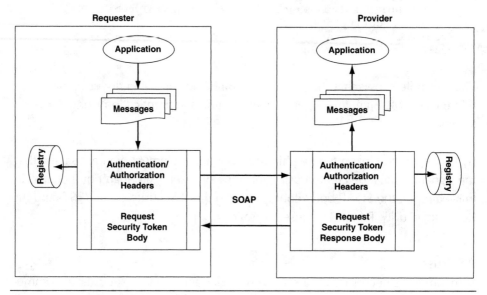

Figure 8-4   WS-Trust defines SOAP messages to issue, renew, and validate security tokens.

WS-Trust defines a namespace used to identify messages used to carry out the trust protocol:

```
xmlns:wst="http://schemas.xmlsoap.org/ws/2004/04/trust"
```

The security model defined in WS-Trust is based on a process in which a Web service provider can require that an incoming message from a requester estab-lish a set of credentials (user name/password, key, permission, capability, and so on). If a message arrives without the required credentials, the provider rejects the message with an error. The service provider can assert the credentials it requires using WS-SecurityPolicy. WS-Trust defines the message exchange pat-tern and format of the credentials information that may need to be exchanged between provider and requester in order to fulfill the policy assertions.

Security tokens are requested using the `<RequestSecurityToken>` message defined in the WS-Trust specification.

Security tokens are returned using the `<RequestSecurityTokenResponse>` message defined in the WS-Trust specification.

WS-SecureConversation

WS-SecureConversation defines a shared security context across multiple message exchanges. It defines a new security context token for the `<wsse:Security>` header block, and it defines a binding for WS-Trust. Instead of having to include the same security credentials in each SOAP message, a provider and requester can use WS-SecureConversation to agree on sharing a common security context. For example:

```
<SecurityContextToken wsu:Id="...">
<wsc:Identifier>...</wsc:Identifier>
</SecurityContextToken>
```

The namespace is as follows:

```
xmlns:wsc="http://schemas.xmlsoap.org/ws/2004/04/security/sc/sct"
```

The context has a unique identifier and can be used to temporarily or persistently store any combination of authentication, authorization, or encryption information that two or more Web services need to share.

As illustrated in Figure 8-5, WS-SecureConversation defines a SOAP message protocol for propagating and establishing common copies of security context at the requester and provider nodes so that they do not have to (for example) exchange authentication information on each Web service invocation request.

The shaded areas indicate shared security context used across multiple message exchanges.

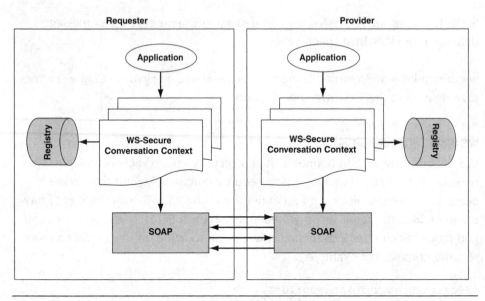

Figure 8-5   Secure conversation establishes shared security context.

WS-Federation

WS-Federation defines how to establish trust relationships across security domains. WS-Trust assumes a single security domain within which the service requester authenticates with the service provider's authentication service. WS-Federation defines a binding of WS-Trust that allows a service provider to accept authentication credentials that come from a different security domain. When an identity is authenticated and access is controlled within a given domain such as an enterprise, department, or execution environment, it may also be necessary to handle these problems for multiple domains because Web services can provide interoperability solutions that cross multiple domains.

The WS-Federation specification defines a message exchange protocol that service requesters and providers can use to establish federation of security domains across multiple trust boundaries. The WS-Federation specification builds on WS-Security, defining a profile of WS-Trust for obtaining and exchanging identity information, a specialized security token service called the Identity Provider (IP), a new policy assertion language syntax called RelatedService, and protocols for interacting with attribute and pseudonym services. An attribute service provides the means to obtain information about a principal (that is, an authenticated subject).

A pseudonym service is a specialized attribute service that maintains alternate identity information about a principal. WS-Security, WS-PolicyAssertions, and WS-Trust can be used in combination to accomplish the federation of security trust domains. In other words, WS-Federation takes WS-Trust a step further and establishes a mechanism for exchanging credentials across trust boundaries, not just within a trust boundary.

Accessing services provided on multiple machines or executable software domains may require additional authentication, unless the authentication operations are federated, as they can be for example in a Windows domain via the Windows Active Directory. Like Active Directory for the Windows environment, WS-Federation can be used to support single sign-on protocols for extended security domains. For example, an authentication check can be forwarded to a third party for validation.

The WS-Federation specification defines an integrated model for federating identity, authentication, and authorization across different trust realms. This specification defines how the federation model is applied to active requestors such as SOAP applications. It also defines how pseudonyms can be used to help preserve secrecy when identities need to be protected across domains.

Security tokens are requested using the `<RequestSecurityToken>` message defined in the WS-Trust specification. Security tokens are returned using the `<RequestSecurityTokenResponse>` message defined in the WS-Trust specification. If the requester doesn't already have the WS-Policy for the exchange, it can request it using WS-MetadataExchange.

Security Assertion Markup Language (SAML)

The Security Assertion Markup Language (SAML) from OASIS is an XML application designed to support single sign-on and propagate authorization information. For example, SAML allows a user to log on once to a Web site and then access affiliated Web sites without having to log on again. The affiliated Web sites need to be able to recognize the original user name (or identity). The same mechanism can be used to provide single sign-on for Web services that access different services. The WS-Security SAML profile defines how to use SAML with SOAP, but SAML can be used independently of SOAP and independently of WS-Security, if necessary.

To accomplish single sign-on, SAML defines three basic components: assertions, protocol, and binding. SAML also defines profiles (Browser/Artifact Profile and Browser/POST Profile), which specify how to convey SAML tokens with application requests. Assertions can be one of three types:

- **Authentication**—Validates that the specified subject was authenticated by a particular means at a particular time.

- **Attribute**—A statement by a security authority that supplies qualifying information about the subject.

- **Authorization**—A statement by an authorization authority that grants permission to a subject to perform a specified action on a specified resource.

The protocol defines how applications communicate with a SAML authority to request authentication and authorization decisions. SAML bindings are defined for SOAP and HTTP.

SAML assertions provide security information about subjects, where a subject is an entity (either human or computer) that has an identity in some security domain. A typical subject is a person, identified by user name. A typical assertion conveys information about the authentication of a subject, including any attributes associated with the subjects. The assertion also provides information about authorization decisions that determine whether or not subjects are allowed to access resources.

A SAML assertion is represented using XML and supports nesting so that a single assertion might contain several different internal statements about authentication, authorization, and attributes. (Note that assertions containing authentication statements can carry the results of an authentication that happened previously.) An assertion is issued by a SAML authority, including authentication authorities, attribute authorities, and authorization authorities.

SAML defines a protocol by which requesters can obtain an assertion from a SAML authority, which might be implemented using a security server product such as Netegrity Siteminder of Tivoli Access Manager. A SAML authority can use various sources of information in creating their responses, such as external policy stores and assertions that were received as input in requests. Thus, requesters use the protocol to interact with SAML authorities to obtain assertions, providers use the protocol to interact with SAML authorities to validate assertions, and SAML authorities can be both producers and consumers of assertions.

SAML is different from other security mechanisms because of how it uses assertions about subjects. Other mechanisms rely on a central certificate authority, which naturally raises the issue of trust for the certificate provider. With SAML, any point in the network can assert that it knows the identity of a user or piece of data. It is up to the receiving application to accept whether or not it trusts the assertion, which sometimes will mean that additional authentication information is needed.

When SAML assertions are used with WS-Security, they can be referenced using the `<wsse:SecurityTokenReference>` element. SAML assertions can also be placed directly inside the `<wsse:Security>` header block. When using the token reference, the `<saml:Assertion>` element is not embedded in the `<wsse:Security>` header. SAML assertions take the format of `<saml:Assertion>` and typically start with a UUID. The remainder of the information is typical SAML information, including information about the SAML issuer. The Web service receiving the SAML assertion can find the assertion issuer and check the assertion.

Use SAML on Its Own or with WS-Security?

This question naturally arises when a technology is available both as a standalone, independent technology and as an integral part of another technology. As a general rule of thumb, the answer is typically determined by the amount of coding necessary to accomplish the task and by the degree to which interoperability can be assured. Whenever a technology such as SAML is profiled inside another technology such as WS-Security, conforming implementations of WS-Security are required to support SAML (assuming the conformance includes the SAML profile, of course). If you are using a Web services platform or a set of Web services products that support WS-Security, the simplest and most interoperable choice is to use SAML within WS-Security. If all you require is SAML, on the other hand, it may make more sense to simply use SAML directly and require services in your platform (and your trading partners' platforms, if any) to also support SAML.

An authentication assertion identifies the subject (using a `NameIdentifier` and/ or a `SubjectConfirmation`), and it contains an authentication statement that specifies when and how the subject was authenticated. Role information may be associated with the subject using an attribute statement. Authorization information may be associated with the subject using an authorization statement. All three types of assertion statements may be included in a single `<saml: Assertion>` element, but they are still three different types of statements.

SAML assertions can also have version numbers and signatures. SAML assertions can also specify condition elements for credential expiration dates. SAML defines a protocol and behavior of the assertion providers. SAML requires SSL certificates to provide digital signing and encryption of SAML assertions.

SAML can provide protection from replay attacks by requiring the use of SSL encryption when transmitting assertions and messages. Additionally, SAML provides a digital signature mechanism that enables the assertion to have a validity time range to prevent assertions from being replayed later.

XACML: Communicating Policy Information

The Extensible Access Control Markup Language (XACML) is an XML application for writing access control polices.

Access control security mechanisms have two sides: the side that performs the check to see whether a user is authorized to access the Web service, and the side that defines and manages the information that the access control mechanism checks. In other words, the access control information needs to be defined in order for it to be checked.

The XACML specification provides an access control language to define access policies and a request/response protocol to request authorization decisions. XACML can also be used to connect disparate access control policy engines.

XACML defines a set of rules for the XML encoding of what data a person is allowed to read. For example, it could define which HR records you can access from the HR Web site based on whether you are the employee, the authorized parent or guardian of the person in the HR records, or the physician or other authorized HR agent who can update the records.

XML Key Management Specification (XKMS)

XKMS is an XML-based mechanism for managing the Public Key Infrastructure (PKI).

PKI uses public-key cryptography for encrypting, signing, authorizing, and verifying the authenticity of information, including Web services messages. Public and private keys can be used in XML Encryption and XML Signature, for example, and to provide additional levels of authentication for an HTTP connection.

The XKMS specification defines a set of Web services to manage the task of key registration and validation, based on the use of a third-party "trust" utility that manages public and private key pairs and other PKI details. In other words, XKMS defines Web service interfaces to key management systems so that Web service applications can access and use their facilities. Otherwise, key management requires a manual process of generating keys, placing them in their proper directories, and publishing their location.

XKMS works with any PKI system, such as those provided by Verisign and Entrust, passing the information back and forth between it and the Web service. XKMS is a W3C specification.

Essential to the public/private key mechanism is the ability to manage and distribute key pairs. If a third party generates the associated key pairs, a management facility such as XKMS is necessary to ensure that the right keys end up in the right place.

Data-Level Security

XML Signature and XML Encryption are fundamental security specifications for protecting Web services data. Because Web services specifications are all applications of XML, the specifications themselves can be protected using these core XML technologies. For example, if you want to protect your WSDL files against unauthorized access, you can encrypt them. If you want to protect your WSDL files against tampering, you can sign them.

These specifications, along with SAML, XACML, and XKMS, are not specific to Web services because they are general to XML and are not specifically adapted to SOAP and WSDL the way the other specifications in this chapter are.

XML Signature defines how to verify that the contents of an XML document have not been tampered with and arrived unchanged from the way they were sent. XML Encryption describes how to encrypt all or part of any XML document so that only the intended recipient can understand it.

It's especially important to consider using these XML security technologies when the XML data needs to be protected outside the context of a SOAP message and when the Web services metadata needs to be protected from unauthorized access. WS-Security uses XML Signature and XML Encryption to help ensure confidentiality and integrity of SOAP messages, but it does not describe how to use these XML technologies outside the context of SOAP and WSDL, which may be important for some applications, especially those storing XML in a kind of intermediate format between transmissions. If a purchase order (PO) has to be stored in the middle of a business process, for example, XML

Encryption can be used to guard against unauthorized access to its contents, and XML Signature can be used by the next step in the business process to ensure that the PO has not been tampered with.

XML Encryption

Encryption of the XML payload when carried over HTTP can be accomplished using SSL, but sometimes that's not enough. When carrying XML over other transports, potentially over multiple transports, or when storing XML documents in a file or in a database, it is helpful or even necessary to have a specific mechanism for encrypting the XML documents.

When encrypting an XML element or element content, the EncryptedData element defined in the XML Encryption specification replaces the element or content (respectively) in the encrypted version of the XML document. As with many things related to XML, encryption works at any level of nesting. Either the entire document (except the encryption headers) or any element within it can be encrypted.

Selective encryption is useful when only part of a document needs to be kept private. It's possible to encrypt the tags as well as the data so that no one can see what the data is supposed to contain, such as hiding a <creditcard> tag within a <CipherData> tag.

For example:

```
<?xml version='1.0'?>
  <PaymentInfo xmlns='http://www.iona.com/artix/paymentService'>
    <Name>Eric Newcomer</Name>
    <CreditCard Limit='50,000' Currency='USD'>
      <Number>5555 5555 5555 5555</Number>
      <Issuer>Example Bank</Issuer>
      <Expiration>04/02</Expiration>
    </CreditCard>
  </PaymentInfo>

<?xml version='1.0'?>
  <PaymentInfo xmlns='http://www.iona.com/artix//paymentService'>
    <Name>Eric Newcomer</Name>
    <EncryptedData Type='http://www.w3.org/2001/04/xmlenc#Element'
    xmlns='http://www.w3.org/2001/04/xmlenc#'>
      <CipherData>
```

```
        <CipherValue>A23B45C56...</CipherValue>
      </CipherData>
    </EncryptedData>
  </PaymentInfo>
```

This example illustrates both plain and encrypted versions of the same data. Encrypted data is contained with the `CipherData` element. If an application requires all information to be encrypted, the whole document can be encrypted as an octet sequence. This applies to arbitrary data including XML documents. For example:

```
<?xml version='1.0'?>
<EncryptedData xmlns='http://www.w3.org/2001/04/xmlenc#'
  MimeType='text/xml'>
  <CipherData>
    <CipherValue>A23B45C56</CipherValue>
  </CipherData>
</EncryptedData>
```

The `<EncryptedData>` element can't be nested, but an `<EncryptedData>` tag can be used at the same level as another `<EncryptedData>` tag, causing already encrypted data to be encrypted again. This is convenient for developers who don't want to worry about the presence of another `<EncryptedData>` tag in the documents they're encrypting.

The `EncryptionMethod` is typically a secret key mechanism such as triple DES or RC4, or sometimes an RSA public key or similar algorithm, depending on the level of protection required.

A reference list contains all encrypted items within the document. A URI can be used to point to the encrypted data.

XML Signature
XML Signature[5] ensures that the provider knows that the part(s) of the document that have been signed haven't been changed between the time it was sent and received. The receiving application (such as a Web service provider) has no obligation to understand what's been signed, but if it can understand the signed

---

[5] XML Signature was developed jointly by the W3C and the IETF (RFC 2807, RFC 3275).

part of the document, it can use the signature to determine whether that part's contents are unaltered and to authenticate the document's author. Applications can sign multiple data objects, some of which may not be XML.

An XML Signature may be applied to the content of one or more parts within an XML document. Because XML documents can contain or reference binary objects and multimedia types, XML Signature has been designed to support those types of objects in addition to XML elements and attribtues.

A signed object is guaranteed by the presence of the signature either to be unaltered or to provide a mechanism for the receiver to determine whether or not the signed object has been tampered with.

The XML Signature associates a key with referenced data objects but does not specify how keys are associated with persons or institutions,[6] nor the meaning of the data being referenced and signed. Key management for XML Signature, as for other aspects of key-based security, is assumed to be handled by another technology, such as a key registry, XKMS application, or other directory service.

The data objects are canonicalized and digested before being sent. Digesting runs a hash algorithm over the data object, and canonicalization removes all white space and formats the document according to the canonicalization algorithm. You must canonicalize the data before signing it to ensure that you get the same results each time. Then you digest it and sign the digest:

```
<Signature ID?>
    <SignedInfo>
        <CanonicalizationMethod/>
        <SignatureMethod/>
        (<Reference URI? >
            (<Transforms>)?
            <DigestMethod>
            <DigestValue>
        </Reference>)+
    </SignedInfo>
    <SignatureValue>
    (<KeyInfo>)?
    (<Object ID?>)*
</Signature>
```

---

[6] Which is why WS-Security may be needed.

This example from the XML Signature specification illustrates the XML Signature syntax structure. The `<CanonicalizationMethod>` tag identifies the mechanism used for distilling the information.

Signatures are associated with data objects using URIs. Within an XML document, signatures are related to local data objects via fragment identifiers. Such local data can be included within a signature or can enclose a signature.

The specification defines a schema for capturing the result of a digital signature operation applied to arbitrary data. XML signatures add authentication, data integrity, and support for non-repudiation to the signed data.

XML Signature can be used to sign only specific portions of the XML tree rather than the complete document. This is important when a single XML document needs to be signed multiple times by a single or multiple parties. This flexibility can ensure the integrity of certain portions of an XML document, while leaving open the possibility for other portions of the document to change. Signature validation mandates that the data object that was signed be accessible to the party interested in the transaction. The XML signature must indicate the location of the original signed object.

Summary

Security is a complex field awash in technologies and protocols to meet an ever-growing series of threats to data and programs. Protecting data against unwanted access typically involves encrypting Web services messages, and a variety of options exist for doing so. It's important when selecting an option to determine compatibility with the services you're interacting with, and to ensure that the overall SOA supports a consistent technology, or set of technologies. Often, more than one encryption technology is needed to handle the variety of services arriving from a variety of sources in an SOA, and mechanisms are available for this purpose.

Protecting against unwanted access to programs and IT resources involves using potentially strong authentication techniques combined with authorization checks to restrict access to only those who need it. Again, a variety of technologies exist for authentication, and picking the right one or set is important for the smooth and efficient functioning of an SOA. When exposing services externally, it may be necessary to support a choice of authentication mechanisms for different consumers.

Whenever decisions are made concerning the selection of the most appropriate security technology, it's important to codify and formalize them in policies. A good security solution starts with a well-reasoned and thoroughly researched statement of policy. Web services provide mechanisms for expressing those policies in machine-readable form, but it's important to thoroughly document the overall security policy and the threats it's designed to guard against.

With security, it's easy to think that you never have enough, but striking the right balance is important because each security technology comes with a built-in performance penalty. The stronger the encryption, the more processing power it takes to encrypt and decrypt, for example. Use only as much security as you really need.

Chapter 9

Advanced Messaging

This chapter describes advanced messaging features, including reliable messaging and extended message exchange patterns for event notification and publish/subscribe. This chapter also covers advanced messaging techniques for mobile workers who operate under "occasionally connected" computing scenarios.

Reliable Messaging

One of the biggest obstacles to the adoption of Web services for some types of mission-critical applications is the use of unreliable network transports, such as HTTP, and the lack of reliable message delivery. By adopting a reliable messaging specification for Web services and adding reliability headers into SOAP messages, Web services can be used for a broader range of applications, and application development can be simplified.

Reliability for Web services is usually discussed with respect to messaging because HTTP is not a reliable communications transport in the way that more traditional middleware transports (such as WebSphere MQ and JMS) and B2B protocols (such as RosettaNet and EDI) are reliable. When Web services are used to replace or supplement traditional middleware, EAI, and B2B applications, a more reliable transport is typically among the application requirements.

Reliability for Web services is defined independently of the transport as a series of SOAP messages exchanged within a group or sequence and some processing rules governing the use of acknowledgments and message numbers to ensure that all the messages are received, that (optionally) duplicates are eliminated, and that (optionally) message ordering is preserved.

Of course, overall application reliability requires more than reliable messaging and messaging is only one part of a comprehensive solution. Security, transactions, and execution environments, such as clustering and redundant storage, may also have a role to play.

Overview

After you have defined your interoperability requirements, the data you want to share, and your requirements for reliably delivering the data, you can consider how to use the various SOAP MEPs to connect the systems. Whether reliable messaging is appropriate for a particular situation usually depends upon the business rules associated with the transactions or business processes at hand. Several business, administrative, and technical factors usually indicate that reliable messaging is needed (see the section "Concepts and Technologies").

Reliable messaging technology requires a piece of software infrastructure deployed on both ends of a connection. The reliable messaging agent handles errors in the transmission of messages from one computer to another over a (potentially unreliable) network. Typically, the agents are symmetrical implementations so that whatever is added to the processing of a message by the requester can be understood by the provider in the reciprocal processing needed to implement the reliability handshake.

The reliable messaging agent assigns a sequence ID to a group of related messages and message IDs to the individual messages within the group. The requester's agent marks the last message in the group, and the provider's agent returns an acknowledgment to indicate whether all messages in the group were received. If one or more message IDs is missing from the acknowledgment, the missing message (or messages) is re-sent until the provider's agent returns an acknowledgment containing all the message numbers in the group.

The sequence IDs and message IDs can also be used to prevent duplicate mes-sage processing and to require that messages be processed in the order they were sent, if that's important to the application. These numbers and associated processing options are included within SOAP headers. Reliable messaging mechanisms can be used with any SOAP MEP.

Figure 9-1 illustrates the basic architecture for reliable messaging: A reliability layer is introduced between the transport and the application that interprets and executes a series of message acknowledgments, typically working together with a persistence mechanism, to implement a reliability policy such as once-and-only-once guaranteed delivery. Acknowledgments let the SOAP requester know when the provider has received the message or set of messages and which ones were received. Persistence, although not typically defined by the Web services reliable messaging specifications, is necessary for achieving consistent reliability levels by storing the message in a file or database before and after sending it, and deleting the original only when the reliability layer acknowledges that it's been successfully transmitted to the receiver.

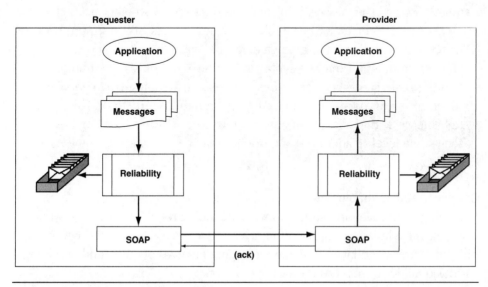

Figure 9-1   Reliable messaging architecture.

The two major specifications that define implementations of this architecture for Web services are:

- WS-ReliableMessaging.

- WS-Reliability.

Both specifications define a very similar set of features and functionality, and eventual consolidation or a mechanism to bridge the two is expected.

One Standard or Two?

When there are two (or sometimes more) specifications in a given area of functionality, such as reliability, it is natural to wonder which one will survive. As a general statement, specifications proposed by Microsoft and IBM tend to be the ones that most people want to implement. This is partly because they are good specifications but perhaps primarily because Microsoft and IBM have been leading the Web services movement since the beginning. But it's also very possible that multiple specifications will continue to exist, each gaining sufficient market share to remain in products for some time to come. This always brings up the question of whether it's better to merge the specifications or simply to create bridges and transformations when you need them to interoperate. It's all XML, after all, which is reasonably transformable from one syntax to another—but only if the transformation is purely syntactical and does not require mapping between slightly different capabilities. In the case of reliability, it looks like WS-ReliableMessaging is way out ahead. However, ebXML messaging has also seen some level of adoption, and bridges may be necessary in some cases.

Concepts and Technologies

Reliability can be defined at many levels, including reliability at the network layer, message layer, and application layer—here we are concerned with reliability at the message layer. Reliable messaging involves defining and providing various qualities of services for message delivery.

Traditionally, reliable messaging includes some or all of the following features:

- Guaranteed message delivery.

- Notification of message status.

- Duplicate elimination.

- Message ordering.

Standard SOAP over HTTP does not provide any of these qualities of services, and it does not provide any of the following delivery cardinality guarantees, which are also often desirable when reliable messaging is required:

- At least once.

- Once and only once.

- At most once.

- More than once.

By providing these qualities of service, reliable messaging is a natural fit for many types of systems, including the following:

- Transactions that do not require an immediate response (e.g., SubmitCustomerOrder).

- Application integration and data synchronization.

- B2B (business-to-business) integration.

- Portals for mobile and untethered users.

- Environments facing unreliable communication infrastructure.

Whether reliable messaging is appropriate for a particular situation usually depends upon the business rules or policies associated with the application or

business process. Several business, administrative, and technical factors typically indicate that reliable messaging is needed:

- **Business**—Reliable messaging may be required to help satisfy business
  rules, policies, or business agreements. For example, reliable messaging
  is important in B2B scenarios because the service-level agreements governing the relationship among the partners may impose penalties for lost
  orders.

- **Administrative**—Reliable messaging is often used when integrating systems under the control of different administrative organizations because
  the different administrators may not have the same schedules for taking
  systems offline for preventive maintenance. For example, requests to
  transfer patient data from a doctor to a hospital may be queued for
  transmission whenever the hospital system isn't fully loaded.

- **Technical**—Reliable messaging is often used to compensate for technical
  factors such as unreliable network connections—for example, delivering
  expense documents over the Internet from occasionally connected mobile devices to the corporate data center.

Many standards, technologies and products provide reliable messaging, such
as reliable file transfer, Electronic Data Interchange (EDI), MSMQ, WebSphere
MQ, Java Messaging Service (JMS), and ebXML messaging. Any of these environments could provide a good basis for implementing Web services reliable
messaging, and some usage patterns for Web services reliable messaging may
involve interoperability between two or more of these execution environments.

Guaranteed Message Delivery
In terms of messaging, reliability usually involves guaranteed message delivery in
the face of partial or complete system failure. A simple messaging system consists
of a sending application, a destination application, messaging agent software on
each computer, and a network connection between the two computers.

Reliable messaging guarantees that a message sent from the sending application
to the destination application will (eventually) arrive in spite of a temporary
failure of the messaging layer, of either of the computers, or of the network
connection.

Retries

A fundamental part of a reliable messaging solution involves persisting a message and providing the ability to retry a transmission should the service provider not return an acknowledgment within a specified period of time. A reasonable timeout is set depending on the network topology and the expected latency between the service requester and provider, perhaps from a few seconds to a few minutes. Retries open up the possibility that the same message may be sent more than once though, because the acknowledgments may not be received within the timeout window.

Message IDs

To help address message reliability requirements, messages are typically assigned unique ID numbers using UUIDs, GUIDs, URIs, or another similar mechanism. The IDs can be checked to ensure that all messages within a group are received, to correlate request and reply messages, to process messages in order (if desired), and to avoid processing duplicates.

Duplicate Elimination

Due to multiple retries, it's possible for the provider to receive duplicate messages. Therefore, a common feature of many reliable messaging systems is eliminating duplicate messages to provide at-most-once delivery semantics or to detect duplicates to ensure that a given message is processed only once.

For example, it is important to a bank customer that each and every DebitAccount transaction is delivered only once to the account-processing application because you don't want to debit the account twice.

Once-and-only-once delivery can be achieved by combining guaranteed message delivery (at-least-once delivery) and duplicate elimination (at-most-once delivery).

Message Ordering

Under normal conditions, it is possible for messages to be received out of order, especially when reliable messaging mechanisms are being used that retry message transmission. For a variety of applications, it is convenient or mandatory that messages be received or processed in the order in which they were sent.

For example, stock trading systems are obligated to process purchases in the order that they were received. For this reason, a common feature of many reliable messaging systems is a sequence number that delivers or processes messages in the same order they were sent.

Message ordering is orthogonal to guaranteed message delivery and duplicate elimination, and it can be offered along with either or both of them. However, the combination of guaranteed messaging and ordering is the only way to guarantee that all messages will be received and processed in the right order.

Message Priority

Normally, messages are delivered on a first-come-first-served basis. For a variety of applications, it is convenient or mandatory that messages be received in priority order. For this reason, a common feature of many reliable messaging systems is delivering messages in priority order, in which a message field or some destination-defined criterion (such as sender ID) defines the priority. Although this feature is not directly required for reliable transmission, many messaging systems provide it because it may be important to the application's view of reliability.

Message Status

This is a facility that allows applications to query the status of reliable messages and determine, at a minimum, if they were received and when they were received.

Message status is essential for business users, customer service representatives, and system administrators who need to review and report upon the status of a transaction. For example, a bank customer may need a reply to indicate that a deposit was processed and the funds are available for paying a bill.

Message Correlation

This is a facility that allows applications to correlate response messages with request messages. Many RPC-oriented technologies provide this facility as a built-in or automatic feature. Because the core Web services standards do not define how to automatically correlate request and reply messages, an extended specification is necessary.

Reply Address

This is a facility that allows a sending application to specify for a destination application where any response messages should be sent. This is typically handled using WS-Addressing.

Benefits of Reliable Messaging

The introduction of reliable messaging technologies can achieve significant benefits for applications, including:

- **Looser coupling**—In general, the availability of reliable messaging technology at the SOAP level reduces the coupling between systems. Without reliable messaging, the requester and provider applications would have to know intimate details of each other's implementations (such as how they handle message acknowledgments) and implement reliable messaging at the application level.

  When the requester and provider applications don't need to be aware of each other's implementation details, it's easier to change either the requester or provider application without affecting the other.

- **Simpler application code due to separation of concerns**—Reliable messaging makes it much easier to separate the business logic in the application code from the underlying qualities of service that are required to satisfy the business requirements. Without reliable messaging, the application code must include specialized non-business logic to replace the reliable messaging layer. Pushing this layer into the infrastructure makes the application easier to develop and maintain.

- **Simpler administration**—When integrating systems under the control of different administrative organizations, reliable messaging is often used to allow the administrators of the respective organizations to take their systems offline for preventive maintenance without directly affecting the other systems.

- **Enables asynchronous communication**—Reliable messaging can be useful when no synchronous connection is available between the requester application and the provider application, or when a synchronous connection is lost due to computer or network failure. Reliable messaging allows asynchronous communication to operate with a high degree of autonomy while guaranteeing that messages will be delivered eventually, providing a useful alternate communications path when synchronous connections are unavailable.

- **Ensures transport independence**—Defining reliable messaging at the SOAP level allows the reliable quality of service to be defined in a transport-independent fashion. If the underlying transport changes (e.g., from WebSphere MQ to HTTP), the quality of service is maintained, and the application code is unaffected.

  Considerable code refactoring would be necessary if an application was first written to send SOAP over WebSphere MQ (relying on WebSphere MQ facilities such as persistent message queuing for providing reliable messaging), but then had to be modified to provide exactly the same reliable messaging features using HTTP (implementing its own message persistence scheme).

- **Compensates for unreliable networks**—Many applications operate over unreliable networks (such as the Internet), and reliable messaging can alleviate the complexity associated with building these types of applications.

Using WS-ReliableMessaging, WS-Reliability, or ebXML messaging solutions with SOAP can help achieve these benefits for SOA-based applications.

Usage Scenarios for Reliable Messaging

Figure 9-2 illustrates some of the most common usage scenarios for reliable messaging.

Long-Running Business Transactions (#1 in Figure 9-2)

Many business transactions take hours or days to complete and do not require an immediate response. For example:

- **SubmitCustomerOrder**—Fulfilling the customer's order may take hours or days, and no immediate response is expected, except an acknowledgment that the order has been successfully submitted.

- **ApproveInsuranceClaim**—Approving an insurance claim usually involves several people in different departments (or different institutions) who are responsible for reviewing and approving different aspects of the insurance claim. This process can take hours or days.

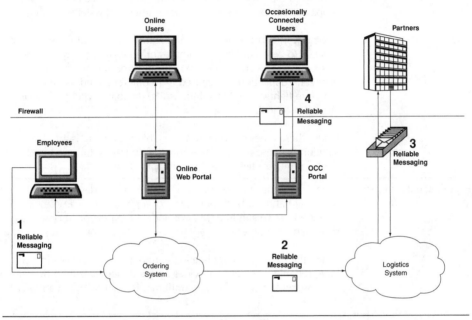

Figure 9-2   Usage scenarios for reliable messaging.

Reliable messaging provides the guaranteed delivery facilities that ensure that these types of business transactions will be delivered to the appropriate system without requiring the customer or employee to wait until the transaction is complete and also ensure that the answers are returned.

These types of transactions are also ideal candidates for Web services orchestration (see Chapter 6, "SOA and Business Process Management").

Application Integration and Data Synchronization (#2 in Figure 9-2)
Asynchronous reliable messaging is a key enabler for application integration. To understand why, we first must review some of the key application integration challenges and how reliable messaging fits into the overall solution (see Table 9-1).

Table 9-1   **Integration Challenges and Role of Reliable Messaging**

Integration Challenge	Role of Reliable Messaging
Data synchronization	A common integration scenario is data synchronization across applications. For example, a call center agent updates a customer's address in the CRM application, and this data needs to be propagated to ordering systems and fulfillment systems.
	Typically, this sort of data synchronization is not real-time—rather, it needs to be completed in minutes or hours (but not necessarily in seconds). This sort of data synchronization might take place between applications purchased from different vendors, and therefore tightly coupled solutions like database synchronization are not practical.
	Under these types of conditions, reliable messaging is an ideal solution because it guarantees that the update is delivered but does not require tight coupling of applications.
Handling data bursts	Data synchronization scenarios like the one just described and ones that handle a burst of orders (for a popular new DVD, for example) may result in a flood of update requests occurring in a short period of time.
	When the destination application cannot process updates in real time, reliable messaging provides an ideal mechanism for flow control and buffering the data until the destination application can process it.
Batch/bulk data operations	It often makes sense to batch up large numbers of updates and send them to remote sites as bulk data transfers. Reliable messaging is ideal for this type of scenario because you can capture the data once and forward it many times.
	For example, this issue would be relevant to a global electronics manufacturer that has call centers around the world, chip fabrication sites in the Far East, and regional headquarters in the U.S. and Europe because they must ensure that certain updates to planning applications occur at each site.
Administrative boundaries	Data synchronization scenarios like the one just described often take place across departmental and administrative boundaries.
	In these cases, the source and destination departments may use different run-time platforms (e.g., .NET Framework versus mainframe) from different vendors, and reliable messaging using SOAP can be used to bridge these differences, to ensure that the systems do not become tightly coupled, and to allow the different departments to evolve their infrastructures independently.

Business-to-Business Integration (#3 in Figure 9-2)

Asynchronous communication and reliable messaging are key enablers for B2B activities and supply chain management systems. These applications face numerous challenges that are difficult to solve using the standard SOAP over HTTP approach, including:

- The sending application and destination application are administered by different organizations.

- There are no guarantees that the sending application and destination application will be online and operating simultaneously.

- Interoperability is required because different development teams have developed the sending application and destination application.

- Business is often conducted over the Internet, which is an inherently unreliable communication network.

Although reliable messaging provides the guaranteed delivery required for B2B interactions, the WS-Reliability and WS-ReliableMessaging specifications do not define any of the extended functionality normally required for successful B2B, such as the following:

- Security (encryption, integrity, non-repudiation, and so on).

- Process management.

For B2B scenarios, it may be necessary to combine reliable messaging with other extended technologies such as WS-Security and WS-BPEL.

Mobile Workers and Occasionally Connected Users (#4 in Figure 9-2)

Advances in wireless networks (such as Wi-Fi) are creating a new class of occasionally connected mobile workers who need to access enterprise systems across the Internet but who are not well-served by existing browser-based systems.

Reliable messaging is a key enabler for Occasionally Connected Computing (OCC) because OCC requires guaranteed delivery of documents over potentially unreliable and intermittent connections. Reliable messaging simplifies the development of OCC solutions by masking the distinction between being connected or disconnected and between different open protocols such as HTTP, FTP, and SMTP that are often used for OCC systems.

Web Services Reliable Messaging Specifications

The WS-ReliableMessaging and WS-Reliability specifications are very similar and offer comparable levels of features and functionality. They both use SOAP headers to exchange message grouping and identification information between requester and provider so that their respective implementations of the reliability layer can guarantee message delivery, eliminate duplicates, and preserve message order. Both specifications strongly recommend the use of WS-Security to sign the reliability headers.

Why Are There Two Reliability Specifications?

There are two reliability specifications because of competition in the specification writing process. Oracle, Sun, and others got tired of waiting for Microsoft and IBM to address the problem, so they published WS-Reliability and submitted it to OASIS. Later, Microsoft, IBM, BEA, and others completed WS-ReliableMessaging and published it, but as of this writing, it still has not been submitted to a standards body. The specifications are actually more similar than different, making it likely that one of them will win out in the end. The IBM and Microsoft specifications are most often the winners in these competitions, but competition can be good, especially when it furthers the goals of achieving an open specification process.

The WS-ReliableMessaging and WS-Reliability specifications described in this section do not interoperate.

WS-ReliableMessaging

The Web Services Reliable Messaging Protocol (WS-ReliableMessaging) was originally published in March 2003[1] by BEA, IBM, Microsoft, and Tibco

---

[1] And updated in March 2004.

Software. WS-ReliableMessaging is designed to work in combination with other specifications to provide secure, reliable, transacted Web services.

The namespace for WS-ReliableMessaging is as follows:

```
xmlns:wsrm="http://schemas.xmlsoap.org/ws/2004/03/rm"
```

Therefore, in SOAP messages, the prefix wsrm identifies the reliable messaging header.

Action URIs for WS-ReliableMessaging have the following format:

```
http://schemas.xmlsoap.org/ws/2004/03/rm/SequenceAcknowledgment
```

Action URIs can be interpreted by servlets or other action URI APIs to perform an action associated with the URI, such as the SequenceAcknowledge command, which directly follows the slash (/) character of the namespace URI and directs the provider to immediately return an acknowledgment. Other ReliableMessaging commands can also be used.

Reliable messaging systems use message IDs, sequence numbers, acknowledgments, and retransmission when messages are lost. For example, here's an extract of a SOAP header that includes reliable messaging information:

```
<wsrm:SequenceNum number="0" status="Start"
   Expires="2005-02-02T03:00:33-31:00" />
<wsu:Identifier>
   www.iona.com/artix/examples/reliability
</wsu:Identifier>
<wsrm:MessageNumber> 3 </wsrm:MessageNumber>
<wsrm:LastMessage/>
...
</wsrm:SequenceNum>
```

This example uses the reliable messaging namespace wsrm and illustrates the concepts of message ID (using a URI derived from www.iona.com), message number, and sequence number.

WS-ReliableMessaging syntax and semantics allow Web service implementa-tions to provide several types of message delivery guarantees:

- **At most once**—Meaning that messages will be delivered without dupli-cation, although some messages might not be delivered.

- **At least once**—Meaning that messages will be delivered at least once, but possibly more than once.

- **Exactly once**—Meaning that messages will be delivered once and only once, without duplication.

- **In order**—Meaning that messages will be delivered in the order in which they were sent by the requester.

These assurances are based on what the reliability layer will provide to the application in the way of reliable messaging guarantees.

For WS-ReliableMessaging to work, both the requester and the provider have to implement the reliability layer, and the requester needs to be able to obtain a valid endpoint reference for the reliability layer on the provider's node (using WSDL or WS-Addressing). The requester also must understand and be able to generate messages conforming to the reliability policy stated by the provider (using WS-Policy)—in other words, the requester needs to be able to obtain the provider's metadata that includes the reliability policy.

The requester generates a unique sequence ID and assigns message numbers in whole integers, incremented by one, starting with 1. Acknowledgments returned from the provider must include the message numbers of messages received and must exclude the message numbers of any messages not received.

The requester initiates a reliable message exchange by sending a SOAP message with a sequence header. For example:

```
<wsrm:Sequence>
<wsu:Identifier>
   http://www.iona.com/artix/examples/bank/aaa
</wsu:Identifier>
```

```
<wsrm:MessageNumber>
   5
</wsrm:MessageNumber>
<wsrm:LastMessage/>
</wsrm:Sequence>
```

The Sequence requires a unique URI for the entire sequence (no matter how many messages might be in the sequence) and a message number for each message within the sequence. The last message in the sequence also must have a LastMessage element. In this case, the sequence has five messages, and the reliability layer will send an acknowledgment after it receives all of the messages. For example:

```
<wsrm:SequenceAcknowledgment>
<wsu:Identifier>
   http://www.iona.com/artix/examples/bank/aaa
</wsu:Identifier>
<wsrm:AcknowledgmentRange Upper="5" Lower="1"/>
</wsrm:SequenceAcknowledgment>
```

This acknowledgment means that the provider has received all five messages in the sequence and the requester can forget about this sequence. If the provider returned an acknowledgment indicating that a message in the sequence was not received, the requester would retransmit that message. For example:

```
<wsrm:SequenceAcknowledgment>
<wsu:Identifier>
   http://www.iona.com/artix/examples/bank/aaa
</wsu:Identifier>
<wsrm:AcknowledgmentRange Upper="2" Lower="1"/>
  <wsrm:AcknowledgmentRange Upper="5" Lower="4"/>
</wsrm:SequenceAcknowledgment>
```

This acknowledgment message indicates that the provider did not receive message 3, and therefore, the requester will retransmit.

The provider returns another acknowledgment following the retransmission. For example:

```
<wsrm:SequenceAcknowledgment>
<wsu:Identifier>
   http://www.iona.com/artix/examples/bank/aaa
</wsu:Identifier>
```

```
<wsrm:AcknowledgmentRange Upper="2" Lower="1"/>
  <wsrm:AcknowledgmentRange Upper="5" Lower="3"/>
</wsrm:SequenceAcknowledgment>
```

This acknowledgment indicates that all messages in the sequence were received, indicating the end of this particular reliable message exchange, which allows the reliability layers to clean up temporarily stored messages.

WS-ReliableMessaging provides some additional options for the requester and provider. A timeout can be set for the sequence to expire. In other words, if the protocol doesn't complete within the timeout period, the timeout value effectively completes the protocol by timing it out. This is to prevent situations in which the requester may endlessly retransmit a failed message due to a processing error on the provider side or some other unrecoverable networking error (such as an invalid TCP address or a server failure).

A requester may request an immediate acknowledgment response message at any point without waiting for the provider to send one by sending an <AckRequested> message to the provider (that is, a SOAP header containing the <AckRequested> element). For example:

```
<wsrm:AckRequested ...>
<wsu:Identifier>
    http://www.iona.com/artix/examples/bank/aaa
</wsu:Identifier>
<wsrm:MessageNumber>
    5
</wsrm:MessageNumber>
...
</wsrm:AckRequested>
```

The <AckRequested> element must include the sequence ID and the highest message number sent within the sequence.

The provider can also send a negative acknowledgment to shortcut the normal acknowledgment process and eliminate some network traffic. The provider has the option to send the requester a message stating that a certain message number was not received. For example:

```
<wsrm:SequenceAcknowledgment>
<wsu:Identifier>
```

```
   http://www.iona.com/artix/examples/bank/aaa
</wsu:Identifier>
<wsrm:Nack>
   3
<wsrm:Nack/>
</wsrm:SequenceAcknowledgment>
```

The provider has been keeping track of the message numbers received, and after it detected that message 3 was missing, it decided to send a negative acknowledgment to the requester to notify the requester to immediately retransmit rather than waiting for a timeout to expire.

WS-ReliableMessaging optionally allows the provider to manage the sequence instead of the requester, which saves an acknowledgment message at the end of the protocol because the provider doesn't have to tell itself when it has received all the messages in the sequence.

The WS-Policy framework defines policy assertions for a service provider implementing WS-ReliableMessaging. In particular, the provider can assert:

- The specification version supported. (When new versions of WS-ReliableMessaging are published, requesters and providers will have a way to discover if they both support the same version of the specification.)

- Whether the provider is going to be responsible for creating the sequences (that is, whether the requester or provider will have to create the initial sequence URI and manage acknowledgments for ensuring that the sequence is completed).

- An expiration value to set the potential duration of the message exchange.

- A timeout value for canceling the message exchange if there's no activity within the specified period.

- A retransmission interval after which the requester will automatically retransmit a message if no acknowledgment is received.

- An acknowledgment interval that sets the delay before returning an acknowledgment message after receiving messages in a sequence.

These optional policies are attached to individual sequences or to sequences according to a match on a common URI prefix using the `<SequenceRef>` expression to reference a policy attachment. Policies can be discovered using WS-MetadataExchange (see Chapter 7, "Metadata Management," for further information on policies and metadata discovery).

WS-ReliableMessaging defines `faultcodes` to be returned using the SOAP fault mechanism. WS-ReliableMessaging headers require the `MustUnderstand` header flag to be set to true.

Some of the features in WS-ReliableMessaging, such as message ordering, do not require an acknowledgment to be returned to the requester. In that case, there's an option to set the protocol to poll on the requester side, which means that the provider will not automatically return an acknowledgment unless specifically asked to do so.

The WS-ReliableMessaging specification recommends the use of WS-Security for signing the headers and body.

Web Services Reliability
The Web Services Reliability (WS-Reliability) specification was released in January 2003 by Fujitsu, Hitachi, NEC, Oracle, Sonic Software, and Sun Microsystems and subsequently was submitted to the OASIS Web Services Reliable Messaging Technical Committee.[2] WS-Reliability borrows concepts from ebXML messaging but is specifically adapted for use with Web services.

Like WS-ReliableMessaging, the WS-Reliability specification defines a protocol for exchanging SOAP messages with guaranteed delivery (including a system of acknowledgments and retransmissions) that supports the elimination of duplicate messages and guarantees message ordering using sequence numbers. Like most extended Web services features, WS-Reliability defines SOAP header extensions and contains a binding to HTTP.

---

[2] WS-Reliability 1.1 was released in August 2004.

The namespace for WS-Reliability is as follows:

```
http://docs.oasis-open.org/wsrm/2004/06/ws-reliability-1.1.xsd
```

WS-Reliability works very similarly to WS-ReliableMessaging. Instead of a sequence, WS-Reliability has a group, but they function the same. Both have message numbers. WS-Reliability uses a different XML syntax and supports some different options. For example:

```
<Request
  xmlns="http://docs.oasis-open.org/wsrm/2004/06/ws-reliability-
  ➡1.1.xsd"
  xmlns:soap="http://schemas.xmlsoap.org/soap/envelope/"
  soap:mustUnderstand="1">
<MessageId groupId="mid://20040202.103832@wsr-sender.org">
  <SequenceNum number="0"
   groupExpiryTime="2005-02-02T03:00:33-31:00" />
</MessageId>
<ExpiryTime>2004-09-07T03:01:03-03:50</ExpiryTime>
<ReplyPattern>
  <Value>Response</Value>
</ReplyPattern>
<AckRequested/>
<DuplicateElimination/>
<MessageOrder/>
</Request>
```

This example shows a WS-Reliability message for SOAP 1.1, including the `mustUnderstand` true header, a message `groupID`, and a `SequenceNum` starting with 0 (meaning it's the first message in the group).

The example illustrates the WS-Reliability options for message expiration in addition to the group expiration, a specific request for an acknowledgment message, and the elimination of any duplicate messages that might be received. Also, the message order is to be preserved, meaning message processing doesn't start until all messages have been received and put in their proper order. WS-Reliability provides acknowledgment indicating not only that the provider received the message, but also that the provider processed it. Here is the response:

```
<Response
    xmlns="http://docs.oasis-open.org/wsrm/2004/06/ws-reliability-
    ➡1.1.xsd"
    xmlns:soap="http://schemas.xmlsoap.org/soap/envelope/"
```

```
    soap:mustUnderstand="1" replyPattern="Callback">
    <NonSequenceReply groupId="mid://20040202.103832@
    ➥oasis-open.org" />
    <NonSequenceReply groupId="mid://20040202.103811@oasis-open.org"
       fault="wsrm:PermanentProcessingFailure" />
    <SequenceReplies groupId="mid://20040202.103807
    ➥@oasis-open.org/">
       <ReplyRange from="1" to="4" />
       <ReplyRange from="5" to="5" fault="wsrm:InvalidRequest" />
       <ReplyRange from="6" to="42" />
    </SequenceReplies>
</Response>
```

The response indicates which messages arrived and which did not and includes a fault message within the WS-Reliability header indicating that a fault occurred when processing message 5. WS-Reliability provides extended options for fault handling beyond what is defined for WS-ReliableMessaging, but it does not define how to map its faults to the SOAP fault mechanism.

Some of the features in WS-Reliability, such as duplication elimination and message ordering, do not require an acknowledgment to be returned to the requester, and in that case, there's an option to set the protocol to "poll" on the requester side, which means that the provider will not automatically return an acknowledgment unless specifically asked to do so.

WS-Reliability defines how to use SOAP with Attachments (a feature shared with ebXML messaging), which WS-ReliableMessaging does not. WS-Reliability explicitly supports request/response and callback MEPs, while WS-ReliableMessaging relies on external addressing information (such as that provided by WSDL or WS-Addressing).

When there's only one message in a group, the group ID can be used as the message ID. When there's more than one message in a group, the message ID consists of the group ID plus the message number.

The following requirements are supported:

- At-least-once delivery.

- At-most-once delivery.

- Duplicate elimination, or exactly once delivery.

- Guaranteed message ordering.

In other words, WS-Reliability supports the same delivery assertions that WS-ReliableMessaging supports.

ebXML Messaging Service

ebXML, sponsored by the United Nations Centre for Trade Facilitation and Electronic Business (UN/CEFACT) and OASIS, defines an open XML-based architecture and a suite of specifications that enables enterprises to conduct complex business-to-business (B2B) scenarios.

Isn't ebXML Dead Yet?

Web services now pretty much replace everything that ebXML provides, but because the extended specifications are taking some time to mature, and because few products are available that implement them, people are turning back to ebXML for another look. And ebXML hasn't been standing still, either. The messaging and registry functions have both improved considerably. The original vision of ebXML was part of its problem—it was too much of a stretch to imagine that you could really derive all you needed to generate a B2B interaction by defining a high-level process flow. In fact, the original ebXML idea was to decide first on the documents to be exchanged between companies (remember that ebXML was conceived as a replacement for EDI), and then by capturing the flow of the exchange, everything else could be automatically generated down to the physical implementation level. This was just too grand a scheme, no matter how interesting or plausible it sounded. But after everyone realized that this grandiose dream wasn't going to happen, they started focusing more on the bits and pieces of ebXML that could still add value in the Web services-dominated world. ebXML does use SOAP, so there is a common foundation, but the similarities often end there. But while the world waited for WS-ReliableMessaging to be completed and submitted to a standards body, ebXML messaging was progressing toward V2 and toward some (although limited) adoption. The

continues

longer it takes for Web services specifications to get into standards bodies, the more opportunity there will be for ebXML, especially its reliable, secure messaging and more functional registry.

The primary objective of the ebXML Message Service (ebMS) is to facilitate the exchange of electronic business messages within the ebXML framework. However, ebMS can be used independently of the rest of the ebXML specifications, and often it is. The ebMS is a set of extensions to SOAP and SOAP with Attachments that provides for secure and reliable communications over any available communications protocol. The ebMS specification includes bindings for HTTP and SMTP.

ebMS directly uses the SOAP-defined mechanism for extensibility. The following is a partial list of the SOAP header extensions, which are defined by ebMS for reliable messaging:

- **From and To**—These elements are useful for identifying the originator and intended recipient of the message.

- **ConversationId**—The ConversationId element is a string identifying the set of related messages that make up a conversation between two applications. It is used during long-running business transactions where multiple messages are being exchanged so that both parties can uniquely identify the business transaction that a particular message is related to.

- **MessageData (MessageId, Timestamp, TimeToLive)**—The ebMS layer uses the MessageData elements to implement guaranteed message delivery and to indicate when a message is stale and should be ignored.

- **DuplicateElimination**—The DuplicateElimination element is used by the sending application to guarantee that duplicate messages are suppressed.

In addition, ebMS uses the SOAP Messages with Attachments specification for packaging the business documents (or payload) and each business document in a separate MIME part, which are considered attachments to the SOAP envelope.

Comparing the Specifications

Table 9-2 shows a side-by-side comparison of the Web services specifications for reliable messaging.

Table 9-2   Comparison of Web Services Specifications for Reliable Messaging

	ebXML Message Service	WS-Reliability	WS-ReliableMessaging
Standards body	OASIS	OASIS	No
Guaranteed delivery	Yes	Yes	Yes
Duplicate elimination	Yes	Yes	Yes
Message ordering	Yes	Yes	Yes
Message status	Yes	Yes	No
Application-level message correlation	No	No	No
SOAP binding defined in spec	Yes	Yes	Yes
HTTP binding defined in spec	Yes	Yes	No
SMTP binding defined in spec	Yes	No	No
Error handling		Yes	SOAP faults
Security	Persistent digital signature Non-persistent authentication Persistent signed receipt Non-persistent integrity Persistent confidentiality Non-persistent confidentiality Persistent authorization Non-persistent authorization Trusted timestamp	Defers to other specifications, including WS-Security	Defers to WS-Security

continues

Table 9-2 **Comparison of Web Services Specifications for Reliable Messaging (continues)**

	ebXML Message Service	WS-Reliability	WS-ReliableMessaging
Policy assertions	Uses Collaboration Protocol Profile and Collaboration Protocol Agreement as defined by the ebXML Collaboration Protocol Profile and Agreement Specification	No	Leverages WS-Policy family of specifications

Comparing Web Services Reliable Messaging and Asynchronous Message Queuing

Asynchronous message queuing is one of the cornerstones of integration and EAI. It is interesting to compare the WS-ReliableMessaging specification to IBM's WebSphere MQ to understand the differences between the reliable messaging technologies designed for Web services-based interoperability, SOA, and BPM solutions and a more traditional, single-technology middleware system (see Table 9-3). It's important to understand features that are not present in Web services technologies when designing interoperability solutions.

Table 9-3 **Comparison of WebSphere MQ and WS-ReliableMessaging**

Integration Feature	WebSphere MQ	WS-ReliableMessaging
Core abstraction	Queues	Messages
Guaranteed delivery	Yes	Yes
Duplicate elimination	Yes	Yes
Message ordering	Yes	Yes
Interface/contract definition	None	WSDL and SOAP headers
Interface/contract registry	None	UDDI and WS-MetadataExchange
Message format	Unstructured ASCII or EBCDIC message buffer.	SOAP message headers

Integration Feature	WebSphere MQ	WS-ReliableMessaging
Message id	Yes—Message id attribute.	Yes
Correlation id	Yes—Correlation id attribute and various policies for generating correlation ids.	Yes
Reply address	Yes—Reply Queue attribute.	Yes
Message priority	Yes—Priority attribute can be used to receive messages in priority order.	No
Transactional queuing	Yes—Messages can be processed in a transaction to ensure it is handled as part of an atomic operation.	Combine with WS-AtomicTransactions
Message status and reporting	Yes—Sender can specify reporting options and be notified when a message arrives, is delivered, expires, and so on.	Yes—partial
Undeliverable messages	Yes—Deadletter queues.	No
Application activation	Yes—Trigger queues.	No
Security	Limited support for user name and password.	WS-Security
Administration	Yes—Complete set of administrative and management tools, some provided by third parties.	No—out of scope
Cross-vendor interoperability	None	Open specification for interoperability across vendors

This comparison illustrates that Web services reliable messaging technologies do not define administrative functions or provide for dead letter services (i.e., they do not define error queues) and do not provide hooks for application activation. This is of course an "apples to oranges" comparison between a product that could be used to provide an implementation of an interoperability specification and a proprietary product implementation of messaging technology, but it is interesting to note where the line is drawn between multivendor interoperability solutions and single-vendor value-added features.

One of the reasons for this is that the definition of persistence is out of scope for the Web services specifications, even though implementations of reliable messaging need to persist messages to meet the required behavior. This illustrates the principle in specifications of ensuring compatibility across multiple implementations by abstracting the definition of the syntax and the required behavior from any specific implementation environment.

Notification

Notification provides a mechanism to publish messages about events so that subscribers can retrieve them independently of any relationship between provider and requester. Notification is a feature of many current distributed computing systems, including message-oriented middleware (MOM) and CORBA.

For example, a failure in a telephone-switching element generates an event that is passed to the notification system to post a message to a topic to which a network management console subscribes. When the message is received, the network management console knows to take corrective action. A connection is not required between the telephone-switching element and the management console in order to send the message notifying the management console of the failure.

The separation between requester and provider allows a provider to send a message based on a defined trigger and the requester to monitor a topic for messages relevant to it, while other requesters monitor other topics they're concerned with.

Notification systems often include the use of an intermediary (such as an event broker or temporary storage channels) to which the message can be sent for later (i.e., asynchronous) retrieval by the consumer. Notification systems do not always require an intermediary, however, because the message providers can also support the temporary storage requirements necessary for an implementation.

For Web services, two notification specifications are proposed:

- **WS-Eventing**—By BEA, Computer Associates, IBM, Microsoft, Sun, and Tibco Software.
- **WS-Notification**—Submitted to the OASIS WS-Notification Technical Committee by Akami Technologies, IBM, Tibco Software, Fujitsu Software, SAP, Sonic Software, Computer Associates, Globus, and HP.

WS-Eventing is much smaller than WS-Notification (which is actually three specifications) and includes only very basic publish/subscribe technology. WS-Notification is part of a larger effort by IBM and others to provide messaging and resource management technologies for grid computing based on Web services.

Both specifications rely upon WS-Addressing for the format of the endpoint references.

Why Did Microsoft and IBM Split over Notification?

The spilt over the notification specification represents the first (and only) time since IBM and Microsoft seriously started collaborating on specifications[3] that the two Web services leaders went their separate ways. The best explanation is probably a difference of opinion over the importance of Web services for grid computing. Unlike IBM, Microsoft is not very active in promoting the use of Web services for grid computing. The fact that WS-Notification is being proposed as a part of a larger effort (Web Services Resource Framework) around the grid would tend to make WS-Notification less attractive to vendors for whom the grid is not a high priority. In addition, however, WS-Notification is considerably more complex. Since the

continues

---

[3] Microsoft and IBM had originally proposed different solutions for service description and orchestration before combining them into WSDL and WS-BPEL, respectively. But since those events, IBM and Microsoft had joined forces on every other specification until notification.

initial publication of WS-Eventing, a new version was published that included IBM (and Sun) among the authors. However, as of this writing, the two specifications remain separate, and no clear reason has been given other than the rationale that one is complex (WS-Notification) and the other simple (WS-Eventing).

WS-Eventing

WS-Eventing is a simple specification that defines how to subscribe to a notification message, including a protocol for generating a confirmation response to a subscription request.

For example:

```
<wsa:Action>
 http://schemas.xmlsoap.org/ws/2004/01/eventing/Subscribe
</wsa:Action>

<wsa:ReplyTo>
<wsa:Address>
 http://www.iona.com/Newcomer/StockOptions
</wsa:Address>
</wsa:ReplyTo>
```

This simple example illustrates the WS-Eventing namespace wsa and the action to subscribe to an event (not shown) that, when it occurs, is published to Newcomer's event sink for stock option notices.

More than these simple headers are involved in notifications. The notification actions are modeled as an exchange of SOAP messages to set up and confirm the subscription, and then a second set of SOAP MEPs (either broadcast or publish/subscribe, depending on how the notification actions are defined) executes the subscription fulfillment when an event occurs that causes an event to be published to the topic.

WS-Notification

WS-Notification is the name for a family of three specifications that are being developed within the Web Services Resource Framework (WSRF) set of specifications. WSRF is centered on the concept of providing references to data and related resources such as persistent storage mechanisms. The WS-Notification specifications define simple to complex mechanisms for tying events to messages. The specifications include:

- **WS-BaseNotification**—Defines interfaces for notification providers and requesters (called *producers* and *consumers* in the specification) and defines related MEPs. This specification covers the simple notification use case of point-to-point notification. This is the core specification on which the others depend.

- **WS-Topics**—Defines the *topics* mechanism, which is a way to categorize and organize subscriptions for different types of information (i.e., different message types). WS-Topics adds to WS-BaseNotification various use cases for publish/subscribe MEPs and specifies an XML model for metadata associated with pub/sub services.

- **WS-BrokeredNotification**—Defines the interface for a notification broker, which is an intermediary that manages the point-to-point and publish/subscribe MEPs.

Altogether, WS-Notification defines a complete notification system, supporting various MEPs such as point-to-point and publish/subscribe, along with interface definitions for a topics mechanism and a broker.

Mobile Workers and Occasionally Connected Computing

Dramatic advances in wireless connectivity and the availability of laptop computers and hand-held devices is sparking a mobile workforce revolution, which is prompting organizations to look for ways to improve the productivity of mobile workers. Now, an entire population of sales representatives, consultants, field technical specialists, and other mobile workers carry computers as part of their jobs.

Here are some of the key challenges faced by organizations trying to improve the productivity of mobile users and untethered workers:

- Occasional connectivity because the worker may be outside of the range of the wireless network for hours or days. In fact, the worker may spend more time disconnected from the network than connected to the network.

- Temporary network failures due to unreliable network connections and spotty network coverage.

- Multiple connection speeds as workers connect via broadband, Wi-Fi, and dial-up.

Because of these factors, it is difficult to extend existing business processes, enterprise applications, and web portals to the unique needs of mobile users and untethered workers. Today, most applications for mobile users are designed with the assumption that they are wired into the network. Switching to a connected/disconnected model, which today's hardware and wireless connectivity capabilities allow, causes these applications to show erratic behavior and does not support the users' requirements.

These applications also typically assume that the mobile user will rely on a thin client—a laptop application, like a Web browser or an email package, with limited functionality—for all interactions with corporate IT systems. Unfortunately, thin-client UIs are poorly suited to supporting mobile workers because they assume that all information can be accessed via a Web server. A mobile worker needs the information stored on her laptop so that she can access it when she is not connected to the network.

Occasionally Connected Computing (OCC) refers to the technical infrastructure required to improve the productivity of mobile users and untethered workers. Here are some of the key elements required for supporting OCC:

- **Reliable, asynchronous messaging**—OCC requires reliable, guaranteed delivery of documents over potentially unreliable and intermittent connections.

- **Intelligent, adaptable messaging**—OCC solutions must be able to adapt their behavior in response to connection status and network speed. Some issues include automatically starting data transfers when connections are detected, resuming unexpectedly interrupted data transfers, and throttling data transfers when network traffic is heavy. Currently, none of the Web services standards address adaptive messaging.

- **Open standards**—Open standards are required for OCC because OCC solutions need to operate across a wide variety of public and private networks and need to interoperate with different products from different vendors. Reliable messaging using SOAP over FTP or SOAP over SMTP combines open standards with the store-and-forward approach needed for OCC.

OCC solutions help mobile workers in the following ways:

- They mask the distinction between being connected and disconnected, allowing mobile workers to make full use of their occasionally connected computers and productive use of down time.

- They eliminate the latency problem of Web-based applications—where users spend most of their time waiting for information to appear—by automatically exchanging content and data whenever a connection is detected.

- They exhibit great flexibility and adaptability by shifting the computing burden from enterprise servers to the mobile workers' own machines.

- They provide intelligent, reliable connectivity, with the ability to sense the type and speed of the connection and transmit documents when appropriate.

Summary

Reliable messaging is one of the cornerstones of SOA and BPM integration for mission-critical applications. The various specifications for Web services advanced messaging (ebXML, WS-ReliableMessaging, WS-Reliability,

WS-Eventing, and WS-Notification) offer solutions for most of the capabilities normally associated with reliable asynchronous message queuing and publish/subscribe solutions found in traditional middleware environments.

Both WS-Reliability and WS-ReliableMessaging lack many features provided by sophisticated products such as WebSphere MQ or MSMQ. However, the reliable messaging specifications are not designed to replace these systems but rather to provide interoperability for Web services mapped to execution environments such as these. Some of the missing capabilities are provided by other Web services specifications such as WS-Security, WS-Policy, and WS-Addressing.

Chapter 10
Transaction Processing

Transactions ensure that a group of Web services achieves a common result. Web services often depend upon each other to complete a complex application request, such as updating a customer record (which might update multiple customer databases) or processing a purchase order (which might update multiple inventory management databases). Transactions use various protocols to ensure that the results of these interdependent services are formally coordinated so that when the failure of one service impacts the success of another, or of the composite application as a whole, the system handles it, rather than the application.

The relationship of a transaction to a Web service might be as simple as delegating a transaction to an existing transactional execution environment. It may also be as complex as coordinating a single transaction across multiple participants in a long-running business process across arbitrary execution environments. The various possible combinations of Web services within a transaction tend to require the use of multiple protocols and an external coordinator capable of bridging disparate execution environments.

Transactional protocols work with reliable messaging and security technologies to help ensure predictable and safe operations on data. Transaction messages can be sent reliably, and it may be important to secure the transaction-processing infrastructure to protect against unwanted results. Especially when coordinating transactional operations across the Internet, it may be necessary to guard against false commit or rollback messages, for example.

Implementations of transaction processing technologies range from synchronous messaging systems using remote procedure calls (RPCs), to asynchronous message queuing systems, to long-running business process management solutions. Transaction management technologies are present in TP (transaction processing) monitors, application servers, database management systems, and packaged applications. Web services transactions may need to work with any, all, or any combination of these systems. Web services transaction technologies are really only necessary when interoperability requirements include transactions; therefore, when a Web service accesses only a single transactional execution environment, Web services transaction technologies aren't needed.

Web services-based interoperability presents significant challenges for transaction processing systems because their loosely coupled interfaces can be mapped to widely disparate systems with widely different transaction protocols and models. Yet those widely disparate systems, when used in combination with Web services, are still usually expected to reliably return predictable results to the people who use them and the businesses that rely upon them, regardless of operating system, hardware, network, or application failures. Transactions therefore represent a key aspect of Web services for SOA-based applications.

Overview

Web services transaction processing technology derives its major concepts from proven transaction processing middleware concepts, such as the independent coordinator and shared context management. Web services transaction processing technology also defines new transaction protocols beyond those typically used in middleware systems, such as compensation-based and business process management protocols. New protocols are being added to existing protocols in order to better handle Web services applications such as SOA-enabled, long-running business processes over wide area networks.

As shown in Figure 10-1, the primary technology in Web services transactions is a coordinator (illustrated using the shaded ellipse), with which the root Web service (that is, the Web service initiating the transaction) registers and other participating Web services enroll for a given transaction protocol type. The root Web service invites other Web services to participate in a transaction by passing the transaction context in a SOAP header. (The coordinator provides the transaction context to the root Web service when the root Web service initiates the transaction so that the root and subsequently called Web services can use the context to register with the coordinator.)

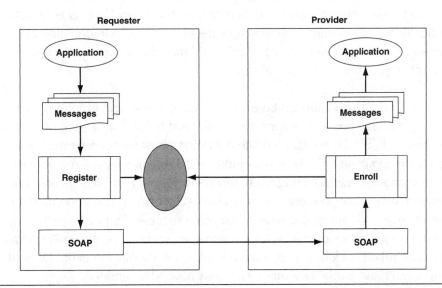

Figure 10-1   Transactions register and enroll Web services within a coordinator.

Two major phases of execution characterize a Web services transaction:

- **Enrollment**—Starts with the first "begin" operation from a Web service to a coordinator to initiate a transaction and return a context, and continues for as long as it takes to enroll other Web services into the transaction.

- **Termination**—Starts when a Web service or a coordinator signals that the work being protected by the transaction is completed, and the transaction protocol is executed to determine the result of the activity.

Subsequent sections in this chapter describe the major concepts and protocols in more detail and summarize the major specifications, including the WS-Transactions family from IBM and Microsoft and the WS-Composite Application Framework family from OASIS.

The Transaction Paradigm

The transaction paradigm coordinates multiple operations on data to speed recovery from failure, to ensure high availability, and to provide a consistent view between a business and its data management system. Transactions automatically execute system-level functions necessary to keep information at a known or easily discoverable state and avoid manual recovery actions such as querying a database for partial results.

The transaction paradigm can be explained using the simple example of purchasing a book from a bookstore. The book must be paid for and removed from inventory—both of these data update operations must succeed for the transaction to be completed. Partial results indicate that the transaction did not take place because it was not completely recorded. Transaction implementations therefore must either preserve the temporary state of each operation until it can confirm that both operations have taken place successfully or restore the original state when either operation fails. If either operation fails, the other operation has to be rolled back or compensated—that is, the transaction either takes place or it doesn't and partial or temporary results have to be undone.

Computers that implement transaction-processing systems have to behave exactly as the real world would and accurately record the reality of the cash drawer contents and bookshelf inventory—the cash must be in the drawer and the book off the shelf for the transaction to have taken place. Mistakes and discrepancies are expensive to track down and fix, as is manually determining the state of the computer-managed data following a crash. In the case of a debit-credit funds transfer, the money can't be (or shouldn't be) in both accounts at the same time.

Transactions are challenging to implement because they are expected to produce consistent results like these despite any type of system failure that may occur at any time. Transactions must often support scaling up to tens of thousands of executions per minute and still manage to avoid errors. Transaction processing systems run business operations and have to be secure, reliable, and highly performant.

Web services transactions are expressly designed for interoperability across various execution environments and are not intended to provide an implementation of the transaction processing paradigm by themselves—they are only useful in the context of other technologies that actually carry out the properties specified in the various protocols—but in accomplishing interoperability goals, Web services transactions remain subject to the same challenging requirements because they become part of the overall solution.

Impact of Web Services on Transactions

Web services use HTTP as a kind of default or always-present transport option for interoperability, meaning that all Web services specifications have to work over HTTP. HTTP is a very loosely coupled transport designed to work on a wide area network (i.e., the World Wide Web). Traditional transaction processing technologies were originally designed to work on a single machine and then were adapted for use within a tightly coupled local area network environment. Now they are being extended with new protocols designed to meet the requirements for Web services for use in service-oriented environments over wide area networks.

Traditional distributed transaction processing solutions rely on a network-level feature called a *persistent session* or *conversation* to share transaction context. This feature stores context information, such as a transaction ID, and associates the context with a communication session so that it can be reused for multiple message exchanges over the same session. When a communications session is lost, a transaction can be safely and automatically rolled back.

HTTP, on the other hand, supports only a single request/response message exchange over the same session and drops the session immediately after the response is returned (or if any error occurs). When multiple operations on data are required to complete a transaction, as is typically the case (otherwise transactions aren't really needed), HTTP provides no mechanism for storing the temporary, persistent state required to execute a rollback in the case of communications or other processing failure, or to enforce a commit should the multiple operations succeed.

For Web services, therefore, transaction context has to be passed on every message exchange, and coordinators have to be extended to work better with asynchronous network transports. Additional context management solutions are required, including a mechanism to coordinate transactions without persistent sessions at the transport level, along with the definition of new protocols on top of the context. Because Web services often represent the entry point to a long-running activity such as an automated business process, context management protocols also have to be extended specifically for that type of application.

When a transaction is managed entirely within a single execution environment, Web services transactions have no role to play. Web services transactions are only useful when the results of more than one Web service execution need to be coordinated into a larger unit of work. However, some cases exist when a Web service may or may not need to be included in a transaction started by another Web service, and it may be necessary for the Web service provider to handle a request to join a transaction.

For example, a self-contained transaction to book a seat on a flight doesn't need to coordinate transactional context. However, when the self-contained transaction is executed within a larger transaction that also includes booking a hotel room and a rental car, the flight Web service may have to accept a transaction context and enroll in the coordinated unit of work. Thus, Web services transactions need to support composable transaction models.

Protocols and Coordination

Because Web services map to a broad variety of software systems, it's necessary to consider the usefulness of multiple transaction protocols for different application styles and types. An application consisting of Web services that are co-located (that is, running within the same address space, or close enough to each other that network latency isn't very great) and that are executed using similar software systems (i.e., both in the same application server container or by a close application server container of the same type) may find benefit in using the classic two-phase commit protocol to ensure that the Web services succeed or fail as a unit.

An application that consists of Web services that are executed in systems far apart in the network, such that latency is a problem, or that are executed using widely different software systems, such as an application server and a message queuing system, may benefit from a protocol better adapted to extended network or application latencies. Furthermore, SOA-based and BPM applications need a protocol capable of running over an extended period of time, something that the two-phase commit protocol isn't good at.

Activity

For Web services transactions, an *activity* represents the execution flow for which transaction coordination is required. An activity is defined externally to the transaction protocol, typically using an SOA, WS-BPEL, or another composite application mechanism. Web services that call each other to share transaction context are considered to be executing within the same activity.

Web service transaction contexts and protocols are associated with activities of different types. The bits and pieces of technology required to coordinate operations on data across multiple, typically distributed Web service invocations, are therefore aligned with an execution scope defined externally to the transaction protocol. Transaction context is associated with the activity by sharing a context ID and protocol type.

A very simple activity such as updating two databases on the same computer might use the AtomicTransaction protocol, while a complex BPM activity such as processing a purchase order might use the Business Process management protocol (see the section "Protocol Types" later in the chapter).

Web services in an activity initiate the activity by requesting a context and registering with the coordinator for a specific protocol type. When the activity ends, the coordinator drives the protocol type across the set of Web services sharing the activity environment and context by initiating the message exchange defined for the protocol. Different types of activities require different types of protocols and different message exchange patterns.

Context

A context is a data structure that carries an identifier unique to the activity so that operations within the same transaction can easily be identified. The context also includes information about the location of the coordinator responsible for issuing, tracking, and cleaning up the context instance at the completion of the transaction. For example, a context header looks like this:

```
<wscoor:CreateCoordinationContextResponse>
    <RequesterReference>
        <Address>
            http://myApplicationProgram
        </Address>
    </RequesterReference>
    <CoordinationContext>
        <Identifier>
            http://myCoordinationService/ts/activity1
        </Identifier>
        <CoordinationType>
            http://xml-soap.org/2003/09/BusinessActivity
        </CoordinationType>
        <RegistrationService>
            <Address>
                http://myCoordinationService/tm/
            ➥myRegistrationService
            </Address>
        </RegistrationService>
    </CoordinationContext>
</wscoor:CreateCoordinationContextResponse>
```

The context header in the example includes the registration address, coordination ID, protocol type (BusinessActivity), and coordination service address.

In general terms, the context data structure can also be used to carry execution environment data for the activity's execution instance, such as user IDs, device IDs, database and file handles, and results of individual Web service executions. The context can also be extended to carry implementation-specific information such as resource manager configuration settings and additional status results.

Distributing transactions across multiple Web service executions requires maintaining shared, persistent context so that common, consistent results can be achieved from the execution of the protocol. Context provides information required by the protocol to function properly. Context is the mechanism by which an activity is associated with a transaction. Different transaction protocol types (see the section "Protocol Types") have different context types. Developers need to ensure that they are using the appropriate transaction context and protocol type for the application.

Addressing

Addressing is important to allow the transaction protocol messages to know where to go and how to correlate with other messages within the same protocol; it also allows them to share the same context instance for the same activity.

When a Web service registers with a coordinator and receives a context data structure including the transaction ID and associated information (which may be specific to a protocol or to an implementation), the Web service also receives the address of the coordinator in order to exchange further messages, especially during termination. The Web service initiating the transaction also needs to be able to pass the address of the coordinator to any other Web service joining the transaction.

For example:

```
<wscoor:RegistrationService>
  <wsa:Address>
   http://www.iona.com/artix/transactions/registration
  </wsa:Address>
  <wsa:ReferenceProperties>
   <openA:UsingBPEL> reference/to/WSDL </openA:UsingBPEL>
  </wsa:ReferenceProperties>
</wscoor:RegistrationService>
```

This example illustrates the use of WS-Addressing for returning the URL for the WSDL of the coordinator service provided by IONA for transaction registration, along with some reference information that this transaction is being coordinated within a WS-BPEL execution instance.

Policy

Policy information about the transaction requirements for a given service is essential to achieve interoperability. Does a Web service always require a transaction context? Is a transaction context optionally supported? Is a transaction context never supported? The policy information, similarly to the way in which transactional properties are identified for a .NET object or an EJB, is part of the service contract, and it helps Web services be composed into transactions and helps to prevent errors from occurring when transactions are not supported. When a Web service requester wants to enroll a Web service provider in a transaction, it's good to be able to determine in advance whether that can happen by checking the provider's WS-Policy information. For example:

```
<wsp:SpecVersion
wsp:URI="http://schemas.xmlsoap.org/ws/2003/09/wsat"
wsp:Usage="wsp:Required"/>
```

This example illustrates a policy asserting a requirement for a Web service requester to use the WS-AtomicTransaction protocol.

Coordination

Coordination is a fundamental concept for distributed computing and for Web services transactions in particular. A *coordinator* is a software agent external to the application that assumes responsibility for executing a given completion protocol to ensure consistent results across multiple executions.

Coordinator examples include the Object Transaction Service (OTS)[1] used in J2EE and CORBA and the Distributed Transaction Coordinator (DTC) used in the .NET Framework. For Web services transactions, the role of these and other

---

[1] The Java Transaction Service (JTS) is a Java API to OTS used in J2EE.

coordinators is expanded to implement additional protocols and take on additional responsibilities for interoperability, in particular for bridging various protocols and transaction models across the various execution environments that support Web services.

The extended Web services transaction coordinator is a generic state machine for which various protocol types and associated context types can be defined, created, and managed. Coordinators can talk to each other, and a sub-coordinator can register with a root coordinator as a participant in a transaction to conserve network resources and to support extended protocols.

As shown in Figure 10-2, the typical distributed transaction coordinator responds to a begin operation by returning a transaction protocol context to the service requester. The coordinator generates and returns a transaction ID and a context associated with the ID (which includes some other related information such as the coordinator's address). The ID uniquely identifies the transaction instance. The ID and the associated context is included in the SOAP header when the requester invokes a remote Web service, thereby passing the information the remote service needs to register with the coordinator for the same transaction. (The remote service may also register with a local coordinator instead of the remote coordinator for efficiency or interoperability—this is called *interposition* or a *proxy coordinator*.)

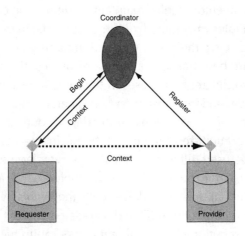

Figure 10-2   Basic coordinator architecture.

To understand why a coordinator is necessary, let's look at an example of a multi-resource transaction. A resource capable of transactional behavior needs to include a transaction manager to track changes to data for a given transaction instance. A typical example of a multi-resource transaction occurs when a message is dequeued from an asynchronous message queue and a database is updated using the message contents in the same transaction. For example, consider a funds transfer from one bank to another. The transfer request is placed into a persistent queue when it arrives over the banking network. When the transfer request is processed, it is dequeued using the queue's transaction manager and the amount of the transfer is added to the recipients' bank account using the database's transaction manager. When a failure occurs, a rollback needs to delete the transfer amount from the database and replace the transfer request on the queue so that the transaction can be restarted. The coordinator ensures that the transaction managers within the queue and the database either both commit or roll back so that the transfer doesn't occur twice.

Figure 10-3 illustrates in more detail what happens when multiple resources are involved within the same transaction. Instead of issuing `begin transaction` directly to the resource, the program issues `begin transaction` to the coordinator so that the coordinator can start a global transaction to ensure that the operations of the transaction managers within each resource manager are tied to each other.

The example shows inventory tables maintained within one database (Oracle perhaps) and order tables maintained within another database (SQL Server perhaps). Both databases have their own transaction managers (and associated logs) because they are both transactional data resources. Because it knows it will be accessing two different databases in the same transaction, the application first calls the independent transaction coordinator to get a transaction ID before it executes any of its operations on the data resources. (The example shows a distributed or multi-resource transaction using two different databases, but it could also have used different application servers or message queues.) In the same way, a Web service that knows it will include one or more other Web services in a transactional unit of work first calls the Web service transaction coordinator to obtain a transaction ID and associated context to pass to the next Web service in the execution chain so that it can enroll in the same transaction.

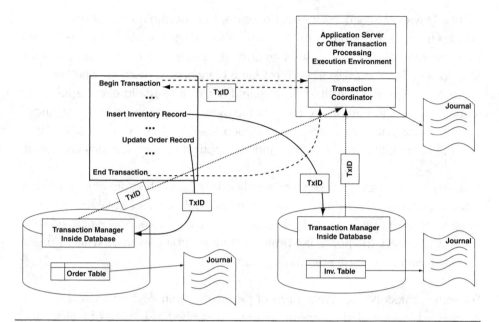

Figure 10-3   Transaction coordinator architecture.

In this example, when the inventory management database receives the request to update the inventory tables, the application includes the independent trans-action ID (and the network address of the coordinator) to indicate that an inde-pendent or external transaction has already been started. (This type of transaction is also sometimes called a *foreign* transaction because it originated outside of the local transaction manager and often uses a different ID format.) When the database receives a foreign transaction ID, it knows that it has to register with the coordinator that started the transaction in order to receive com-pletion messages, and it uses the coordinator address provided in the request message to do so. In the same way, Web services subsequent to the one initiat-ing the transaction use the ID and context received from the first Web service to register with the coordinator.

When the application accesses the order database, it also passes the transaction ID to allow the order database to register with the coordinator. The coordinator keeps a journal of all resource managers involved in the transaction. It does not log database changes; each database transaction manger still performs that duty locally. However, when the transaction ends, the coordinator is notified and initiates the two-phase protocol to commit the changes or use the journal to roll back the transaction in the case of an error or failure. The coordinator is responsible for sending messages to both resource managers to discover whether a commit is possible or a rollback is required because of a failure to complete the requested operation on one or more of the transactional resources. Upon successful completion of the two-phase protocol used for this example, both databases are committed and in synch, and the application data remains consistent.

In a very similar way, Web services enrolled in a transaction are able to achieve a common result by sharing context among all Web services involved in the same transaction. Because multiple protocols are available, however, the Web services also have to choose the protocol they are going to share when a protocol other than two-phase commit is required.

For some protocols or optimizations of protocols, multiple coordinators are needed, which is called *interposition* and is described as the use of intermediaries or proxy coordinators. Figure 10-4 illustrates the case in which a transaction has a root coordinator, which represents the originator of the transaction. The transaction may also have an interposed coordinator, which represents the sub-participants. Coordinators are depicted using ovals.

The typical solution for bridging transactions involves a coordinator that can take responsibility for coordinating the actions of multiple recoverable resources. First, the resources, such as databases, files, and queues, need to be able to understand transactions. Second, an independent coordinator needs to be able to coordinate the actions of multiple resources into a single unit of work. Third, the set of coordinator, resources, and Web services need to be able to share a common protocol type.

The coordinator assigns a transaction ID for the context and protocol type to be associated with the specific transactional unit of work. All operations on data within the scope of the transaction will be associated with that ID and therefore become part of the activity for that protocol. Multiple coordinators may be needed to optimize network traffic or bridge disparate transaction protocols.

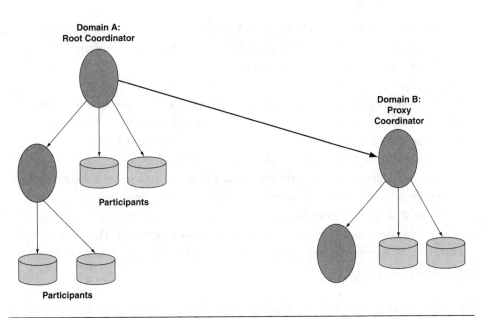

Figure 10-4   Interposed or proxy coordinator architecture.

Protocol Types

In the world of complex Web services, SOA, and BPM, a variety of transaction protocols are needed in order to handle the variety of application requirements, execution environments, and network connectivity options.

The protocols developed for Web services transactions include the following:

- **Generic context management**—Separating the role of context from transactional protocols so that it can be used to support a variety of other requirements for lightweight coordination (i.e., without a formal coordinator agent).

- **ACID or atomic transaction**—A definition of the classic two-phase commit protocol with an emphasis on interoperability.

- **Compensation-based or business activity**—A definition of the Saga[2] concept in which intermediate commits are possible and are undone using compensation rather than rollback.

---

[2] Saga is a word used in transaction literature to describe long-running transaction models.

- **Business process management**—A protocol designed specifically to bridge other protocols across arbitrary execution environments in a long-running business process flow.

All of the specifications covered in this chapter share this perspective on the problem. All are derived to a greater or lesser degree from the pioneering work at the OMG in the *Additional Structuring Mechanisms for the OTS Specification*, or *Activity spec*, as it's known. The main innovation of the Activity specification was to define the concept of an activity and separate the coordinator from the protocol, allowing additional, new protocols to be added as plug-ins to a generic coordinator for handling different types of activities (such as long-running flows or automated business processes). The generic coordinator is a generic state machine driver, and the protocols define the state machines to be driven.

The main issue is how to correctly model the concept of a transaction in a Web services world, in which Web services are mapped to multiple execution environments with potentially widely different characteristics, and therefore design an appropriate protocol. No single protocol will fit all use cases for Web services; therefore, it's necessary to ensure that you choose the right protocol for the job. The protocols involved in Web services transactions provide:

- **Atomic transactions**—The all-or-nothing-style transactions that suspend completion of an activity until it's committed and changes to data are made permanent. At any time up to the moment at which the commit record is logged, the results of the activity could be rolled back; that is, cancelled or undone. Primarily used for interoperability across existing atomic transaction protocols and for Web services located close to each other in the network. Examples include WS-AtomicTransactions and the ACID transaction protocol in the WS-TransactionManagement specification.

- **Compensation-based protocols**—Providing the ability to undo a change that was previously made permanent by a prior commit. Compensation is like returning an item you purchased for credit. The transaction was completed but now has to be undone by performing another transaction that basically cancels the results of the first. Compensation actions can be automatically executed using compensation handlers, but the compensation logic cannot be automatically generated and therefore relies upon application-specific business logic. Examples include WS-BusinessActivity and the Long Running Actions protocol in the WS-TransactionManagement specification.

- **Business process management (BPM)-based protocols**—These include the use of atomic, compensation, and other subprotocols to provide an overall transaction coordination function aligned with a business process flow. Each task in the subprocess flow is permitted to implement its own transaction subprotocol, depending upon the particular technology used within the execution environment. The overall Business Process management protocol extends the pluggable state machine concept of the coordinator with a coordinator-coordinator protocol that spans execution environments and notifies humans if something goes wrong that can't be automatically fixed. The Business Process transaction protocol in the WS-TransactionManagement specification is an example.

In general, the traditional atomic transaction (also known as two-phase commit protocol) is the most widely used and implemented distributed transaction-processing protocol today. However, it is not very well suited to Web services because it relies on maintaining temporary locks on data, preventing anyone else from accessing the same or related data (such as indexes) until the transaction is concluded, and locking is not well-suited to loosely coupled environments that might involve long message latencies and span multiple organizations. Even in LAN environments, transaction programmers are instructed to keep locks for as short a duration as possible and never to allow the user to hold locks open while on a coffee break or during other interruptions because doing so inhibits concurrency and therefore decreases performance.

Achieving Consensus on Transaction Specifications

Transaction processing specifications have always been difficult to achieve consensus on because TP system implemntations tend to be hard to change. However, the specifications described in this chapter do not require changes to fundamental TP system artifacts—they are modeled entirely as extensions to existing technologies, in particular to the coordinators that already exist within J2EE, .NET, and CORBA environments, to name a few. Coordinators are present wherever two-phase commit is supported, and that's pretty much everywhere. The problems tend to come in the area of the higher-level protocols. Some people think that higher-level protocols aren't necessary or that basing the higher-level solution on extending the coordinator won't work. Others think that we still haven't defined the right set of protocol types. Everyone agrees that transactions are ultimately required for loosely coupled SOA and BPM solutions to be truly reliable, however.

Compensation-based protocols have been used informally for a long time because they are a part of everyday life. Whenever goods are returned after purchase, compensating transactions repay the credit card or provide store credit and restock the item in store inventory. However, automating compensation-based protocols has limits because it is effectively impossible to implement recursive compensation—that is, if an automatic compensation program fails, it is not really possible to anticipate how to compensate for the failure because it may fail in the middle. In addition, some operations on data simply can't be compensated for or undone, such as firing a missile or printing a boarding pass.

Although neither atomic nor compensation-based transaction protocols can meet every requirement, it's possible that a combination of the two, together with some additional coordinator-based protocols, can. Thus, the need exists for a third protocol that can bridge the two and more. The third protocol is actually a kind of meta-protocol whose job is to discover the results of the sub-protocols and tie those results together into a larger unit of work.

Transaction Specifications

A Web service transaction can be implemented using a wide variety of technologies and techniques. To indicate that a transaction is required, policy assertions can be defined to express the requirements of a particular service for a particular protocol or to declare whether the Web service requires or allows a transaction context.

Still Basically an Unresolved Problem

Despite the variety of proposals, protocols, and approaches represented here, transaction processing remains basically an unresolved problem area for Web services because beyond the classic two-phase commit protocol, none of the additional transaction protocols have been widely implemented or adopted in production environments. This is true for a variety of reasons, including the fact that it's hard to coordinate what happens within an interoperability layer and map it down to executable environments, and also the fact that Web services are loosely coupled whereas existing transaction processing technologies were designed for tightly coupled environments. In addition, transaction processing technologies tend to be tightly integrated with their platforms and require considerable low-level interactions with operating systems and hardware to ensure reliability and to avoid data corruption errors. These technologies have been in place in some cases for more than 30 years. One way to attack the problem is to assume that software will be added to every integration endpoint to translate between a standard protocol and a technology-specific protocol such as XA, OTS, DTC, or RRMS. Another approach, taken by the currently proposed specifications, is to extend the coordinator for multiple protocols and models. It isn't clear yet which approach will end up gaining widespread adoption because a lot of practical issues still have to be resolved.

Several specifications have been proposed for transaction processing with Web services, including:

- **WS-Transactions**—A family of specifications including:

  - **WS-AtomicTransactions (WS-AT)**—A two-phase commit protocol for Web services interoperability.

  - **WS-BusinessActivity (WS-BA)**—An open nested protocol for long-running business processes.

  - **WS-Coordination (WS-C)**—A pluggable coordination framework supporting WS-AT and WS-BA.

- **WS-Composite Application Framework**—A family of specifications including:

  - **WS-Context (WS-CTX)**—A generic context management mechanism.

  - **WS-CoordinationFramework (WS-CF)**—A pluggable coordination framework supporting WS-AT, WS-BA, and the three protocols in WS-TXM.

  - **WS-TransactionManagement (WS-TXM)**—A two-phase commit protocol for Web services interoperability (ACID), a compensation-based protocol for long-running activities (LRA), and a business process management protocol (BP).

The WS-Transactions family of specifications was developed by BEA, IBM, and Microsoft and released originally in conjunction with WS-BPEL in August 2002. The specifications were updated in September 2003 when WS-BusinessActivity was broken out into its own specification. The original WS-Transactions specification was also renamed WS-AtomicTransactions at that time.

WS-AT, WS-BA, and WS-C define a protocol for a traditional two-phase commit, another one for longer running compensations, and a generic coordinator for registering Web services, managing context, and executing them.

The WS-CAF family of specifications was developed by Arjuna, IONA, Oracle, Fujistu, and Sun and was submitted to the OASIS WS-CAF Technical

Committee in October, 2003. Similarly to the WS-Transactions family, the WS-CAF family centers on the concept of an extended coordinator and pluggable protocols. However, WS-CAF also defines generic context management as a separate function, usable without a coordinator, and defines an additional pluggable protocol type (the business process protocol) beyond those defined in WS-Transactions. The WS-CAF family also supports the WS-Transactions protocols.

Aside from their common approach to Web services transaction management, WS-CAF and WS-Transactions have considerable overlap. Proponents of each have suggested convergence, which would of course be good for the industry. Both families of specifications center around the concept of extended coordination and a pluggable software service that can drive a variety of protocols for handling various transaction processing requirements, such as two-phase commit, compensation, and business process transactions. Participants in a transaction register with the coordinator and specify the protocol type so that the coordinator can drive the appropriate protocol for the Web services that register for it.

The overall model is described using the concept of coordination; we highlight individual protocols and differences among specifications in the following sections.

Branches of the Same Tree

The WS-Transactions and WS-CAF specification families have a common ancestry inasmuch as both are derived from the *Additional Structuring Mechanisms for the OTS Specification* at OMG, which was the first specification to define the concept of a generic "activity" whose participants might have operations that need to be coordinated. However, the specifications have taken divergent paths, which highlights the problem caused in the marketplace by a lack of leadership for Web services specifications. If an independent body were leading the standardization process, the specifications could be combined because they are more similar than different. This situation, as much as any in the Web services specifications arena today, illustrates the political nature of the standardization process.

The Web Services Coordinator

If you want to do anything with the WS-Transactions family of specifications, you first need an implementation of WS-C because both WS-AT and WS-BA require it.

WS-CAF also defines a coordinator in the WS-CoordinationFramework specification, which is central to its use of protocol types. Examples shown in this section apply equally to both coordination models. Following the general explanation of coordination are separate sections on each of the individual protocol specifications.

The act of coordination involves an enrollment or registration phase during which Web services in a common activity (whose results need to be coordinated according to a certain protocol) establish the fact that they are all in the same unit of work. After all Web services have joined the transaction (of whatever type) and completed their work (typically operations on data that need to be coordinated), the protocol can enter the completion phase, during which the rules of the protocol are enacted through the exchange of specific messages defined for the protocol. Although the large number of messages might seem to cause significant additional overhead for the Web services that participate in a transaction, implementations are likely to piggyback the protocol messages for better efficiency.

Coordination involves three major elements:

- **Activation**—During which a transaction is created.
- **Registration**—During which one or more Web services sign up for the transaction.
- **Coordination**—During which the results of Web services signed up for transaction are coordinated.

These elements relate to the basic coordination architecture and the sequence of events that occur during Web services transaction processing.

As illustrated in Figure 10-5, a Web service mapped to a transactional execution environment begins the transaction by creating an activity, thereby initiating the transaction. The act of creating an activity is essentially the same as the example in the previous section of how an independent coordinator works, except that the Web service also needs to specify the protocol type and use Web services conventions for structuring the context and representing the coordinator address.

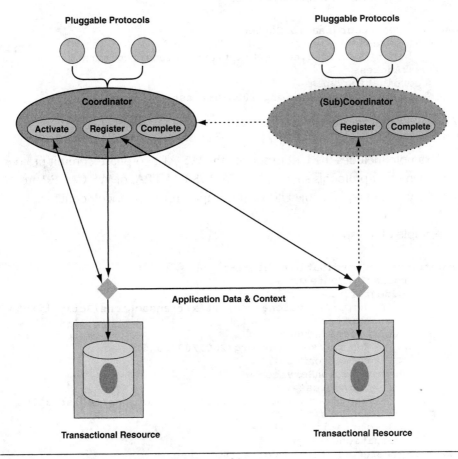

Figure 10-5   Web services coordination architecture.

After the activity is started and the Web service has received the context for the requested protocol type, the Web service registers itself for the transaction and then calls another Web service mapped to a transactional execution environment, passing application data (to be updated by the transactional resource) and the context information. The Web service being called uses the context data to register with the coordinator for the same transaction (or optionally to register with an interposed coordinator, which then would register with the root coordinator on behalf of the second Web service).

An example of a registration message is:

```
<wscoor:CreateCoordinationContext>
   <wsa:Address>
       http://www.iona.com/artix/transactions/registration
   </wsa:Address>
    <CoordinationType>
        http://xml-soap.org/2003/09/wast
    </CoordinationType>
</wscoor:CreateCoordinationContext>
```

This example includes the URI to specify the WS-AT two-phase commit protocol. When other protocols such as WS-BA, WS-CAF LRA, or WS-CAF BP are used, they would replace this URI with the appropriate protocol identifier.

An example of a response message is:

```
<wscoor:CreateCoordinationContextResponse>
    <CoordinationContext>
        <Identifier>
            http://www.iona.com/artix/transactions/ActivityXyZe
        </Identifier>
        <CoordinationType>
            http://xml-soap.org/2003/09/wast
        </CoordinationType>
        <RegistrationService>
           <wsa:Address>
            http://www.iona.com/artix/transactions/registration
           </wsa:Address>
        </RegistrationService>
    </CoordinationContext>
</wscoor:CreateCoordinationContextResponse>
```

This example illustrates the ID of the activity, or context ID, for the transaction along with the coordination protocol type and address of the coordinator. This information is needed to pass along to the next Web service in the activity so that it can join the same unit of work and register with the same coordinator in order to receive the protocol messages on completion of the activity.

Figure 10-6 illustrates the general sequence of events involved in the relationships between the Web service application, the coordinator, and the transactional resource. The application initiates the transaction by issuing a `begin` operation for the activity (specifying the protocol type) and registers with the coordinator after receiving the context. When the application starts performing operations on data managed by a transactional resource, the Web services transaction context is mapped to the execution environment context. Finally, when the activity is ended, messages are exchanged between the execution environment, the Web services layer, and the coordinator to ensure that either the desired outcome was achieved (success) or some recovery operation is required (rollback, compensation, or other) in order to complete the activity.

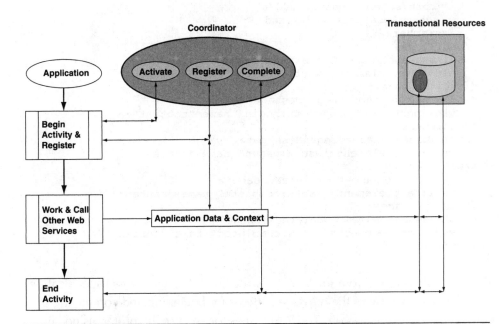

Figure 10-6   Sequence of operations in transaction coordination.

(Note that these are generic examples for the purpose of explaining the overall model. Specific XML for the different protocols and specifications will vary.)

Web services transactions specifications include WSDL definitions of the message exchange patterns they support. For example:

```
xmlns:tns="http://www.webservicestransactions.org/wsdl/wsctx/
➡2003/03"
xmlns:wsctx="http://www.webservicestransactions.org/schemas/wsctx/
➡2003/03"
xmlns:xs="http://www.w3.org/2001/XMLSchema"
xmlns:soap="http://schemas.xmlsoap.org/wsdl/soap/"
xmlns:wsdl="http://schemas.xmlsoap.org/wsdl/"
targetNamespace="http://www.webservicestransactions.org/wsdl/
➡wsctx/2003/03">
  <wsdl:types>
   <xs:schema>
      <xs:import namespace=http://www.webservicestransactions
      ➡.org/schemas/wsctx/2003/03
       schemaLocation="wsctx.xsd"/>
   </xs:schema>
  </wsdl:types>
  <wsdl:message name="ContextMessage">
    <wsdl:part element="wsctx:context" name="content"/>
  </wsdl:message>
  <wsdl:message name="BeginMessage">
    <wsdl:part element="wsctx:begin" name="content"/>
  </wsdl:message>
  <wsdl:message name="BegunMessage">
    <wsdl:part element="wsctx:begun" name="content"/>
  </wsdl:message>
  <wsdl:message name="CompleteMessage">
    <wsdl:part element="wsctx:complete" name="content"/>
  </wsdl:message>
  <wsdl:message name="CompletedMessage">
    <wsdl:part element="wsctx:completed" name="content"/>
  </wsdl:message>
```

This example is taken from the WSDL for the WS-CAF WS-Context specification and illustrates the use of the message patterns for beginning and completing a context management session. The WSDL files for each of the protocols detail the messages defined for that protocol. (See the section "WS-Context" later in the chapter for further information on WS-Context.)

SOAP bindings for transaction messages must use the document-oriented style for Web services with callback MEPs that correlate asynchronous messages. Any coordination context, such as the WS-AT context, must flow on all application messages involved with the transaction, when the context is passed by reference (something WS-CAF supports).

When a context isn't included in a registration, a new transaction is created, and a new transaction context is returned to the Web service. If a current context is included with a new registration, the target coordinator interprets this action the way a transactional resource manager responds to the appearance of a foreign transaction ID—namely, it registers with the root coordinator.

A coordination context may include a timeout attribute that can cause a transaction to be terminated because it's taking too long. Timeout is often set to ensure that deadlocks or other unanticipated errors can be resolved without holding a transaction open interminably. The coordinator can roll back or cancel the transaction on timeout.

It's also important to define security policies and attributes for transaction protocol messages. It's important to secure the coordinator from unauthorized access and to sign (or otherwise protect) the context in the SOAP headers and ensure proper identification for the senders of the protocol messages. Maintaining and enforcing a list of authorized participants is an important aspect of securing the transaction-processing environment.

WS-AtomicTransaction

The WS-AtomicTransactions (WS-AT) specification defines a protocol that can be plugged into WS-Coordination to provide a Web services adaptation of the classic two-phase commit protocol. It's often said that two-phase commit isn't well adapted to Web services, but as with most aspects of technology, that all depends upon what you're doing with it. For interoperability across short-lived, co-located Web services that need to ensure consistent, all-or-nothing results for a transaction, two-phase commit works fine. Thus, every Web services transaction suite includes support for this basic and foundational protocol because there are cases in which it is very useful.

Two-phase commit, or *atomic* transactions, are typically designed to be short in duration and to execute within the same security domain. The atomic transaction model is implemented in Web services to enable existing two-phase commit applications to be represented as Web services and to extend Web services interoperability capabilities to this type of application. It's also very possible that Web services will be designed and developed independently and yet be used within the same transaction (and possibly even be co-located). In these cases, such as when an inventory service and an order management service happen to be tightly coupled enough to benefit from it, two-phase commit is the right answer.

But it's equally true that while some use cases will support the technology, others will require very different transitional protocols, and that's why protocols such as WS-BusinessActivity and WS-CAF's Long Running Actions and Business Process exist.

The atomic transaction or two-phase commit is not really intended as a foundational or suitable model for SOA. In SOA terms, the two-phase commit model is something that typically executes within the same software domain, within the same application, or inside an interface composed of other interfaces. This protocol is intended primarily for compatibility with existing systems.

WS-AT includes volatile and durable versions of 2PC (two-phase commit). Participants in the volatile 2PC must respond to the prepare phase before any durable participants respond. The idea is to coordinate any transactional operations on in-memory data before coordinating transactional operations on disk, for example, so that an in-memory application server cache can be flushed to disk before driving the commit operation on persistent data. Volatile participants may not receive notification of a transaction's outcome (because by definition, volatile transactions do not have a durable log).

Upon receiving a commit notification in the termination stage, the root coordinator begins the prepare phase of all participants registered for the volatile protocol. All participants registered for this protocol must respond before any prepare message can be issued to a participant registered for the durable protocol.

Participants register for this protocol using one of the following protocol identifiers:

```
http://schemas.xmlsoap.org/ws/2003/09/wsat#Volatile2PC
http://schemas.xmlsoap.org/ws/2003/09/wsat#Durable2PC
```

After successfully completing the prepare phase for volatile participants, the root coordinator begins the prepare phase for durable 2PC participants. All participants registered for this protocol must respond prepared or read only before a commit notification is issued to a participant registered for either protocol.

WS-BusinessActivity

The BusinessActivity (WS-BA) specification defines a protocol that can be used with WS-Coordination to drive consistent results for long-running composite applications. WS-BA also provides the option for the application to drive the completion protocol instead of the coordinator.

Activities allow for nesting and define a way in which some participants can opt in or out for the coordination of the results. In this way, a kind of commit optimization can be defined with participants choosing to take themselves out of the transaction if it doesn't look like they will be able to participate in the commit.

The business activity protocol is designed to encompass both ACID transactions and compensations for rollback and undo operations that might be necessary to achieve consistency. The WS-BA protocol is designed for use with long-running transactions that may access multiple data sources and perform multiple operations that need to be taken into account. Unlike the WS-AT protocol, WS-BA does not assume a need for quick results.

The WS-BA specification provides the definition of a business activity protocol type used to coordinate activities that apply business logic to handle business exceptions. Actions (such as commit) can be applied immediately and made permanent. Compensating actions can then be invoked when it's necessary to correct an error or undo an action. WS-BA enables existing business process and workflow systems to wrap their proprietary mechanisms and interoperate across trust boundaries and different vendor implementations.

WS-BA is designed for transactions that have the following characteristics:

- May consume many resources over a long duration.

- May involve a significant number of atomic transactions.

- Results for individual tasks can be seen prior to the completion of the overall activity because their results may have an impact outside of the activity.

- Responding to a request may take a very long time. Human approval, assembly, manufacturing, or delivery may have to take place before a response can be sent.

- Exception handling mechanisms may require business logic, for example in the form of a compensation task, to reverse the effects of a completed task.

- Participants may be in different domains of trust where all trust relation-ships are established explicitly.

WS-BA defines a protocol in which all state transitions are reliably recorded, including application state and coordination metadata. All notifications are acknowledged in the protocol to ensure a consistent view of state between the coordinator and participant.

The coordination type for WS-BA is as follows:

```
http://schemas.xmlsoap.org/ws/2004/01/wsba
```

When this URI appears in the create coordination context request, a context type for WS-BA is returned to the Web service initiating the activity.

WS-Context
The WS-Context specification in WS-CAF defines a mechanism for handling generic context information for various execution environment contexts such as

user IDs, device IDs, database and file IDs, session IDs, and so on. Execution environments generate and manage many different kinds of short-lived context data.

As we have mentioned, it is often said that Web services are immature and missing some features compared to other distributed computing development environments such as .NET, J2EE, or CORBA. Many features and functions of distributed systems depend upon persistent sessions, including secure sessions, conversations, and load balancing and failover mechanisms. One way to think about persistent sessions in general is that they provide the ability to return to where processing left off in a remote program on a subsequent call, such as maintaining the pointer of the first operation on a database while waiting for the next to arrive.

WS-Context provides a generic mechanism for Web services to share persistent session state, which is required to support conversational interactions, single sign-on, transaction coordination, and other features dependent upon system-level data items such as IDs, tokens, and so on. Context provides a way to correlate a set of messages into a larger unit of work by sharing common information, such as a security token exchanged within a single sign-on session.

Through the use of shared context, Web services from different sources can effectively become part of the same execution environment by sharing common system information. A classic example is a single sign-on mechanism that allows a user or an application to present authentication credentials to access to a set of cooperating Web services. Application-level context, such as a shared document, can also benefit from a generic context management service.

WS-Context defines a unique context identifier, the type of the context (e.g., transaction or security), and a timeout value (how long the context can remain valid). For example:

```
<ContextType> MyContext </ContextType>
  <context-identifier>
   www.webservicestransactions.org/example/Activity1oY
  </context-identifier>
  <child-contexts>
    <child-context>
```

```
   <user-name> EricN </user-name>
   <password> ******** </password>
</child-context>
<child-context>
   <database-name> SQL-DB </database-name>
   <file-name> Index-S-file </file-name>
   <display-address> PocketPc25 </display-address>
</child-context>
<child-context>
   <transaction-type> BusinessProcessManagement
   ➡</transaction-type>
   <transaction-mode> Required </transaction-mode>
</child-context>
</child-contexts>
```

This example context structure includes "children" that can be used to share information needed to process a request on behalf of the user of a composite Web service. The example illustrates user information that obtains a security token and passes the token as a single sign-on feature for the composite application. In other words, the context could be provided as input to the first Web service in a WS-BPEL defined flow. The first Web service in the flow then could check the username and password (the asterisks are used to indicate opaque data in the example) and retrieve an authentication token to use in checking whether the user is authorized to access each subsequent Web service in the flow. Such an authentication token could be placed back into the context data structure as an augmentation to the original structure.

Other child contexts define data management characteristics of the execution environment and indicate the requirement for using a business process protocol type.

WS-Coordination Framework

Like WS-Coordination in the WS-Transactions family, the definition of a coordinator in the WS-CAF family's WS-CoordinationFramework (WS-CF) specification is extended with a plug-in mechanism that supports multiple protocol types, such as the classic two-phase commit protocol, long-running actions with compensation, and complex business process and orchestration flows.

The WS-CF specification coordinator is capable of driving a variety of context types and transaction protocols (including those defined in WS-AT, WS-BA, WS-TXM, and potentially others).

```
<env:Envelope xmlns:env="http://www.w3.org/2002/12/soap-envelope">
  <env:Header>
    <n:Composite xmlns:n="http://example.org/
    ➥CompositeApplication">
      <n:Coordinator>
       http://www.webservicestransactions.org/example/interface
       ➥CoordinatorURI
      </Coordinator>
    </n:Composite>
  </env:Header>
...
  <env:Body>
</env:Envelope>
```

In this example, the coordinator URI points to a Web service interface that defines the SOAP message pattern for interactions between the coordinator and the Web service execution. The coordinator then manages any user-defined context and generates and propagates the context for use within the operations of the composite application, including each registered Web service in the recovery protocol, if any is specified. When multiple Web services register with the coordinator to use the same context type, the message exchange pattern includes all Web service executions within the composite. In other words, the scope for a given context type is determined by the Web services that register with the coordinator to share it. The context type can be one of the transaction protocols or a generic context management type.

The message exchange pattern described for the Web services in the application isn't changed. By registering with the coordinator, however, a separate message exchange pattern is established as a secondary, system-level interaction to handle the context propagation and recovery operations. The two message exchange patterns are linked using the context ID passed in the SOAP header and given to the coordinator upon registration.

Headers are also used to indicate the protocol choice when multiple protocols are available. For example:

```
<wscaf:protocolType>
http://www.oasis-open.org/ws-caf/ws-txm/2004/09/ACID
</wscaf:protocolType>
```

```
<wscaf:Completion ... />
<wscaf:TwoPhaseCommit ... />
```

The example illustrates the WS-CAF namespace `wscaf` and shows the kind of SOAP header necessary to enroll the Web service in a classic two-phase commit style (or ACID) transaction. It also illustrates how a completion message might be sent to the coordinator to terminate the transaction with a two-phase commit protocol.

WS-Transaction Management

The WS-CAF family's WS-TransactionManagement (WS-TXM) specification defines three transaction protocols that can be plugged into WS-CF, including:

- A classic two-phase commit protocol called ACID.

- A compensation-based protocol called Long Running Action (LRA).

- A protocol specifically designed for use with automated business process flows called Business Process (BP).

The right protocol can be selected for the right job by including the appropriate registration request in a SOAP header talking to the coordinator. The BPM protocol includes ACID and LRA as potential sub-protocols.

ACID

The ACID protocol in WS-TXM is essentially the same as WS-AT without the volatile version of the protocol and including heuristic error reporting to address the uncertainty state.

The ACID protocol in WS-TXM is also designed specifically to support interoperability across multiple variations of the two-phase commit protocol that exist in current and proposed systems.

LRA

The Long Running Action (LRA) protocol in the WS-TXM specification is very similar to WS-BA. LRA is designed specifically for business interactions that occur over a long duration. An LRA is intended to reflect business interactions that are compensatable: All work performed within the scope of an application must have a compensation action defined in order for it to be undone in the case of an error. The LRA protocol defines the triggers for compensation actions and the conditions under which those triggers are executed, but not the compensation actions themselves.

For example, when a user reserves a seat on a flight, the airline may immediately book the seat and debit the user's charge card, relying on the fact that most of their customers actually buy the seats they book. The compensation action for this would be to un-book the seat and credit the user's charge card.

Business Process Transactions

In the Business Process (BP) transaction protocol defined in WS-TXM, all parties involved in a business process reside within *business domains,* which use business processes to perform work. Business process transactions are responsible for managing interactions *between* these domains. A business process (business-to-business interaction) is split into *business tasks,* and each task executes within a specific business domain. A business domain may itself be subdivided into other business domains (business processes) in a recursive manner.

Because each business domain typically provides different transaction protocols within different execution environments, a business task has to provide execution-specific error recovery. The controlling application may request that all of the business domains checkpoint their state such that they can either be consistently rolled back to that checkpoint by the application or restarted from the checkpoint in the event of a failure. The BP protocol is designed to interoperate across any combination of TP systems, whether a single resource manager system, multi-resource manager system, or more complex TP monitor or application server system, relying first on execution environment-specific recovery mechanisms and second on a coordinator-coordinator protocol to assemble execution environment information into an integrated, higher-level protocol to determine an overall outcome.

Figure 10-7 illustrates how the proxy coordinator model can be used to bridge across disparate transaction systems, such as between a synchronous request/ response transaction and the asynchronous messaging model used in asynchronous message queuing systems. This is an important aspect of the BP protocol. The coordinators exchange messages according to the BP protocol, which lets the root coordinator know the result of the transaction, while the proxy coordinator delegates execution of the actual transaction and recovery mechanism to the underlying execution environment, whatever it may be.

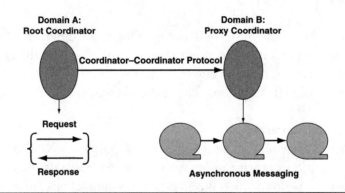

Figure 10-7   Bridging disparate transaction models.

Composite applications take advantage of the ability to invoke one Web service from another, and new applications are easily created from stitching multiple Web services together into an automated business process or workflow. When this happens in the context of transactional systems, there needs to be a way to combine the protocols and results of individual transaction executions across different TP system implementations.

The BP protocol allows the transactions to run to completion in each of the sub-domains bridged with a proxy coordinator, unless a participant raises a synch-point event (that is, a request to checkpoint the transaction). Any participating coordinator (on behalf of one of the sub-domains) can raise a synchpoint event at any time to the root coordinator, which in turn triggers the coordinator-coordinator protocol to assess the current status of the transaction. When the status signals that a recovery action is needed, the protocol triggers appropriate recovery mechanisms such as rollback, compensation, and roll forward (from replay logs) defined for each domain. When recovery isn't possible, the protocol sends a message to an error queue or to an operator to ask for further instructions, such as to seek an alternate path that might have a better chance of success or to log a permanent error for manual correction.

As shown in Figure 10-8, BPM solutions can include multiple types of TP technologies, especially when crossing organizational boundaries. A classic example is a PC manufacturer scheduling a manufacturing run for the next day based on the current day's orders. The manufacturer needs to order the right number of CPUs, memory chips, disks, displays, and so on. Different suppliers need to be contacted to place the orders for each of the different components. The suppliers of CPUs, memory chips, disk drives, displays, and so on are very likely to have implemented their order entry systems using different transaction processing platforms such as JMS, WebSphere MQ, CORBA, EJB, .NET Framework, SAP, and Siebel.

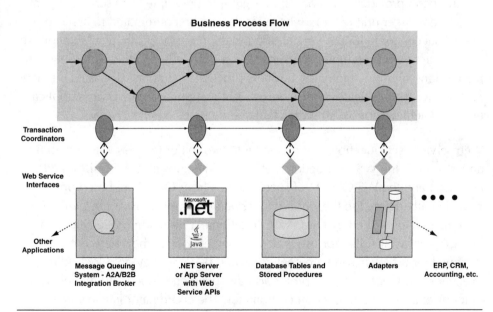

Figure 10-8   Business process transaction architecture.

The PC manufacturer initiates the BP transaction protocol to find out whether the manufacturing run for the following day is possible, given the availability of parts from the various suppliers. If the supplier of displays is out of the 17-inch monitors requested, the manufacturer might receive a message from the BP protocol to ask whether 15-inch monitors are an acceptable substitute, allowing the order to complete. If not, the entire order is cancelled via a system of compensations, rollbacks, and notifications.

Because transaction models vary across different types of TP systems, the ability is needed to express the transaction context in a way that's meaningful to the Web services overlay, or orchestration layer, and in a way in which it can be mapped into and out of the variety of underlying systems. The BP protocol accomplishes this by using interposed coordinators. Each type of software system is treated as a foreign software *domain* represented by a sub-coordinator. The coordinators talk to each other to communicate the results of the transaction across the domains.

Summary

A transaction provides a mechanism for grouping multiple Web services operations into a larger unit of work whose results can be coordinated to achieve overall success or failure. A variety of transaction protocols are available for use with different types of applications, ranging from tightly coupled to loosely coupled to long-running automated business process executions. Choosing the right protocol for the application helps ensure that composite Web services applications can achieve consistent, predictable, and reliable results.

Web services specifications are divided into two major families with a common ancestry. Both the WS-Transactions set of specifications from BEA, IBM, and Microsoft and the WS-CAF set of specifications from OASIS are based on concepts initially defined in the *Additional Structuring Mechanisms for the OTS Specification* published by the OMG. Traditional transaction processing technology is not well suited for use with Web services since they were not designed for use over wide area networks and because they hold locks during execution, and therefore new protocols have been developed and modeled as plug-ins to a generic transaction coordinator. The coordinator is a feature of existing distributed transaction management environments, making it a logical choice for handling this extended Web services feature.

Bibliography

Books

Barry, Douglas K. *Web Services and Service Oriented Architectures: The Savvy Manager's Guide.* Morgan Kaufmann, 2003.

Bernstein, Philip A. and Eric Newcomer. *Principles of Transaction Processing.* Morgan Kaufmann, 1997.

Chatterjee, Sandeep and James Webber. *Developing Enterprise Web Services: An Architect's Guide.* Upper Saddle River, NJ: Prentice Hall PTR, 2004.

Conlkin, Peter and Eric Newcomer. "The Keys to the Highway." In *The Future of Software,* ed. Derek Leebaert. MIT Press, 1995.

Erl, Thomas. *Service-Oriented Architecture, A Field Guide to Integrating XML and Web Services.* Upper Saddle River, NJ: Prentice Hall, 2004.

Harold, Elliotte Rusty. *Processing XML with Java: A Guide to SAX, DOM, JDOM, JAXP, and TrAX.* Boston, MA: Addison-Wesley, 2003.

Hohpe, Gregor, Bobby Woolf, Kyle Brown, Conrad F. D'Cruz, Martin Fowler, Sean Neville, Michael J. Rettig, and Jonathan Simon. *Enterprise Integration Patterns: Designing, Building, and Deploying Messaging Solutions.* Boston, MA: Addison-Wesley, 2004.

Kaye, Doug. *Loosely Coupled: The Missing Pieces of Web Services.* Rds Associates Inc., August 2003.

Linthicum, David S. *Next Generation Application Integration: From Simple Information to Web Services.* Boston, MA: Addison-Wesley, 2004.

Manes, Anne Thomas. *Web Services: A Manager's Guide.* Boston, MA: Addison-Wesley, 2003.

Meyer, Bertrand. *Object-Oriented Software Construction.* Upper Saddle River, NJ: Prentice Hall, 1997.

Newcomer, Eric. *Understanding Web Services: XML, WSDL, SOAP, and UDDI.* Boston, MA: Addison-Wesley, 2002.

O'Neill, Mark et al. *Web Services Security.* McGraw Hill, 2003.

Schmelzer, Ron, Travis Vandersypen, Jason Bloomberg, Madhu Siddalingaiah, Sam Hunting, Michael Qualls, Chad Darby, David Houlding, and Diane Kennedy. *XML and Web Services Unleashed.* SAMS, 2002.

Technology References

CORBA
Henning, Michi and Steve Vinoski. *Advanced CORBA® Programming with C++.* Addison-Wesley, 1999.

CICS
Horswill, John. Members of the CICS Development Team at IBM Hursley. *Designing and Programming CICS Applications.* O'Reilly, 2000.

IMS
IMS Primer, IBM Redbooks, Vervante, 2000.

MQ
Websphere Application Server V5 and Websphere MQ Family Integration,
Vervante, 2003.

JMS
Monson-Haefel, Richard and David Chappell. *Java Message Service*.
O'Reilly, 2000.

Kerberos
Garman, Jason. *Kerberos: The Definitive Guide*. O'Reilly, 2003.

LDAP
Specification home page: www.ietf.org/rfc/rfc2251.
Arkills, Brian. *LDAP Directories Explained: An Introduction and Analysis*.
Addison-Wesley Professional, 2003.

Tibco Rendezvous
Tibco web site: http://www.tibco.com/software/enterprise_backbone/
rendezvous.jsp.

Tuxedo
Andrade, Juan M., Mark T. Carges, Terence J. Dwyer, and Stephen D. Felts.
*The Tuxedo System: Software for Constructing and Managing Distributed
Business Applications*. Addison-Wesley Professional, 1996.

X.509
Specification home page: http://www.ietf.org/html.charters/pkix-charter.html.

Articles

Akamai Technologies, Computer Associates International, Fujitsu Laboratories of Europe, Globus, Hewlett-Packard, IBM, SAP AG, Sonic Software, and TIBCO Software. "Publish-Subscribe Notification for Web Services." March 5, 2004, http://www-106.ibm.com/developerworks/library/ws-pubsub/.

Bellwood, Tom. "Rocket Ahead with UDDI V3." IBM: November 2002. http://www-106.ibm.com/developerworks/webservices/library/ws-uddiv3/.

Cabrera, Luis Felipe, Christopher Kurt, and Don Box, "An Introduction to the Web Services Architecture and Its Specifications." September 2004, Microsoft Corp.

Chappell, David. "WS-Security: New Technologies Help Make Your Web Services More Secure." *MSDN Journal,* April 2003. http://msdn.microsoft.com/msdnmag/issues/03/04/WS%2DSecurity/.

Dimitriou, Labro. "An Architectural Blueprint." Pts. 1 and 2. *Web Logic Developers' Journal*, 3, no. 4 and 5, May/June 2004.

Ferguson, Donald F., Tony Storey, Brad Lovering, and John Shewchuk. "Secure, Reliable, Transacted Web Services." October 2003. http://www-106.ibm.com/developerworks/webservices/library/ws-securtrans/.

Ferris, Chris. "The New WS-I Profiles Explained." IBM: August 2004, http://www-106.ibm.com/developerworks/webservices/library/ws-basicprofile11.html.

Freund, Tom and Tony Storey. "Transactions in the World of Web Services." IBM Corporation: August 2002. Part 1: http://www-106.ibm.com/developerworks/webservices/library/ws-wstx1/. Part 2: http://www-106.ibm.com/developerworks/webservices/library/ws-wstx2/.

IBM and Microsoft. "Federation in a Web Services World." Joint white paper, July 2003. http://www-106.ibm.com/developerworks/library/ws-fedworld/.

————. "Reliable Message Delivery in a Web Services World." Joint white paper, March 2003. http://www-106.ibm.com/developerworks/library/ws-rmdev/.

————. "Security in a Web Services World: A Proposed Architecture and Roadmap." Joint white paper, April 7, 2002. http://www-106.ibm.com/developerworks/webservices/library/ws-secmap/.

McCarthy, Vance. "A Developer's Roadmap to Using WS-Security." *Integration Developers News,* Sept. 4, 2004, http://idevnews.com/IntegrationNews.asp?ID=108.

Seely, Scott. "Understanding WS-Security." October 2002. http://msdn.microsoft.com/library/default.asp?url=/library/en-us/dnwssecur/html/understw.asp.

Kaye, Doug, with Jeff Barr of Amazon.com. "An IT Conversation." http://www.itconversations.com/shows/detail31.html.

Specifications

General
SOAP 1.1: http://www.w3.org/TR/2000/NOTE-SOAP-20000508/

WSDL 1.1: http://www.w3.org/TR/wsdl

SOAP 1.2: http://www.w3.org/2000/xp/Group/

SOAP with Attachments: http://www.w3.org/TR/SOAP-attachments

Message Transmission Optimization Mechanism: http://www.w3.org/TR/soap12-mtom/

XML Binary Optimized Packaging: http://www.w3.org/TR/xop10/

Resource Representation SOAP Header Block: http://www.w3.org/TR/soap12-rep/

Web Services Architecture: http://www.w3.org/TR/ws-arch/

XML home page: http://www.w3.org/XML/

WS-I Profiles: http://www.ws-i.org/Documents.aspx

Metadata
UDDI: http://www.oasis-open.org/committees/tc_home.php?wg_abbrev=uddi-spec

WSDL: http://www.w3.org/2002/ws/desc/

WS-Addressing: http://www.w3.org/Submission/ws-addressing/

WS-MessageDelivery: http://www.w3.org/Submission/ws-messagedelivery/

XML Schema: http://www.w3.org/XML/Schema

Relax NG: http://www.oasis-open.org/committees/tc_home.php?wg_abbrev=relax-ng

WS-MetadataExchange: http://www-106.ibm.com/developerworks/webservices/library/specification/ws-mex/

Web Services Policy Framework (WS-Policy): ftp://www6.software.ibm.com/software/developer/library/ws-policy.pdf

Web Services Policy Attachment (WS-PolicyAttachment): ftp://www6.software.ibm.com/software/developer/library/ws-polat.pdf

Web Services Policy Assertions (WS-PolicyAssertion): http://www-106.ibm.com/developerworks/library/ws-polas/

Web Services Policy Language (WSPL): http://www.oasis-open.org/committees/
download.php/3661/draft-xacml-wspl-04.pdf

W3C Web Services Constraints and Capabilities Workshop papers: http://
www.w3.org/2004/09/ws-cc-program.html#papers

Security

WS-Security: http://www.oasis-open.org/committees/tc_home.php?wg_
abbrev=wss

WS-SecureConversation: ftp://www6.software.ibm.com/software/developer/
library/ws-secureconversation.pdf

Web Services Trust Language (WS-Trust): ftp://www6.software.ibm.com/
software/developer/library/ws-trust.pdf

XML Encryption: http://www.w3.org/Encryption/2001/

XML Signature: http://www.w3.org/Signature/

WS-Federation: http://www-106.ibm.com/developerworks/webservices/
library/ws-fed/

Security Assertion Markup Language (SAML): http://www.oasis-open.org/
committees/tc_home.php?wg_abbrev=security

Extensible Access Control Markup Language (XACML): http://
www.oasis-open.org/committees/tc_home.php?wg_abbrev=xacml

XML Key Management Specification (XKMS): http://www.w3.org/TR/xkms/

Secure Sockets Layer/Transport Layer Security (SSL/TLS):
http://www.ietf.org/html.charters/tls-charter.html

HTTP Authentication: ftp://ftp.isi.edu/in-notes/rfc2617.txt

HTTP Digest Authentication: http://www.w3.org/Protocols/rfc2069/rfc2069

Reliability
ebXML Messaging: http://www.oasis-open.org/committees/tc_home.php?wg_abbrev=ebxml-msg

WS-Reliability: http://www.oasis-open.org/committees/tc_home.php?wg_abbrev=wsrm

WS-ReliableMessaging: ftp://www6.software.ibm.com/software/developer/library/ws-reliablemessaging200403.pdf

Notification
WS-Eventing: http://ftpna2.bea.com/pub/downloads/WS-Eventing.pdf

WS-Notification: http://www.oasis-open.org/committees/tc_home.php?wg_abbrev=wsn

Transactions
WS-CAF: http://www.oasis-open.org/committees/tc_home.php?wg_abbrev=ws-caf

WS-AT: ftp://www6.software.ibm.com/software/developer/library/ws-atomictransaction.pdf

WS-C: ftp://www6.software.ibm.com/software/developer/library/ws-coordination.pdf

WS-BA: ftp://www6.software.ibm.com/software/developer/library/ws-busact.pdf

Orchestration
Web Services Business Process Execution Language (WS-BPEL): http://www.oasis-open.org/committees/tc_home.php?wg_abbrev=wsbpel

Web Services Choreography Description Language (WS-CDL): http://
www.w3.org/2002/ws/chor/#published

Orchestration Historical References
ebXML Business Process Specification Schema: http://www.ebxml.org/specs/
ebBPSS.pdf.

P. Malu, J.J. Dubray, A. Lonjon et al. ebXML Business Process Specification
Schema (BPSS), Version 1.05, 2002.

A. Arkin, S. Askary, S. Fordin, W. Jekeli, K. Kawaguchi, D. Orchard, S. Pogliani,
K. Riemer, S. Struble, P. Takaci-Nagy, I. Trickovic, and S. Zimek. *Web Service
Choreography Interface (WSCI) 1.0.* Published on the World Wide Web by BEA
Systems, Intalio, SAP, and Sun Microsystems, 2002.

A. Arkin et al. *Business Process Modeling Language (BPML),* Version 1.0, 2002.

Assaf Arkin. Business process modeling language—bpml1.0 last call working
draft. Published on the World Wide Web by BPMI.org, 2002.

Satish. Thatte. *XLANG Web Services for Business Process Design*, 2001. http://
www.gotdotnet.com/team/xml_wsspecs/xlang-c/default.htm.

Francisco Curbera, Frank Leymann, Dieter Roller, and Sanjiva Weerawarana.
Web Services Flow Language (WSFL) 1.0. Published on the World Wide Web
by IBM Corporation, May 2001. See also http://xml.coverpages.org/wsfl.html.

F. Curbera, Y. Goland, J. Klein, F. Leymann, D. Roller, S. Thatte, and S.
Weerawarana. *Business Process Execution Language for Web Services*, Version
1.0. Standards proposal by BEA Systems, International Business Machines
Corporation, and Microsoft Corporation, 2002.

WfMC, Wf-XML, and XPDL
http://www.wfmc.org/about.htm

RosettaNet
http://www.rosettanet.org/RosettaNet/Rooms/DisplayPages/LayoutInitial

http://xml.coverpages.org/rosettaNet.html

Other Resources

Microsoft's Developer Network Web services home page:
http://msdn.microsoft.com/webservices/understanding/

IBM's Developerworks Web services home page: http://www-136.ibm.com/
developerworks/webservices

Java Community Process specifications: http://www.jcp.org/en/home/index

Robin Cover's cover pages: http://xml.coverpages.org/

OASIS symposium proceedings: Reliable Infrastructures for XML: http://
www.oasis-open.org/events/symposium/pre_program.php

Amazon.com Web services: http://www.amazon.com/gp/browse.html/
102-8845530-0831331?node=3435361

Google's Web services APIs: http://www.google.com/apis/

SOAPBuilders (interoperability testing results): http://www.soapbuilders.org/

Index

A

abstractions, service contracts, 112
access
    multi-channel access, 216-217, 219
        obsolete infrastructure
            elimination, 202
        service-oriented architectures,
            202-214
        staffing cost reductions, 202
        Web services, 26-28
    occasionally connected architecture, 28
    services, 12
account applications, declining, 231
account information
    collecting, 229
    repairing, 231
    validating, 230
ACID, 397
activity, transactions, 389
addressing
    multi-transport addressing, 294
    transactions, 391
    Web services, 39
ADS (Microsoft Active Directory
    System), 126

alternative transports, 145-146
    SOAP over CORBA IIOP, 148
    SOAP over IBM WebSphere MQ, 147
    SOAP over JMS, 147-148
    Tibco Rendezvous, 149
    WDSL, 146
Amazon.com, Web services, 279
API/method-driven integration, 168
application architectures, 57
application integration, 166
applications
    composite applications, developing,
        214-216
    consolidation, 163
architecture
    WDSL service contracts, 114-115
    Web services, 149-150
assertions, WS-Policy, 302-305
assign task (WS-BPEL), 249
asynchronous message queuing,
    WS-Reliable Messaging, compared,
    374-376
asynchronous messaging, 82
    service requesters, 83
    stateless services, 82

X-Z

informIT

<section>www.informit.com</section>

YOUR GUIDE TO IT REFERENCE

Articles

Keep your edge with thousands of free articles, in-depth features, interviews, and IT reference recommendations – all written by experts you know and trust.

Online Books

Answers in an instant from **InformIT Online Book's** 600+ fully searchable on line books. For a limited time, you can get your first 14 days **free**.

Safari
TECH BOOKS ONLINE
POWERED BY

Catalog

Review online sample chapters, author biographies and customer rankings and choose exactly the right book from a selection of over 5,000 titles.